More Votes That Count

More Votes That Count:
A Case Study in Voter Mobilization

Robert Benedetti, editor

Berkeley Public Policy Press
Institute of Governmental Studies
University of California, Berkeley
2012

Library of Congress Publication Data

More votes that count : a case study in voter mobilization / Robert Benedetti, editor.
        p.m.
    ISBN 978-0-87772-441-4
  1. Campaign management—United States—Case studies. 2. Political campaigns—United States—
Case studies. 3. Voting—United States—Case studies. I. Benedetti, Robert Reed, 1942-
    JK2281.M65 2012
    324.7—dc23
2012011673

Contents

Preface

Patrick Johnston[1]

With the election of a president at stake, the nation hung on the question of the hanging chads of Florida in November of 2000. My mind, however, kept drifting back 20 years to the cramped San Joaquin County Registrar of Voters office in the decrepit old Stockton Hotel.

I was a candidate for the California State Assembly in November 1980 and I had just lost a nail-biter by a scant 18 votes out of more than 70,000 cast to Adrian Fondse. But wait! A recount was possible even in the new age of electronics. A computer could only count what a light passing over a hole in a voter's ballot where a tiny rectangle of card stock has been punched out to designate a candidate preference scans.

After 10 days of hand counting with occasional disputes over individual ballots, I emerged the winner by 25 votes. The opposition challenged the outcome in court arguing that County Registrar Ralph Epperson should not have counted votes where there was a "hanging chad." Judge Bill Dozier found that the standard to use in counting votes was: what is the voter's intent and can it be determined? Applying that standard meant that the question of whether to count a vote did not turn on whether one, two, or three corners of the chad were detached from the card. Rather, the question was could the registrar clearly observe one and only one choice that the voter was making in jabbing at the card with the sharp object?

The story of my election continued to Secretary of State March Fong Eu's office where I received a Certificate of Election, then a challenge in the 3rd District Court of Appeals, and finally a vote in the State Assembly that seated me and removed Fondse on a strictly partisan vote.

The experience of that 1980 recount in San Joaquin County motivated the Board of Supervisors to change the system of voting in hopes of guaranteeing uncontested election results. Twenty years later the same punch-card style ballots were at the center of the Florida controversy that would determine who would be president. And, again, when the dust had settled and George Bush had taken the oath of office, there were calls to "reform" the election process.

Congress acted and the states reacted. This volume is the story of one crucial California county's efforts to meet the challenge of improving the election system. San Joaquin County and the Universi-

---

[1] Patrick Johnston served 20 years in the California Legislature, 10 in the Assembly, and 10 in the Senate. Currently, he is the president and CEO of the California Association of Health Plans and a member of the Delta Stewardship Council. He is a graduate of St. Patrick's College and holds a master's degree from CSU Sacramento.

ty of the Pacific's Jacoby Center partnered to do the job with the primary goal of increasing voter participation.

Today the issues are different. Electronic voting machines have been tried, but confidence in their reliability is not widespread. Instead there is a new emphasis on making the old paper ballot more understandable and more accurate. One option that is popular with voters is voting by mail. In fact, Oregon has gone to vote by mail as its primary election system. Other strategies are to devise marketing campaigns to inform voters on election procedures and to improve the training of poll workers. Voter errors do occur, so it is necessary to explore ways to catch the mistakes and assure that the voter's will is reflected in the official count.

This book provides insightful perspectives on the issues surrounding contemporary voting systems and behaviors. Furthermore, it offers both a scholarly overview and a practical guide to remaking the act of voting for the 21st century. Many of the recommended fixes are inexpensive.

The laboratory for this examination of voting is San Joaquin County, a jurisdiction with historically low turnouts. The county's in-migration—from the gold rush to the more recent influx from Mexico, Southeast Asia, and the San Francisco Bay Area—has generated a diversity of languages and household incomes that is a challenge beyond what many locales face. Hence, San Joaquin County is a good place to try making the electoral system work better—and measuring the effort.

In sum, serious students of the American democratic experiment should read this book as part of America's continuing struggle to complete its democracy. As a former candidate and legislator, I know studies like this one generate better public policy.

Acknowledgements

This book was written under the auspices and with the support of the Jacoby Center for Public Service and Civic Leadership at the University of the Pacific. The project would not have been possible without the cooperation of the staff at the San Joaquin County Registrar of Voters, especially Registrar Austin Erdman.

ל

Chapter 1

Introduction: Anatomy of a Case Study

Robert Benedetti[1]

From the outset, this project was an experiment. In 2007, the Registrar of Voters of San Joaquin County was the epicenter of dramatic change in electoral policy after the California secretary of state decertified electronic voting machines that had been purchased by the county. The timing of this decision was particularly challenging as the registrar faced a year (2008) in which three (February, June, and November) elections were scheduled including both a presidential primary and a presidential election.

In order to ease the return to paper ballots, the registrar sought to increase vote by mail, to improve poll-worker training, and to discover practices that might reduce voter error. Fortuitously, the secretary of state made Help America Vote Act (HAVA) funds available to counties to help implement the return to paper balloting. The registrar was able to access these funds and negotiate a two-year contract with the Jacoby Center for Public Service and Civic Leadership at the University of the Pacific in Stockton, California, to undertake research focused on these three areas of concern.

The Jacoby Center assembled an interdisciplinary team including four political scientists, four members of the Department of Communication, a graphic designer, and a director from the Department of Theatre Arts. The team used the February election as a trial run for a limited number of experimental "treatments." These included television ads, changes in poll-worker training and poll-station signage in an effort to educate the public and to respond to the registrar's three areas of concern. It also commissioned three surveys of the electorate in San Joaquin County, one following each election, to evaluate reactions to the changes that had been implemented and to learn more about public perceptions of the voting process generally and vote by mail specifically.

In subsequent elections, the team worked with Registrar of Voters staff on revisions to the sample ballot and in preparing mailings to encourage vote-by-mail registration. It also created television ads to recruit poll workers, supervised a trial program using college students at polling stations, and designed alternative media campaigns to distribute key information about voting to the wider public. Finally, one team member undertook the analysis of "spoiled" ballots for several elections to gain a better understanding of how voter errors occur.

The team completed assignments individually, but met regularly to discuss procedures and findings. The Registrar of Voters and his staff were frequently part of these discussions. While faculty

---

[1] Executive Director, Jacoby Center for Public Service and Civic Leadership, University of the Pacific.

supervised the analysis, data were often collected and discussed by undergraduate and graduate students at the University of the Pacific. In every way possible, this project was structured as a learning experience for students as well as an exercise in applied communication and political science theory.

I

This set of essays is the result of an interdisciplinary effort to assist a county Registrar of Voters to improve the accuracy and efficiency of the electoral process. The primary purpose of the authors' conclusions is to suggest best practices in regard to vote by mail, voter information, poll-worker training, and voter error.

However, the essays are also relevant to longstanding general conversations regarding the act of voting in America, the efficacy of political reform, and the implementation of public policy. Following the 2000 election, politicians and political scientists turned their attention from problems of voter decision making and voter access toward the challenge of voting accuracy or the assurance that one's vote counts as intended. Clearly, these issues are not fully separable from one another. However, earlier scholarship had seen the way voters decide and the way voting systems deny access to classes of voters as of greater relevance than the accuracy with which votes are recorded. These latter questions were only raised when clear claims of corruption were lodged against a particular jurisdiction. This changed in 2000, and these essays reflect these new directions in the way the act of voting is conceptualized.[2]

The essays are also reports from the front lines of a political reform. When electoral contests become close and the electorate is divided, every vote counts and all parties are concerned that they may be denied victory by administrative mistakes. Among the lessons of the Florida election in 2000 was the realization that recording of ballots is not a straightforward process and might benefit from new technology. Public interest groups, political parties, and politicians joined in their call for change. In fact, some authors suggest that the result was a rebirth of the Progressive movement's call for electoral reform in the name of popular control:

> At the beginning of the twenty-first century, we are again in a period of repeated calls for a new progressivism to reevaluate America's electoral institutions.[3]

However, unlike other reform movements that run their course at the state and local level before receiving national attention, voting reform was quickly placed on the congressional agenda. Even in a legislature dominated by the Republican Party, usually skeptical of electoral change, a new and national reform was forged in the Help America Vote Act. Once passed, this initiative faced the challenge of implementation in 50 states and American territories. Because the scope of the legislation was large and required the cooperation of both state and local officials, it offers a significant opportunity to assess the implementation and compliance mechanisms currently available to ensure that Washington's will is worked on Main Street.[4]

While this introduction cannot detail the extent of the scholarly treatment of voting, reform, and implementation, it is important to at least provide a general outline of the directions these separate lines of inquiry have taken and to place these essays in the context of current scholarly discussions.

---

[2] For a sample of how this new interest in voting procedures is driving fresh research agendas, see "Symposium—2008 and Beyond: The Future of Election Reform in the States," *PS: Political Science and Politics* 40, no. 4 (2007): 631–86, and Bruce Cain, Todd Donovan, and Caroline J. Tolbert, editors, *Democracy in the States* (Brookings: Washington, D.C., 2008).

[3] Caroline Tolbert, "Editor's Introduction," *Symposium, ibid.,* 632.

[4] See, for example R. Michael Alvarez and Thad E. Hall, "Rational and Pluralistic Approaches to HAVA's Implementation: The Cases of Georgia and California," *Publius. The Journal of Federalism* 35, no. 4 (2005): 559–77.

II

The voting act is at the core of what has been called the American science of politics. This preferred position is justified in several ways. The vote is an expression of the voice of the people, the foundation on which a democracy rests. However, some also consider it a weak link. Since Athens, people of substance have questioned whether the average citizen can make an informed decision on public matters.[5]

Of equal interest is the fact that American citizens treasure their individualism and have not behaved as citizens in other democracies by developing strong preferences for a particular political party over a lifetime. Their selections at the ballot box are not simply a party line and therefore require investigation to understand.[6]

As a vote is cast secretly, survey research has been relied upon to unmask the reasoning that leads voters to behave as they do. The discovery of how voters decide requires a careful research strategy and clear-eyed analysis. Such analysis allows for the use of quasi-experimental research designs and can claim a measure of validity from following a scientific methodology rigorously. Therefore, voting studies have often been the poster child for a political science that can rival the surety of the natural sciences.[7]

Finally, voting most perfectly matches the way liberalism, still a powerful force in American political thought, suggests that individuals decide.[8] Voting is conceptualized as a free act in which the citizen considers alternatives and makes a selection based on some calculus of satisfaction or at best enlightened self-interest. This fit with the American creed may in part explain why the study of voting began with the voter rather than the context in which the voter behaves.

Early studies focused on choice and assumed that the voter, indeed, had choice. These studies found that voters chose according to particular cues including the opinions of perceived leaders, party affiliation, and economic well-being.[9] Since that time, they have matured to realize that certain structural realities intrude to complicate such choices and limit the determination of cues, namely the nonexistence of competition, the lack of third parties, the lack of ethnic diversity among candidates, the length of campaigns, and the shortage of voter education materials and voting opportunities.[10] As a consequence of findings that validate the reality of these impediments to meaningful individual choice, there have been cries for reforms: more competitive districts, greater flexibility in registration and voting procedures, rules stimulating third parties, more candidates of color and gender diversity, and better media coverage. Like the Progressives before them, these reformers hope that structural tinkering can ensure that the public has meaningful choices.[11]

Particularly serious has been the realization that certain legal and social structures have been put in place systematically to limit the access of some citizens to the voting booth. While the drumbeat for reforms that expand choice continues, the post–WWII generation of reformers has focused on a

---

[5] Even strong defenders of democracy like Robert Dahl find that the voter can best be trusted where the choice is between the team that represents the current state of affairs and a team proposing change. See Robert Dahl, *Preface to Democratic Theory* (Chicago: University of Chicago, 1956).

[6] A good summary of the "golden age" of voting studies and their results is provided in Stanley Kelley, Jr., and Thad W. Mirer, "The Simple Act of Voting," *The American Political Science Review* 68, no. 2 (June 1974): 572–91. They concluded that the voter's attitudes towards individual candidates are determinative if they clearly discriminate between the candidates. Only if the voter does not have a clear preference based on attitudes toward one candidate or another does the voter rely on party labels.

[7] For a discussion of political science as science, see Bernard Crick, *The American Science of Politics* (New York: Routledge, 2003).

[8] For a discussion of the current state of liberalism in America, see Alan Wolfe, *The Future of Liberalism* (New York: Vintage, 2010).

[9] Kelly, Jr., and Mirer. *passim.*

[10] See Bruce E. Cain, "Reform Studies: Political Science on the Firing Line," *Symposium*, 635–38.

[11] *Ibid.*

call for open access to the polls. The Voting Rights Act of 1965 created a bumper crop of academic studies and court cases exposing the way electoral procedures and boundaries were preventing black and other citizens from exercising their rights fully.[12] Sensing that their candidates had the most to benefit from the enfranchising of such citizens, the Democratic Party has led the way in championing access to the ballot box.

More recently, concerns about the accuracy of the voting process have come to the forefront. While there have long been concerns of corruption at the ballot box in big cities, the cumulative impact of carelessness in state and local administration became most evident when magnified by the use of sophisticated technologies. The 2000 election and the exposé of Florida's practices educated the nation and the academy on the scale of the problem. It is also increasingly clear that the public at large has serious questions about the accuracy of the voting process and that the doubts that result from such questions can have a chilling effect on voter participation.[13] Realizing that a failure to ensure accuracy could harm Republican as well as Democratic voters, a Republican majority in Congress supported the Help America Vote Act to provide technical and financial assistance to states with the goal of ensuring a voting system that accurately translated voter preferences into ballot results. The essay by Randall S. Collette, Ben Goodhue, and Nathan Monroe tell this story below.

While this case study focuses primarily on attempts to respond to the challenge of accuracy in one county in California, San Joaquin, the county's efforts are rooted in federal and state actions, particularly as the initiatives undertaken were funded through the Help American Vote Act as administered by the secretary of state of California. That is, San Joaquin County is charged with implementing plans made well beyond its boundaries and without a detailed understanding of its situation. For example, concerns over accuracy in San Joaquin are complicated by lingering doubts about the clarity of the propositions on which Californians vote and the fairness of their electoral districts. In other words, attempts to improve accuracy are not without implications for voter choices and voter access.

III

The concern about accuracy in voting can lead scholars to explore the efficacy of several clusters of reforms. The first involves alternative voting technologies. A second focuses on staff preparation, particularly at the level of the poll worker. The third takes seriously voter education as it relates to the process of voting itself. Though much of current research has focused on the first set of issues, namely the feasibility of a technological fix,[14] this case study examines all three reforms and in the context of attempts to implement HAVA and related statewide mandates.

The rush to print of several books on the potential impact of electronic voting machines as well as the analysis of governmental agencies on the subject has added this growing research literature to the list of considerations Registrars of Voters weigh in implementing reforms. However, the move to electronic voting has been slowed by technological and budgetary—not to mention political—concerns. This has forced those who would implement the spirit of reform as it relates to voting accuracy to explore nonmachine solutions.

---

[12] See, for example, Richard L. Hasen, *The Supreme Court and Election Law: Judging Equality from Baker v. Carr to Bush v. Gore* (New York: NYU Press, 2003).

[13] Paul S. Herrnson, Richard G. Niemi, Michael J. Hanmer, Benjamin B. Bederson, Frederick C. Conrad, and Michael W. Traugott, *Voting Technology: The Not-So-Simple Act of Casting a Ballot* (Washington, D.C.: Brookings, 2008), 47ff. discusses the different levels of confidence inspired in voters by different types of voting arrangements. Interestingly, this study finds that paper balloting does not stimulate the greatest confidence in the voter and hence may itself undermine participation over time more than some machine alternatives.

[14] *Ibid.*, and R. Michael Alvarez and Thad E. Hall, *Electronic Elections: The Perils and Promises of Digital Democracy* (Princeton, N.J.: Princeton University Press, 2008).

As the Early Voting team at Reed College has articulated, the West is particularly taken with vote-by-mail solutions.[15] While there is debate over how much money vote by mail can save, whether it improves turnout, and the degree to which it discriminates against less powerful groups, there is little doubt about its convenience. The essay by Dari Sylvester and Nathan Monroe argues that the particular way a vote-by-mail program is implemented will have an impact on its success in generating higher turnout. They also expose the rationality of the voter in reacting to such cues. They conclude that, when voters are solicited to sign up permanently for vote by mail, they do so in increased numbers. Since California is nonpartisan at the local level, it lacks a robust grassroots party structure to mobilize voters in most districts; it would seem, however, that cues from the Registrar of Voters would help.

Like other public policy, the impact of voting reforms depends on the nature of the implementation process. As Jeffery Pressman argued several years ago, plans made in Washington are drastically modified in state capitols and localities.[16] Keith Smith extends the congressional analysis offered by Randall S. Collette, Ben Goodhue, and Nathan Monroe to investigate the way the state of California reacted to HAVA, in light of its own history of electoral reform. In fact, California's prior experience appears to have made the early and enduring adoption of electronic voting difficult, if not impossible. Further, the impact of budget shortfalls leaves any future investments in expensive reforms in doubt.

Moving to the implementation of reforms in San Joaquin County, the Registrar of Voters faced with a mandate to return to paper ballots, sought alternative strategies to increase voter accuracy. He requested an evaluation of poll-worker training, an analysis of voter education initiatives, and an investigation of voter errors rejected by optical scanning devises.

Jon Schamber and his team undertook a participant observation of poll-worker training during one election cycle and helped redesign the process in regard to a second. His essay is a response to the call by Thad Hall, J. Quin Monson, and Kelly D. Patterson for more research in this area.[17] His analysis does not question the substance of the training as much as the pedagogical practices it employs. In other words, the standardized content communicated to local counties by the Office of the secretary of state can provide a good outline of what needs to be learned, but such outlines do not by themselves teach the material. Again, the social skills necessary to make implementation happen are the keys to success.

While empirical studies examine vote by mail and poll-worker training make use of rational choice theory and learning theories, the study of the impact of ballot design and other aspects of voter information as presented here draw on theoretical constructs from communication and visual arts.[18] The essay by Paul Turpin examines the challenges of any attempted change in the structure of voter information. He explores the ways that existing social systems impede new ideas and the complex interworking of the Registrar of Voter's staff with contractors, consultants, and other governmental agencies.

The essay that follow by Brett DeBoer, Lisa Tromovitch, and Alan Ray documents the development of three types of voter information initiatives: signage and ballot design, video advertising, and radio/media campaigns. They ponder the several challenges that face anyone attempting to apply artistic, public relations, and media best practices to the system of voting.

---

[15] Paul Gronke, Eva Galanes-Rosenbaum, and Peter A. Miller, "Early Voting and Voter Turnout" in *Democracy and the States*, 68–82.

[16] Jeffrey Pressman and Aaron Wildavsky, *Implementation: How Great Expectations in Washington Are Dashed in Oakland or, Why It's Amazing That Federal Programs Work at All, This Being a Saga of the Economic Development Administration as Told by Two Sympathetic Observers Who Seek to Build Morals on a Foundation* (Berkeley: UC Press, 1979).

[17] Thad Hall, J. Quin Monson, and Kelly Patterson, "Poll Workers' Job Satisfaction and Confidence," *Democracy in the States*, 35–51.

[18] Marcia Lausen, *Design for Democracy* (Chicago: University of Chicago Press, 2007).

The final two essays assess future options for reformers. While previous studies have documented the error rates of different technologies and argue for electronic solutions, Qingwen Dong has analyzed in detail the nature of the errors that occur when paper ballots are used with optical scanning devises. This allows him to suggest changes that may, in fact, increase the accuracy of a paper system and therefore challenge one of the "selling points" of a conversion to other types of electronic voting machines. Here he tests some of the conclusions reached by Herrnson, et al. though even their analysis confirms that paper balloting keeps nonvoting at a minimum.[19]

Benedetti and Erdmann end the collection with a reflection on the current passion for reform and discuss future trends in electoral redesign. They applaud the possibility that social scientists will become increasingly involved in the administration of elections and suggest that more analysis should be focused on the social system surrounding the vote rather than the impact of the technology to be used. In other words, the content of voter information provided at every stage in the process, the training and use of poll workers, and the nature of the media campaigns launched deserve ever greater attention.

IV

The literature cited above helps to place this case study of San Joaquin County in the context of the wider field of voting studies. As Stanley Kelly and Thad Mirer wrote several years ago following the conclusions of Anthony Downs, "A comparison of candidates resulting in a choice among them should be one consideration—but not the only one—in the decision about whether to vote. Considerations about efficacy, convenience, and cost of voting should also enter."[20] To be sure, the act of voting is in all probability influenced by a voter's perception of the technology involved, the nature of poll-worker assistance, and the information about the election at hand.

However, the content of this particular case argues it should also be seen as a case study in which political reform and policy implementation intertwine. Caroline Tolbert is persuasive that the current interest in the election process is well understood as a continuation of the reform impulse in American politics: "At the beginning of the twenty-first century we hear repeated calls for a new progressivism to reevaluate America's electoral institutions."[21] Bruce Cain in his discussion of the new progressivism includes a renewed interest in redistricting, direct democracy, multiple parties, and term limits. Cain focuses on state reform opportunities, rather than a federal fix.[22] On the other hand, HAVA was not a state-by-state option, but an attempt to implement reform from the top down. At least part of the story of electoral reform at this time is an account of federal leadership and the nature of the implementation that followed.

While this set of essays can be seen as relevant to a general discussion of voting and reform, more significant may be its testimony about the pitfalls and possibilities of democratic reform when it begins in Washington, untested in the "laboratories of democracy" at the grassroots. For example, while HAVA provided considerable encouragement for localities to purchase electronic voting machines, several of these essays suggest that other electoral procedures not involving electronic machine use by the public can increase participation and lower errors. Mailings inviting vote by mail may raise vote-by-mail registration. There may be ways to instruct voters to make fewer errors, avoiding the purchase of expensive machines. Appropriate advertising may encourage a more competitive pool of poll workers and therefore a more responsive polling place. Media campaigns by Registrars of Voters

---

[19] Herrnson, et al., 81–88. See also, Alvarez and Hall who also discuss errors with optical scan equipment but without the empirical research to report, 21ff.

[20] Kelly and Mirer, 574.

[21] Caroline Tolbert, "2008 and Beyond: The Future of Election Reform in the States—Editor's Introduction," *Symposium*, 623.

[22] Bruce Cain developed the theme Tolbert summarizes in Cain, 635–38.

may be able to substitute or complement the mobilization of political parties in getting out the vote. In other words, reform centrally stimulated may result in expensive changes whose effectiveness could be matched by less extensive adjustments at local levels.

Further, implementation of this federal mandate was indeed slowed by state politics and policies. The purchase of voting machines and their certification provided opportunities for illegal preferences to be given and contributed to the resignation of one secretary of state. Another secretary was persuaded that the current offering of machines was not secure or sufficiently reliable, and suspended machine use except for voters that so requested. In other words, reform from Washington provides resources that invite political horse trading and opens the opportunity for state officials to highjack decisions made above.

However, the initiative from Washington was effective in capturing local attention and stimulating reflection on the accuracy of voting. The San Joaquin Registrar of voters, realizing that electronic machines could not be used in a timely fashion to address accuracy concerns, applied for and was granted HAVA funding to undertake the studies reported here. Though HAVA was launched to speed a technological fix, in San Joaquin it stimulated a sober review of more traditional practices in the hope that they could be repaired rather than abandoned.

In sum, then, HAVA was implemented in San Joaquin County, but not as envisioned in Washington, D.C. Though the county initially spent money on machines (they are currently in storage), it has been pleased with the results of less capital intensive investments in advertising, poll-worker training, and mailers. And the county seems more interested in social science research than electronic engineering. Clearly the seeds of the national impulse for reform have reached these grassroots, but with a more textured outcome than anticipated.

V

As noted above, while the essays in this volume were authored or co-authored separately, all of them are the result of the deliberations of an interdisciplinary team and the staff of the San Joaquin Registrar of Voters office. Given the particular interests of the Registrar of Voters and the regulations that applied to HAVA funding, the effort was focused on practical results rather than theoretical significance. The team did not begin with a particular hypothesis regarding the voter who selects mail or who commits an error. Rather, the challenge was to reach voters who might vote by mail, to lower error rates, and to improve poll-worker selection and training. The authors offer their own best practices relevant to the topic they address. However, there are at least five practices that gain support from the work of several authors.[23]

First, much voter information is structured to comply with legal or traditional mandates. From the signage at polling places to the design of ballots, from advertisement for poll workers to the layout of sample ballots, the focus needs to shift from compliance with preset norms to the quantity of voter turnout and the accuracy with which the vote is recorded. Thus, it is not sufficient to make specific suggestions on ways to improve materials; there needs to be a change in the values that are brought to a discussion of their creation. The shift is, in fact, similar to one occurring in higher education where the paradigm for evaluating outcomes has shifted from resource checklists to evidence of student learning.[24] The staffs of registrars' offices alone are not the only group that could reconsider its perspective toward change. Consulting groups, the Post Office, the secretary of state, and even the legislature need to reorient their analysis to put reaching the voter with correct and understandable information higher on their list, and specifically before technological fixes.

Second, the voters must take responsibility to ensure that their votes are counted appropriately. Voters often fail to ask questions of poll workers and decline to follow written instructions. While the

---

[23] Our suggestions complement those made by Herrnson, et al., 141–52 and Alvarez and Hall, 179–89.

[24] See, for example the *Handbook for Accreditation*, Western Association of Schools and Colleges, 2001.

atmosphere of the polling station may be altered in some fashion to increase the comfort level of those who would ask questions, in the final analysis, the voter needs to be willing to come forward wherever there is confusion.

Third, poll inspectors are key players in the voting system and deserve special attention. Professor Schamber notes that they are the "go to" person for nonroutine questions. Where they are not thoroughly and specially trained, the polling station is substantially weakened, particularly in regard to new voters and voters with disabilities.

Fourth, when attempting to improve accuracy by the use of media, it is a challenge to select images that establish attachments across demographic groups. In other words, the introduction of media into the voting process requires special sensitivity to difference. One solution to this may be the increased use of diagrams, symbols, and animation. Such solutions were introduced by part of the experimentation undertaken by the team and were incorporated into television ads, signage, and sample ballot redesign.

Fifth, electoral systems can be improved prior to the introduction of electronic voting machines and some of the sources of inaccuracy may continue with or without the introduction of machines. For example, the use of machines will not overcome errors made during vote by mail, an increasingly popular practice in the West. The use of machines assumes a level of poll-worker preparation not yet achieved. Even with the most advanced voting machines, voters should be expected to seek help where they have questions. They need to be encouraged and empowered to do so by staff well schooled in whatever technology is adopted.

Overall, the team finds that much of the need for change and improvement in regard to accuracy must occur at the local level and is related to local social conditions. It is difficult to legislate in the areas of voter information, poll-worker training, and the general social atmosphere at a polling place. Since the issues are often ones of intercultural communication and social cues, the use of social science teams to evaluate particular voting arrangements can be particularly helpful in developing concrete strategies.

Part I: The Public Policy of Elections

Chapter 2

Helping America Vote in a New Millennium

Randall S. Collette, Ben Goodhue, and Nathan Monroe[1]

In November 2000, the electoral system of the United States failed to designate conclusively who would become the 43rd president. The focus of the nation's attention fell on Florida and the ambiguity surrounding the assignment of the state's decisive 25 electoral votes. Election mishaps were not, however, limited to Florida. Elections across the country were reportedly held hostage by errors and mistakes. Given the high stakes of the 2000 election, citizens and legislators alike paid particular attention to the shortcomings of the electoral process and discovered an outmoded, flawed system.

For example, some districts in New Hampshire failed to count ballots that were marked for straight party-line ballots. One county in Iowa lost 890 votes for Al Gore in a recount, and another district boasted a 100 percent turnout. In New York, polls did not open on time and some lines at polling places were so long that voters turned away, frustrated. Many parts of New York City used old machines, purchased in the 1960s. When some of these machines broke down, there were not enough back-up paper ballots to accommodate voters.[2] Within Florida, black voters claimed intimidation and police harassment when attempting to reach their polling places; though the minority made up only 11 percent of the electorate, black voters were estimated to have composed 54 percent of disenfranchised voters.[3]

Systemwide, the electoral infrastructure of 2000 seemed crippled; it is estimated that between four million and six million votes were discarded. Every election brings forth allegations of fraud, but the single greatest challenge to effective voting in this election appears to have been funding.

Traditionally, running elections has been managed at the county level, drawing on differing funding sources and a broad array of technologies, ranging from lever-pull machines designed in the 19th century to computer touch screens. The most common form of ballot technology in the 2000 election was the punch card; 34 percent of the jurisdictions nationally used these cards. Florida's infamous butterfly ballot—a "maze" like ballot with names down both sides and punch holes in the center—was part of such a system.

---

[1] Department of Political Science, University of California, Merced.

[2] Howard Troxler, "With Trouble All Around, Florida Gets All the Blame," *St. Petersburg Times*, November 15, 2000.

[3] Andrew Gumbel, "U.S. Presidential Election," *The New York Times,* December 2, 2000.

Counties often lack access to adequate funding sources, particularly in poor areas. The less advanced voting technology used in such neighborhoods had the potential to cause disproportionate disenfranchisement. For example, an outdated punch-card system rejects about four percent of ballots, whereas an optical system more commonly used in wealthy areas and that uses the pencil shading of bubbles, rejects only 1.4 percent of ballots.[4] In sum, with funding for elections unequally distributed between districts across the country, the 2000 election revealed an election system that was hardly an adequate foundation for democracy that boasts equal justice under law.

The Creation of HAVA

Introduction and Early Support

In the aftermath of the 2000 election, a bipartisan effort in the House of Representatives sought the modernization of voting in U.S. elections. Propelled by controversies over invalid and confusing ballots, Congress sought better, more reliable means for citizens to cast their votes in future elections. The result—the Help America Vote Act of 2002 (HAVA)—gave money to states for a full overhaul of the voting system. However, what began and ended as a "bipartisan" piece of legislation did not emerge unscathed from its treacherous, year-long battle through the partisan waters of the U.S. Congress.

The act was launched auspiciously on November 14, 2001, when Representative Robert Ney, a Republican from Ohio, and Representative Steny Hoyer, a Democrat from Maryland, introduced HR 3295. Through HAVA they aimed

> [t]o establish a program to provide funds to States to replace punch card voting systems, to establish the Election Assistance Commission to assist in the administration of Federal elections and to otherwise provide assistance with the administration of certain Federal election laws and programs, to establish minimum election administration standards for States and units of local government with responsibility for the administration of Federal elections, and for other purposes.[5]

Quickly, 172 Representatives—109 Democrats, 62 Republicans, and 1 Independent—co-sponsored the bill. However, this early, overwhelming bipartisan support for the legislation masked an undercurrent of disagreement. While the legislators generally agreed that election reform was badly needed, there were significant differences of opinion over which reforms to emphasize. In large part, this divide was over the implications of reform for the future electoral fortunes of each political party.

Prior Conflict over Voting Reform

Partisan divides over voting procedures, however, are certainly not unprecedented. Congress had a similar quarrel over "motor voter" legislation in the early nineties. Initially proposed in 1992, this legislation sought to make it mandatory for states to offer voter registration at their respective Departments of Motor Vehicles (DMVs). Debate over this bill foreshadowed many of the issues that were to generate partisan conflict over HAVA. Republicans asserted that the passage of the law would make it easier to commit voter fraud, while Democrats argued that making registration simpler and more accessible could increase turnout and be a boon to the democratic process.[6]

---

[4] Michael Kondrake, "Fixing the Machines," *The Washington Times*, December 13, 2000.

[5] "Help America Vote Act of 2001," 2002. <http://thomas.loc.gov/cgi-bin/query/D?r107:13:./temp/~r107LmDLHf::>.

[6] Clifford Krauss, "Senate Passes Bill to Force States to Make Voter Registration Easier," *The New York Times*, May 21, 1992.

The motor voter bill cleared the House easily, but in the Senate the partisan divide was clear: 55 Democrats and only 5 Republicans voted to pass the bill. The issue was especially contentious because elections were on the horizon as the vote was taken. President George H. W. Bush vetoed the Motor Voter Act along with other election reforms proposed that year.

The legislation was given a second chance in the 103rd Congress, after the election of President Clinton. Again there was significant partisan strife over the bill. Republicans mounted a filibuster in the Senate, which was broken when five Republicans joined the 57 Democrats in calling for cloture (i.e., to cut off of debate), but only after Democrats made concessions. Democrats were forced to remove provisions in the bill that would have required registration in welfare and unemployment offices, offices that serve a Democrat-leaning population. By contrast, a Republican amendment was accepted that offered members of the military, who lean Republican, the opportunity to register at the time they enlist.[7]

Partisan Implications of HAVA

Just as with motor voter, on its surface the debate over HAVA was about the best way to ensure fair, effective voting processes. Democrats hoped to enfranchise more voters by improving the voter registration processes and stipulating provisional voting. Republicans wanted to protect elections from voter fraud and corruption. Taken at face value, both goals arguably promote a healthy democracy. However, the health of the system was not the only thing at stake in these reforms.

Improving registration is good for democrats (the small "d" citizenry) because it promotes broader representation in government, an intrinsic goal of citizens who support representative democracy. But, it is also good for Democrats (the big "D" partisans), because more registration opportunities for their constituents mean higher probability of electoral success. Higher voter turnout has historically helped Democratic candidates. Surely, Democrats favored broader registration because of both benefits it yielded, but the latter reality encouraged partisan tension.

Similarly, making the registration process more burdensome to safeguard against fraud reforms makes it more difficult for enemies of fair elections to compromise the integrity of the process (a small "d" goal). But, under some conditions, it also has the potential to make it more difficult for lower socio-economic groups—who are historically more likely to support Democratic candidates—to complete the process and successfully cast ballots. Thus, though it would be unfair to cast Republicans as opponents of fair elections, it would be naïve to ignore the potential electoral side-benefit for Republicans that comes from more restrictive voter-fraud provisions.

One key point of disagreement during the HAVA debates was over a provision that would require everyone who registered to vote by mail, after January 2004, to show identification before casting their first vote. Democrats asserted that this practice would hurt poor and minority populations. However, Republicans insisted that without such protections, voter fraud was imminent. As Senator Bond, a Republican from Kansas, remarked in October of 2002:

> I like dogs and I have respect for the dearly departed, but I do not think we should allow them to vote. Protecting the integrity of the ballot box is important to all Americans [. . .]. This legislation recognizes that illegal votes dilute the value of legally cast votes—a kind of disenfranchisement no less serious than not being able to cast a ballot.[8]

---

[7] Michael Wines, "Senators Approve a Bill that Eases Voter Registration," *The New York Times*, March 18, 1993.

[8] *Congressional Record* 148, no. 136, October 16, 2002. Senate, page S10488–S10516. From the Congressional Record Online through the Government Printing Office <www.gpo.gov>.

On some level, voter-fraud protections are a bipartisan issue. However, it was particularly easy for Republicans to endorse solutions that would burden demographic groups that traditionally vote Democratic. For this reason, these reforms were a hard sell to those on the other side of the aisle.

At that same time, Democratic legislators worked to expand registration in ways that caused discomfort for their Republican counterparts. For example, Representatives Menendez of New Jersey, DeLauro of Connecticut, and Johnson of Texas put together an amendment to allow second language voting and to guarantee the continuation of the motor voter program. On this point, Representative Joseph Crowley noted:

> In my district, the Seventh District of New York, there are native speakers of over 70 languages. These hard working American citizens are just as entitled to a vote as everyone else, and should not be intimidated by the electoral process—something every American should hold dear.[9]

Since making voting more accessible to voters who primarily speak languages other than English would likely draw disproportionately on Democratic constituencies, it is not surprising that the amendment failed to emerge from the Republican-controlled House Committee on Rules.

Another fight arose over a Republican effort to add a provision requiring new voters to put either their driver's license number or the last four digits of their social security number on their voter registration form. Democrats argued that this requirement would burden those without a driver's license, typically the poor. Congressman Charlie Gonzalez, who chaired the Hispanic Caucus's Civil Rights Task Force, voted against the bill because of the implications of the provision:

> The major obstacle to Latino voters in this bill is the inclusion of a new voter identification requirement. This will be the first time in contemporary election law history that an identification requirement is federally mandated. [. . .] the requirements in this conference report would particularly disenfranchise low income people, especially women and the elderly, who, for example, live in multi-person households and are less likely to drive, and therefore do not possess a driver's license, do not receive a utility bill in their name and may not have any of the other forms of identification listed in the bill.[10]

The Democratic emphasis on enfranchisement and the Republican focus on increasing election security are clearly related to the electoral implications of each set of reforms. During the debate on HAVA, Congress was closely divided. The Republicans held a slight 221 to 212 lead in the House, and the Democratic Senate majority rested on a razor thin margin of 50 Democrats, 49 Republicans, and 1 independent (Jim Jeffords, who defected from the Republicans in May 2001). Hence all the legislation passed was of necessity a compromise between these two competing concepts of the best way to improve the election system.

Compromise and Final Action

Despite the potential for partisan disagreement, HAVA passed the House relatively quickly, and without a major fight. Though there were some initial calls by House Republicans to add new safeguards against voter fraud, the bill found overwhelming support in the House, passing less than a month after its introduction by a vote of 362 to 63.[11] The reception of HAVA in the Senate, however, was very different.

The bill's sponsors, Senator Dodd and his fellow Democrats, were pressured by voting and civil rights special interests to drop many of the voter-fraud provisions included in the House bill, and

---

[9] "Help America Vote Act of 2001," 2002, <http://thomas.loc.gov/cgi-bin/query/D?r107:13:./temp/~r107LmDLHf::>.

[10] Congressman Gonzalez, *Congressional Record*, October 11, 2002.

[11] Much of the summary of legislative action and compromise in this section is informed by "New Voting Standards Enacted," *CQ Almanac* (2002): 14-3–14-6.

championed by Senate Republicans. Early Senate floor action in February 2002 stumbled over how first-time voters would have to prove their identities. Democratic Senator Schumer proposed an amendment that would have relaxed the demand on new voters, only requiring them to provide a signature that could be matched against other government records in order to vote. Republican Senator Bond, the main advocate for antifraud provisions in the Senate, attempted to kill the amendment, but the vote failed 46 to 51. Thereafter Republicans dug in for a fight. During the last days of February and the first days of March, they first threatened and then executed a filibuster on the legislation, an effort that withstood two attempts to invoke cloture by votes of 49 to 39 and 51 to 44. Frustrated, Senate Democrats moved on to other legislative business.

Three weeks later, after intense closed-door negotiations, a compromise emerged. Senate Democrats agreed to require some form of identification for first time voters, but persuaded Republicans to allow a variety of options that would count as "identification," such as a driver's license, canceled government issued check, or utility bill. Further, voters would be allowed to cast provisional ballots if they failed to provide identification. These votes could be counted later if eligibility was subsequently proven. Democrats, as a concession to Republicans, dropped a proposal to allow individuals to sue over violations of the election standards set out in HAVA.

This package was proposed as a unanimous consent agreement on March 22, 2002. Two additional weeks of floor action and miscellaneous amendment activity resulted in additional modifications, including the removal of a provision requiring election officials to inform voters if their provisional ballots were counted. The final Senate bill (S. 565) was then substituted for the House version (H.R. 3295), and passed with only one member in opposition.

The fight, however, was not over. Because the House and Senate versions of the bill were not identical, the chambers arranged for a conference committee to consider the legislation. Democrats from both chambers tried to use the conference as a vehicle for relaxing antifraud provisions. However, at the continued insistence of Senator Bond, and with the support of both House and Senate Republicans, the antifraud "identification" requirements agreed to in the Senate remained intact. On October 10, nearly six months after the Senate passed its version of the legislation, the House adopted the final bill by a vote of 357 to 48. The Senate followed suit six days later, with only two no votes. These were cast by Senators Schumer and Clinton, who were outspoken in their opposition to having voters show identification, and believed the bill would contract rather than stimulate turnout.[12]

As he signed the bill into law on October 29, 2002, President George W. Bush noted: "Every registered voter deserves to have confidence that the system is fair and elections are honest, that every vote is recorded, and that the rules are consistently applied. The legislation I sign today will add to the nation's confidence."[13]

Final Form: Provisions and Programs

The bill, as signed into law, made sweeping changes to the electoral process. First, and foremost, it mandated the replacement of old punch card and lever voting systems like those used in Florida in 2000. A clear preference was indicated for electronic machines as they were thought to reduce voter errors and to ensure that every ballot counted.

HAVA also created the Election Assistance Commission (EAC) to "assist the states regarding HAVA compliance and to distribute HAVA funds to the states."[14] The EAC was to be composed of four commissioners, no more than two from any political party. The commissioners were to be appointed by the president and confirmed by the Senate. This commission was charged with monitoring

---

[12] Pear, Robert, "The 2002 Campaign: Ballot Overhaul; Congress Passes Bill to Clean Up Election System," *The New York Times*, October 17 2002, sec. A; National Desk: 1.

[13] "Washington in Brief," *Washington Post,* October 30 2002, sec. A SECTION: A02.

[14] "Help America Vote Act," 2009. <http://www.eac.gov/about/help-america-vote-act>.

voting procedures and operating a voting system certification program, as well as overseeing the use of HAVA funds and reporting annually to Congress.

HAVA authorized several grants to provide money to states for the changes required, including $20 million for voting machines and technology, $30 million for the establishment of the EAC itself, $5 million to encourage college students to work as poll workers, and $10 million for testing voting equipment.[15] This allocation was to jumpstart HAVA. However, to receive funding, states were required to meet minimal equipment standards.

HAVA mandated the development of a system of provisional balloting allowing those not on voting rolls to cast a ballot. The state would later decide eligibility and discard votes if the voter was deemed ineligible. This procedure allowed nearly 800,000 additional votes to be cast in the 2006 election. Only 20 percent were ultimately rejected.[16]

The legislation, at its core, created a new set of election standards intended to be state of the art for fair elections. HAVA provisions required voters to be able to correct any errors privately, and set a maximum error rate for states, to be determined by the EAC. Further, the law required uniform statewide registration lists and multilingual accessibility, and incorporated the hotly debated fraud-protection provision requiring identification for first-time voters that register by mail.

The law anticipated that reform would be accomplished through voter education as well as procedural change. Accordingly, HAVA provided money for educating voters on voting rules and their rights and required signs at polling places explaining the technology in use and the rules of voting. It also authorized funds for educating poll workers on voting procedures and mandated telephone hotlines for voters to report fraud and to request information on registration and polling locations. Finally, HAVA paid special attention to disabled voters, providing assistance for them to reach polling places and insisting that poll workers have the training necessary to help the disabled cast votes successfully.[17]

The enforcement of these provisions was left to states, but HAVA provided an annual allocation of funds for them to carry out the law's provisions. All complaints were to go to the states first. If they were not resolved in 90 days, the Justice Department was authorized to intervene and file civil action against states that failed to meet these provisions. Due to the Senate compromise however, individuals were prohibited from suing the state directly.

Implementation of HAVA

Since passing in 2002, HAVA has had mixed results. For example, election officials in 2004 were not sure how to process provisional ballots. According to Ohio's Secretary of State J. Kenneth Blackwell, "the provisional ballots wouldn't be counted until 11 days after the election. Even then, county election boards composed of two Democrats and two Republicans had little guidance on which ballots to count—and allowing a vote to be counted would have required the agreement of three of the four board members."[18]

Voting machines appeared to be a proven technology when HAVA was passed, but in 2005 HAVA's Pennsylvania administrator said that voting machines were not passing federal standards, and states would not be able to purchase any until they did so.[19] To qualify, voting machines were to

---

[15] Much of the summary of legislative action and compromise in this section is informed by "New Voting Standards Enacted," *CQ Almanac* (2002): 14-3–14-6.

[16] Advancement Project, "Provisional Voting: Fail-Safe Voting or Trapdoor to Disenfranchisement," Advancement Project (2008): 1–5.

[17] "Help America Vote Act," 2009, <http://www.eac.gov/about/help-america-vote-act>.

[18] Nancy Petersen and *Inquirer* staff writer, "Mandate to Buy Voting Machines Proving Elusive," *Philadelphia Inquirer*, October 5 2005: B02.

[19] "Help America Vote," *The Washington Post,* November 10, 2004.

meet three criteria. First, the votes marked by a voter must be verified by the voter before they are cast. Second, upon review, the voter must have the opportunity to edit their ballot before it is cast. Lastly, the machine must tell the voter if they have made an error, such as over voting (i.e., voting for too many candidates in a given race).[20] Originally, legislators planned to install voting machines across the nation with all deliberate speed. However, by 2009, no voting machines had been approved for general use by the EAC.

Voter-education programs were to be mounted only after voting machines were selected.[21] Once passed, HAVA doled out money to states, but left most of the allocation to state legislatures. This decision opened implementation to additional argumentation, particularly over the price tags on alternative machines. For example, in New York, complaints arose when the legislature considered a "full-faced ballot" that would make its machines more expensive than typical machines.[22] Thus, while states received HAVA funds, they found it difficult to use them for their intended purposes, as they became increasingly uncertain what voting machine technologies to select. This, in term, slowed the implementation of voter education programs.

Conclusion

In the wake of the 2000 election debacle, HAVA was a federal response to the wide spread demand for election reform. HAVA set out to standardize the election process across the nation by creating the Elections Assistance Commission and requiring the modernization of voting methods. But what began as a bipartisan mission was sidetracked over issues that were, at least in part, driven by partisan electoral concerns. Democratic efforts to expand registration and Republican efforts to safeguard the system against voter fraud were motivated in part by a desire for a healthy representative democracy. But the side effects of these reforms, the potential emergence of new Democrat-leaning voters, also colored the way each party hoped to craft new electoral processes.

Since the passage of HAVA, the most notable voting legislation that has passed was the renewal of the Voting Rights Act in 2006. Here Congress renewed several of the act's provisions that were due for expiration including the availability of second language voting and extra oversight of southern states with a history of discriminatory polling practices. The legislation went through easily, passing the Senate with a vote of 98–0.[23]

Numerous pieces of legislation dealing with voting integrity have been proposed since the passage of HAVA. Voter verification was brought before the 108th Congress and subsequent sessions, in the form of an amendment to HAVA. Voter-verification legislation would require that there is a paper record of every vote and that this record be verifiable by the voter before the ballot is cast. Though verified voting has not been legislated at the national level, verified voting procedures have been legislated in 31 states.[24]

HAVA is not a perfect solution to the problems that it set out to address. However, partisan fighting and implementation problems aside, it represents a commitment on the part of the federal government, and by the majority of both parties in Congress, to improve the way America counts the votes of its citizens. A modest step, perhaps, but a step nonetheless.

---

[20] "Help America Vote Act of 2001," 2002, <http://thomas.loc.gov/cgi-bin/query/D?r107:13:./temp/ ~r107LmDLHf::>.

[21] "Help America Vote," *The Washington Post,* November 10 2004.

[22] "While We Weren't Looking," *The New York Times,* November 13 2005, sec. 14LI; Long Island Weekly Desk: 15.

[23] Laurie Kellman, "Voting Rights Bill Goes to Bush," *The Boston Globe*, July 21, 2006.

[24] Kibrick, Robert, "Voter-Verified Paper Record Legislation," 2009, <http://www.verifiedvoting.org/ article. php?list= type&type=13>.

Chapter 3

California's HAVA Odyssey

Keith W. Smith[1]

Following the 2000 presidential election, nearly everyone agreed that there was a problem with elections in the United States. However, there was little consensus about what, exactly, the problem was. Some argued that it was low voter turnout—just 50 percent of the voting age population (54 percent of the voting eligible population) cast a ballot for president.[2] Others suggested the problem was poor ballot designs, such as Palm Beach County's "butterfly" ballot.[3] Some pointed to the deleterious effects of the partisan control of election administration.[4] Others focused on the voting technology, specifically the use of prescored punch-card machines and the potential for hanging chads. Still others maintained that there was too much potential for voter fraud. Finally, some emphasized the violations of voters' civil rights.

The way a public policy problem is defined is never neutral; a definition points to a set of appropriate solutions and rules out others.[5] This chapter explores how different problem definitions led to dramatically different electoral reform efforts in California. From 2000 to mid-2003, election reform in California was guided by a belief that there were problems with (a) the machines used, and (b) the ways in which elections were administered. The reform efforts were also motivated by a concern about access to elections, specifically about the ways in which voting technologies affected minority voters. In late 2003, however, the problem definition changed and became focused almost exclusively

---

[1] Department of Political Science, University of the Pacific.

[2] Michael McDonald, "2000 General Election Turnout Rates," United States Election Project, George Mason University, <http://elections.gmu.edu/Turnout_2000G.html>.

[3] Jonathan N. Wand, Kenneth W. Shotts, Jasjeet S. Sekhon, Walter R. Mebane, Jr., Michael C. Herron, and Henry E. Brady, "The Butterfly Did It: Aberrant Vote for Buchanan in Palm Beach County, Florida," *American Political Science Review* 95 (2001): 793–810. See also, Richard G. Niemi and Paul S. Herrnson, "Beyond the Butterfly: The Complexity of U.S. Ballots," *Perspectives on Politics* 1 (2003): 317–26.

[4] See Commission on Federal Election Reform, *Building Confidence in U.S. Elections*, Center for Democracy and Election Management, American University, September 2005, for a review of many of these issues. See also the many reports from the AEI-Brookings Elections Reform Project (<http://www.election reformproject.org>) and the CalTech/MIT Voting Technology Project.

[5] Deborah Stone, *Policy Paradox: The Art of Political Decision Making*, revised edition (New York, N.Y.: Norton, 2002).

on the perceived threat that direct recording electronic (DRE) machines represented to the accuracy of California elections. This chapter explores this shift and the challenge of large reform efforts when a significant number of actors are involved.

While the focus of this chapter is predominantly on post-Help America Vote Act (HAVA) actions, California's attempts to change the administration of elections began two years before this federal legislation passed. Table 1 presents a timeline of the major HAVA-related events in California. The November 2000 presidential election saw the first use of DRE voting machines in California. The timeline ends with December 2009, the expected completion date of the state's voter registration database. As in many policy areas, California was a policy innovator in election reform, and so it is not surprising that the state's efforts began before the federal government became involved.

Pre-HAVA Efforts

Alvarez and Hall identify three frames for election reform after the 2000 presidential election.[6] The first frame focuses on the problem of election administration. Here deficiencies in how elections are administered are assumed to have affected the potential outcome of the election. The second frame focuses on voting as a civil right—because of the voting technologies used in the election, certain segments of the voting public (e.g., ethnic minorities and disabled voters) are more likely not to have their votes count than are others. The third frame focuses on the potential for fraud in elections. Thus it is hypothesized that because the procedures governing the election are faulty, because some eligible voters are denied their votes, or because people vote who should not have done, the outcome of the election might not reflect the true preference of the electorate.

California's pre-HAVA voting reforms were a response to the first two policy frames of election reform: the problem of election administration and the violation of voters' civil rights. These reform efforts were spurred by a set of contemporaneous but unconnected events. The first was a lawsuit challenging the constitutionality of allowing some counties to use prescored, punch-card (PPC) machines to conduct elections while others did not. The second was a legislative effort to keep the problems experienced in Florida from happening in California. The end goal of both initiatives was the same—to replace California's older voting machines with more modern technologies.

In April 2001, the American Civil Liberties Union of Southern California filed suit in federal district court on behalf of Common Cause, the Southwest Voter Registration Education Project, the Southern Christian Leadership Conference of Greater Los Angeles, the Chicano Federation of San Diego, the AFL-CIO, and eight individual voters.[7] The lawsuit, known as *Common Cause v. Jones*, sought to ensure that every voter in California's elections had an equal chance of her vote being counted in the final tally, regardless of where her ballot was cast in the state. The plaintiffs hoped to force the secretary of state (SOS) to decertify the PPC machines used by nine counties.[8] These were

---

[6] R. Michael Alvarez and Thad E. Hall, *Electronic Elections: The Perils and Promise of Digital Democracy* (Princeton, N.J.: Princeton University Press, 2008). See esp. Chapter 1.

[7] *Common Cause et al., v. Bill Jones*, 213 F. Supp. 2d 1106 (C.D. Cal 2002). See also Henry Weinstein, "Suit Seeks Uniformity in State's Vote Counting," *The Los Angeles Times* April 18, 2001, A1, A15. The AFL-CIO retained its own legal representation in the case.

[8] The nine counties were Alameda, Los Angeles, Mendocino, Sacramento, San Bernardino, San Diego, Santa Clara, Shasta, and Solano. A second goal, which did not receive as much press coverage, was to force the Secretary of State to create uniform recount procedures for the entire state.

Table 1. Major HAVA-Related Events

Year	Month	Event
2000	Nov.	Presidential election; Riverside County first in nation to use direct recording electronic (DRE) machines
2001	Apr.	*Common Cause v. Jones* filed in Los Angeles
	Sept.	Secretary of State (SOS) Bill Jones decertifies prescored punch-card machines
2002	Mar.	Prop. 41 (Shelley-Hertzberg Act) passed by California voters
	Oct.	Help America Vote Act (HAVA) becomes law
	Nov.	Statewide election; Kevin Shelley elected SOS
2003	Feb.	SOS Shelley convenes Ad Hoc Touch Screen Task Force
	May	Ad Hoc Touch Screen Task Force publishes recommendations
	Sept.	SOS Shelley publishes *My Vote Counts*; special election temporarily halted by Ninth Circuit Court
	Nov.	Special election to recall Gov. Davis; SOS Shelley announces requirements for Voter Verified Paper Audit Trail (VVPAT)
2004	Mar.	Presidential primary; Alameda, San Diego counties report problems with Diebold DRE machines
	Apr.	SOS Shelley decertifies Diebold DRE machines
	June	SOS Shelley begins recertification of Diebold machines
	Nov.	Presidential election
	Dec.	State Auditor releases audit critical of SOS's HAVA implementation; U.S. Election Assistance Commission calls for audit
2005	Feb.	SOS Shelley resigns

	Mar.	Gov. Schwarzenegger appoints Bruce McPherson SOS
	Aug.	SOS McPherson certifies Automark machines—first certified to meet Jan. 2006 HAVA deadline
	Oct.	SOS McPherson announces new voting machine certification criteria
	Nov.	Memorandum of Agreement with Justice Department about VoteCal system issued
	Dec.	U.S. Office of Inspector General finds $3.86 million in improper HAVA spending by SOS Shelley
2006	Jan.	**Statutory deadline for state compliance with all HAVA requirements**
	June	Statewide primary—Seven counties out of compliance with HAVA requirements
	Oct.	EAC issues final ruling on repayment of CA HAVA funds
	Nov.	Election; all counties in compliance with HAVA requirements; Deborah Bowen elected SOS
2007	Mar.	Preliminary draft of top-to-bottom review circulated for public comment
	July	Top-to-bottom review published; SOS Bowen decertifies DRE machines save for use by disabled voters
	Dec.	VoteCal request for proposals published
2008	Feb.	Presidential primary
	June	State primary
	Nov.	Presidential election
2009	Dec.	Expected deployment date for VoteCal system

counties employing the same kind of voting machines that had stirred controversy during the 2000 election in Florida.[9]

In making their arguments, the *Common Cause* plaintiffs sought to extend the equal protection argument advanced in the U.S. Supreme Court's *Bush v. Gore* ruling.[10] There the Supreme Court held that because elections officials used different criteria for what constituted a vote across counties in Florida, a vote counted in one county might not have been counted in another. As a result, voters did not have an equal chance to have their votes counted. The lack of uniform recount procedures, therefore, violated voters' equal protection rights.[11]

The *Common Cause* plaintiffs argued that the use of different voting machines—particularly the PPC machines—by some counties similarly violated voters' equal protection rights. Following the 2000 election, several political science and policy groups demonstrated that voters using the PPC machines were several times more likely to make errors that would disqualify their ballots than voters using other kinds of machines.[12] The different error rates attributed to the type of machine used meant that voters were not equally likely to have their votes counted.[13] The problem was exacerbated as the counties using the PPC machines tended to have large minority voting populations, and the counties using less error-prone technologies tended to have smaller minority populations. The use of the PPC machines, the plaintiffs argued, meant "that a disproportionate number of votes in some counties are not counted at all, and that a disproportionate number of African-American, Latino, and Asian-American voters in the state do not have their votes counted at all."[14]

Secretary of State Bill Jones, though forced to contest the lawsuit, embraced it. He believed that the lawsuit echoed calls for reform he had made prior to the November election.[15] Even the county

---

[9] Specifically, the counties used the Votomatic and Pollstar machines. Voters using these machines received a ballot (an IBM-style computer card with prescored boxes) that was then inserted into a machine that had the ballot choices (offices, candidates, and propositions) for that district attached to it. Voters turned through the pages on the machine, exposing different columns of boxes, or chads, to punch out with a stylus.

This style of voting machine, especially the Votomatic, was prone to a number of errors. Voters frequently had trouble aligning their ballots in the machines so that the boxes matched the assigned candidates. Confusing ballot designs (e.g., the butterfly ballot) meant that voters sometimes voted for too many candidates in a contest or no candidate at all. Failure to fully punch out and remove the chad (the infamous hanging chad) meant that the vote might not be counted (i.e., processed by the machine).

[10] 531 U.S. 98 (2000).

[11] See Edmund S. Sauer, "'Arbitrary and Disparate' Obstacles to Democracy: The Equal Protection Implications of *Bush v. Gore* on Election Administration," *Journal of Law and Politics* 19 (Summer 2003): 299–344.

[12] See Brady, Buchler, Jarvis, and McNulty, *op. cit.*, and the CalTech/MIT Voting Technology Project, *Residual Votes Attributable to Technology: An Assessment of the Reliability of Existing Voting Technologies*, VTP Working Paper #2 (March 2001), <http://vote.caltech.edu/drupal/files/working_paper/vtp_wp2.pdf>. Even before the 2000 presidential election, numerous problems had been documented with these machines. See especially, Roy G. Saltman. *The History and Politics of Voting Technology* (New York, N.Y.: Palgrave MacMillan, 2006).

A second type of punch card system—Datavote—differed from the Votomatic and Pollstar machines, however, in two key ways. First, voters using the Datavote machine used a hole-punch device to mark the ballots instead of a stylus, significantly reducing the likelihood of a voting error due to a hanging chad. Second, the Datavote ballot had the candidates and propositions printed directly on it, lessening the likelihood of errors due to misaligned ballots.

[13] In their initial filing, the *Common Cause* plaintiffs alleged that in the November 2000 election, 53.4 percent of voters statewide used prescored punch card machines. Yet ballots cast using prescored punch card machines accounted for 74.8 percent of all ballots that did not register a vote for the president of the United States. Prescored punch card machines resulted in an average combined overvote (the machine reading more than one vote and thus disqualifying that vote) and undervote (the failure of the machine reading the punch card to read any vote) rate of 2.23 percent. The combined overvote and undervote, herein referred to as the "error rate," for these machines is more than double the error rate of any other type of machine or system used in California (4).

[14] *Ibid.*, 4.

[15] Weinstein, *op. cit.*

registrars—who were responsible for purchasing and deploying the machines—did not dispute the lawsuit's central claims. Los Angeles County Registrar-Recorder Conney McCormack stated, "Their facts are correct. The remedy is the rub."[16] The case was settled after Secretary of State Jones decertified the PPC machines on September 18, 2001. The decertification order initially required the nine counties to replace over 65,000 machines by January 2006, though the conversion date was later advanced by the Court to March 2004.[17]

Many in California had been disturbed by the prospect of Florida's mechanical problems being replicated in California because it used the same type of machines.[18] Before the *Common Cause* suit had been filed, Assembly Speaker Robert Hertzberg introduced AB 56 on December 4, 2000, to help counties replace their voting machines. As introduced, AB 56 would have made $300 million in state bond funds available to counties through matching grants. The state would provide $3 subsidy to match every $1 spent by a county on new voting machines. AB 56 was passed as the Voting Modernization Bond Act of 2002 (the Shelley-Hertzberg Act) and placed before voters in March 2002 as Proposition 41. Prop. 41 reduced the total amount of funding to $200 million (of which $195 million would be made available to counties) but retained the matching grant formula. The promise of Proposition 41 funds, and the potential for additional federal funds through what would become HAVA, made the September decertification order easier for counties to swallow. Prop. 41 passed with 51.6 percent of the vote.

To disburse the funds to counties, Prop. 41 created the independent Voting Modernization Board (VMB), composed of two members appointed by the secretary of state and three appointed by the governor. The VMB was given authority to develop the funding allocations for counties (based on the number of eligible, registered, and actual voters) and to evaluate county plans for purchasing new machines.[19] Applications from counties began arriving shortly after the VMB released its guidelines in late July (with a deadline of September 3), and counties began receiving Prop. 41 funds in December 2002. (As of spring 2010, funds are still being dispersed).

Thus, even before the federal government passed the Help America Voter Act in October 2002, California was moving to replace its punch-card voting machines. Not only were the problematic machines ordered out of service by March 2004, but California voters committed up to $300 million in county and state funds for upgrading the state's voting technology (the federal government would commit an additional $350 million to California's efforts through HAVA).

---

[16] *Ibid.* Los Angeles was the largest county using the PPC machines. At the time, Registrar-Recorder McCormack estimated that replacing the voting machines in Los Angeles County alone would cost $100 million.

[17] The move to the March 2004 date was opposed by Secretary of State Jones, who argued that counties would be forced to purchase intermediate voting systems since the hoped-for DRE machines would not be ready until 2005.

The issues raised in *Common Cause v. Jones* were revisited when the Southwest Voter Registration Education Project and the Southern Christian Leadership Conference filed suit to halt the 2003 recall election (*Southwest Voter Registration Education Project v. Kevin Shelley*, 278 F. Supp. 1131 (C.D. Cal. 2003)). Again, the issue was the use of prescored, punch-card machines by some counties, in particular Los Angeles County, which had not yet replaced their voting machines. In response to this lawsuit, the federal Ninth Circuit Court of Appeals temporarily halted the 2003 special election over the equal protection concerns, though it later ruled that the election could go forward.

[18] Claudia Buck, "The Florida Backlash," *California Journal*, January 1, 2001.

[19] The allocations ranged from a low of $8,115 for Alpine County to a high of $49,636,590 for Los Angeles County. See Appendix A of the Voting Modernization Board's Statement of Plans and Projects for a complete listing of the expected county allocations (<http://www.sos.ca.gov/elections/vma/pdf/vem/plansandprojects.pdf>).

Implementing HAVA

When Congress passed the Help America Vote Act, it required states to make a number of changes to their electoral systems by January 2006 (see Chapter 2 in this volume for a full description of these requirements). As shown in Table 2, these changes covered a broad spectrum of issues, but the most frequently noted was the requirement to replace all punch-card voting machines with more technologically advanced machines.

In order to receive the federal funds, each state—under the direction of its chief elections officer (in California, the secretary of state)—had to develop and submit a plan to the newly created U.S. Election Assistance Commission detailing how it would implement HAVA requirements. The act provided some guidance for how the state plan should be created. For example, the two largest electoral jurisdictions had to be represented on the planning committee and the plan had to address 13 specific policy areas (e.g., how the state would provide for voter education). On the other hand, the act provided broad discretion (and relatively little guidance) for how states actually chose to spend the federal funds.

By placing responsibility for developing and implementing the state plan in the hands of the secretary of state, HAVA altered the balance of power in California elections administration, albeit qualitatively rather than quantitatively. HAVA gave the secretary agenda-setting authority in an area traditionally dominated by other actors.

In California elections are not the sole responsibility of any one official; they are a cooperative effort between the secretary of state (SOS),[20] 58 separate county registrars of voters,[21] and, for some elections, city officials. Historically, local officials, not the secretary, have been the focal point for elections administration. Local officials make the bulk of decisions affecting who does what, when and how on Election Day. County officials, for example, are responsible for registering and notifying voters of an upcoming election; designing and printing ballots; recruiting, training, and deploying poll workers; and counting ballots cast.[22] In contrast, the secretary certifies candidates for state and federal office, certifies ballot propositions, prepares voting guides for all statewide elections, and compiles and certifies final county vote totals after an election has taken place.

In addition, the secretary is responsible for setting the guidelines under which state elections take place. For example, only voting machines certified by the secretary may be used in an election in California. The secretary is also responsible for setting the procedures governing the training of poll workers, the tabulation of votes, and any necessary recount processes. The secretary ensures that the state's (and nation's) election laws and campaign finance disclosure laws are enforced. Following HAVA's passage, the secretary took a much more active role in exercising its regulatory responsibili-

---

[20] The secretary of state is a partisan office. Candidates from different political parties contest the office, and the secretary is elected on a statewide basis to a four-year term. The fact that the secretary is an elected official means that whoever becomes the secretary campaigns on a platform of issues related to election administration and once in office, like other elected officials, the attempts to follow through on his or her campaign promises. Kevin Shelley, who was elected secretary in 2002, for example, campaigned on a platform of implementing Proposition 41 (a $200 million state program to replace voting machines described herein), allowing voters to register up to Election Day, promoting the use of touch-screen machines, and increasing voter turnout. Debra Bowen, who was elected secretary in 2006, campaigned on a platform critical of the state's process for certifying electronic voting machines and was opposed to requiring photo identification in order to cast a ballot.

[21] Like the secretary of state, most county registrars wear many hats. The registrar may also be the county recorder, clerk, assessor, and auditor. While 45 counties choose their registrar through nonpartisan elections, the remaining 13 counties—including the large counties of Los Angeles, San Diego, San Bernardino, Riverside, Santa Clara, and Alameda—allow the county board of supervisors to appoint the registrar.

[22] Additionally, a registrar's responsibilities include: determining district boundaries for county offices; designing and printing supplemental information guides; organizing election precincts; purchasing, storing, maintaining, and deploying voting machines; and transmitting election results to the secretary of the state.

Table 2. Major HAVA Requirements with Deadlines

HAVA Mandatory Requirements	Effective Date
State voting systems must meet certain requirements, including the following:	January 1, 2006
• Permit voters to verify their votes before their ballots are cast.	
• Allow voters to change their ballot or correct any error before their ballots are cast.	
• Produce a permanent paper record for audit and recount.	
• Be accessible for individuals with disabilities.	
• Provide alternate language accessibility.	
• Comply with Federal Election Commission error rate standards.	
States must implement a single, uniform, official, centralized, interactive, and computerized statewide voter registration list that is defined, maintained, and administered at the state level.	January 1, 2006
States or local elections officials must do the following:	January 1, 2004
• Permit eligible individuals to cast provisional ballots and have free access to a system that will inform them whether their votes were counted and, if not counted, the reasons why.	
• Require individuals to meet certain identification requirements if they register to vote for the first time in a state or jurisdiction by mail.	
• Ensure the public posting of certain voting information at each polling place on the day of each federal election.	

Note: HAVA initially required states to implement the statewide voter registration database by January 1, 2004, but states could receive a waiver postponing the effective date until 2006. California applied for and received such a waiver.

Source: Bureau of State Audits, California State Auditor, *Office of the Secretary of State: Clear and Appropriate Direction Is Lacking in Its Implementation of the Federal Help America Vote Act*, 2004-139, December 2004, Table 1.

ties.[23] Where the secretary may have deferred to counties to make decisions about how voters would cast their ballots before HAVA, after HAVA the office began to prescribe such details.

The tradition of shared responsibility for administering elections, however, created the potential for conflict and delay for would-be elections reformers. One of the key lessons of implementation studies is that the more veto points in a decision process, the less likely an action will be taken.[24] For example, while HAVA placed responsibility for ensuring that a state's punch-card voting machines were replaced in the secretary of state's hands, county registrars (with the blessing of their county board) were responsible for the actual purchase and deployment of the machines. Counties could not

[23] Additionally, after HAVA was enacted, the SOS became responsible for maintaining a statewide database of registered voters—a responsibility previously left to the individual country registrars.

[24] *C.f.* Jeffrey L. Pressman and Aaron Wildavsky, *Implementation: How Great Expectations in Washington Are Dashed in Oakland*, 3d ed. (Berkeley, Calif.: University of California Press, 1984).

purchase the machines, though, until (a) the secretary certified them for use in California elections—based on the recommendations of several advisory committees—and (b) either the Voting Modernization Board released the Prop. 41 funds or the secretary released the HAVA funds to the counties.

Secretary of State Kevin Shelley appointed a 24-member committee, the California State Plan Advisory Committee, to develop California's plan on May 1, 2003.[25] Only the registrars from Los Angeles, Orange, and Shasta counties were appointed to the committee. Thus registrars were but 12.5 percent of the membership of this committee, or about half the average representation of registrars on such committees nationally.[26] A strong labor advocate, Secretary Shelley included six labor-group representatives on the committee. Five of the committee members represented California's major ethnic minority groups. The remaining members were drawn from groups representing other major interests in California, including the League of Women Voters, students, gay-rights groups, advocates for the blind and disabled, an elections law firm, and one academic.[27]

The advisory committee quickly held a series of public hearings throughout the state, and a draft of the state plan was published in mid June. The final version, entitled *My Vote Counts: California's Plan for Voting in the 21st Century*, was published in September. Given the passage of Prop. 41, and the $200 million in state funds to replace voting machines made available through it (as well as the committee membership), it is perhaps not surprising that California's HAVA plan focused more on "restoring confidence in the integrity of the voting process and increasing the participation of informed voters" than on replacing outdated voting machines.[28] The state plan estimated that just $42.6 million to $70 million (12 to 20 percent) in HAVA funds would be used to assist counties replacing their voting machines.[29] The remainder of the money would be spent on other activities, primarily voter education (up to $45 million), election official education (up to $45 million), and poll-worker education (up to $45 million).[30]

My Vote Counts continued what would become a long dialogue regarding the use of direct recording electronic machines in California. California's early efforts at reform had pushed the state toward direct recording electronic (DRE) machines.[31] In resolving *Common Cause v. Jones*, the court nearly

---

[25] California Secretary of State Kevin Shelley, "Secretary of State Kevin Shelley Announces Members of State Plan Advisory Committee to Help Implement the 'Help America Vote Act,'" News Release KS03:024, May 1, 2003.

[26] R. Michael Alvarez and Thad E. Hall, "Rational and Pluralistic Approaches to HAVA Implementation: The Cases of California and Georgia," *Publius* 4 (2009): 559–77.

Shasta's (one of California's smaller counties) registrar was included by virtue of being chair of the California Association of Clerks and Elections Officials.

[27] In addition to the county registrars, the groups represented were: the National Association for the Advancement of Colored People; Chinese Affirmative Action; the League of Women Voters of California; United Farm Workers of America, AFL-CIO; the California Labor Federation, AFL-CIO; the Organization of Los Angeles Workers; the National Association of Women Business Owners; Equality California (a lesbian, gay, bisexual, and transgender advocacy group); the California State Student Association; Exploding Myths, Inc. (an advocacy group for people with disabilities); Protection & Advocacy, Inc. (another disability advocacy group); the National Association of Latino Elected and Appointed Officials; the Asian Pacific American Legal Center; the Mexican American Legal Defense and Educational Fund; the Los Angeles County Federation of Labor, AFL-CIO; the California Council of the Blind; the State Building and Construction Trades Council, AFL-CIO; Coalition for a Living Wage (a labor group); the McKay Foundation; and the CalTech/MIT Voting Technology Project.

[28] *My Vote Counts: California's Plan for Voting in the 21st Century*, September 2003, 1.

[29] *Ibid.*, 25.

[30] *Ibid.*, 26.

[31] DRE machines presented voters with a computerized version of the ballot. Voters indicated their choice by touching the computer screen and were given the option of reviewing their choices before their votes were added to the tally in the machine's memory. DRE machines had already been used in Riverside County in the 2000 elections. Riverside County was the first county in the nation to use DRE machines for national and state elections.

ordered the use of DRE machines to replace the PPC machines. Much of the discussion surrounding Prop. 41 was predicated on the promise of DREs. Finally, disabled advocates saw DREs as a way for their constituents to participate fully in the electoral process.[32]

There is a clear preference for DRE machines in the state plan. The plan declares: "[T]he Secretary of State . . . will . . . support, promote and encourage the use of direct recording electronic (DRE/touchscreen) voting systems, at polling places . . . [and] expeditiously certify new DRE voting systems that are compliant with state and federal law."[33] The plan also intimates the decertification of paper-ballot systems (i.e., punch-card and optical scan), which "are difficult to operate, which are prone to error with respect to voters with disabilities, or which do not provide equal access to the ballot."[34]

Narrowing the Focus to DRE Machines

California's remaining efforts to implement the Help America Vote Act, Prop. 41, and the district court order were motivated by the third electoral reform frame: the potential for fraud to alter election outcomes, specifically because of the machines used to record votes. In early 2003, critics of direct recording electronic machines began to challenge the technology's efficacy. Led by a number computer scientists, such as Professor David Dill of Stanford University, and joined by the California Voter Foundation, these critics argued the machines "pose an unacceptable risk that errors or deliberate election rigging will go undetected, since they do not provide a way for voters to verify independently that the machine correctly records and counts the votes they have cast."[35] The anti-DRE movement quickly gained traction in California.

In response to these concerns, at the same time that the advisory committee began its work on the state's HAVA plan, Secretary Shelley convened an Ad Hoc Touch Screen Task Force to study the effectiveness and security of DRE machines. The focus of the task force was more technical than political, though Professor David Dill was appointed as a member.[36] Its 10 members were charged with addressing four sets of questions:

> (1) *Computer Security*: Whether there is evidence of a security issue with DRE voting systems and, if so, the nature and probability of the security issue; (2) *Administrative Security*: Whether the existing federal, state and local tests are adequate, and whether current security protocols and processes used by DRE vendors are adequate; (3) *Voter Confidence*: How to ensure voter confidence in our voting systems and elections; and (4) *Voter Verification*: Whether verification by voters is useful or not; whether verification by voters is necessary or not?[37]

In evaluating these technical questions, however, the task force had to balance a number of politically sensitive considerations. First, local elections officials need systems that are easy to administer.

---

[32] At about the same time as the Shelley-Hertzberg Act was passed, California also passed AB 2525, which required all voting systems used in California elections to allow disabled voters to cast their ballots unassisted. Advocates for disabled voters argued that PPC machines made it difficult for disabled voters to cast their ballots in private. Other technologies, particularly DRE machines would allow disable voters to cast ballots without the assistance of others, either by reading the ballot choices aloud or marking the ballot for them.

[33] *My Vote Counts, op. cit.*, 10.

[34] *Ibid.*

[35] Henry Norr, "Scientists Question Electronic Voting," *San Francisco Chronicle*, March 3, 2003.

[36] This is not to say that the task force was not a political committee. Secretary Shelley convened the task force in response to political considerations—that is, expressions of public concern about the efficacy of DRE machines. That said, the task force included two computer scientists, the IT Coordinator for the San Diego County Registrar's Office, and the president of a voting technology company. There was no attempt to give voice to major interest groups.

[37] *Secretary of State's Ad Hoc Touch Screen Task Force Report*, July 1, 2003, 4–5.

Second, disabled voters need systems that are accessible for them to use privately. Third, non-English speaking voters must be able to read ballots in their own language. Finally, voting systems vendors require clear guidelines and an adequate time frame for developing and manufacturing new hardware. This latter consideration was particularly challenging because of the cost limitations imposed by Prop. 41 and HAVA and the need to have new systems in place by the March 2004 presidential primary.

The task force focused on two major issues in its review—issues that would be revisited many times before DREs were ultimately decertified in 2007. The first dealt with the integrity of the DRE voting machines themselves. The bulk of the task force's recommendations had to do with ensuring the voting machines' security against errors, hackers, and malicious efforts to alter the outcomes of elections. The question was how to guarantee that a machine's software would accurately record a voter's choice and that the vote could not be altered to change the election results. This challenge was made harder by the fact that DRE manufacturers viewed the source code for their machines as proprietary trade secrets and did not want to open them up to third parties—including the state and local governments—for review.[38] To ensure that the machines could not be hacked and that no malicious code could be added to the machines, the task force made 32 separate recommendations affecting the manufacture and use of DRE machines to be certified in California.

A second major issue was whether to require DRE machines to use a voter-verified paper audit trail (VVPAT).[39] While the task force recommended that a paper copy of each voter's ballot be printed by a local jurisdiction after the polls are closed, it was not able to reach a consensus on whether to require VVPATs on all DRE machines. Some members of the committee were sympathetic to the arguments of the DRE critics, who argued that without a VVPAT there was no way for a voter to ensure that the vote cast on a DRE machine was the same as the vote being stored in the machine's memory. Others were not.

There were a number of problems with requiring a VVPAT. HAVA only required a paper audit trail for each polling place, not a paper audit trail for each voter. Some elections officials believed that requiring a VVPAT would be equivalent to using paper ballots, greatly increasing the cost of administering an election and defeating one of the main purposes for using DREs. The DRE machines already certified and in use by three counties (Alameda, Plumas, and Riverside) did not readily have the capability to attach a printer in order to print each voter's ballot. Finally, advocates for disabled and non-English speaking voter advocates worried that VVPATs would not meet accessibility requirements, making it harder for disabled voters to cast their vote without assistance.

The task force issued its report on July 11, 2003, but Secretary Shelley did not immediately take action on its recommendations. The secretary of state's office was overwhelmed by the need to prepare for the special recall election of Gov. Gray Davis to be held in November 2003.[40]

---

[38] Sequoia even went so far as to fight a lawsuit in Florida seeking access to the machine's software following a contested election.

[39] A VVPAT is a computer printout of the choices made by a voter on a DRE ballot. The ballot is printed at the same time the voter enters her choices, and allows the voter to review her choices (and make changes) before they are entered into the machine's memory. In some states, the VVPAT is a legal ballot—it can be used for vote tabulations. In others, the VVPAT is not a legal ballot but it can be used in the case of a manual recount.

[40] The secretary of state's elections-related activities, though the focus of this chapter, make up a relatively small portion of what the office does. The secretary of state is also responsible for a variety of activities not directly related to elections: registering business and interest group lobbyists and tracking their activities, chartering corporations and maintaining business filings for the state (the largest portion of the office's activities), commissioning notaries of the public, maintaining the California State Archives, serving as a trustee for the California Museum, and administering several state registries (e.g., the Domestic Partnership Registry).

DRE Problems

Despite the distraction of the recall election, counties continued the process of replacing their PPC machines with newer technologies. By the March 2, 2004, presidential primary election, 14 counties were using DRE machines. (See Table 3.)

In the March primaries, Alameda and San Diego counties experienced significant problems with their Diebold TSx (a kind of DRE) machines.[41] In Alameda County, 186 of 763 vote-card encoders (24 percent) malfunctioned, causing delays at voting places; 150 people were not able to vote.[42] San Diego had problems with its encoders, but also with machine batteries. One-third of its precincts were unable to open on time and reported that the machines miscounted almost 3,000 votes.[43]

In response to these malfunctions and similar events in other states, Secretary Shelley decertified all DRE machines for use in California elections on April 30, 2004.[44] The move placed 14 counties in limbo seven months before a presidential election. Ten of the counties would be able to use their touch screen machines in November provided that they implemented a series of security measures.[45] The secretary's order banned the Diebold TSx machines—used by Kern, San Diego, San Joaquin, and Solano counties—outright.[46] These four counties were forced to idle equipment worth approximately $40 million through the November election. Instead, they would of necessity have to use the optical scan devices normally reserved for processing absentee ballots. Secretary Shelley also required any counties approved to use DREs to allow voters to use a paper ballot in the November election if they chose.

The same day, Secretary Shelley announced plans to require a VVPAT on every touch-screen machine in the state.[47] Counties that were in the process of purchasing DRE machines could only purchase machines with VVPAT capabilities beginning in 2005. Counties that had already purchased DRE machines would be required to install VVPAT devices on their machines by 2006. At the time of the order no such technology existed, though the machines' manufacturers believed such a fix could be quickly created. Riverside County estimated that installing these devices would cost the county $4.3 million.

County registrars were incredulous at the secretary's actions. San Bernardino County Registrar Scott Konopasek stated, "We knew it was possible, but I don't think we as county officials ever thought it would come to this, so I guess we're numb."[48] Los Angeles County Registrar-Record Conny McCormack said, "He (Secretary Shelly) put out a report on April 20 saying that touch screens

---

[41] It later came to light that the Diebold machines used in the March 2004 election had not been certified for use by the federal or state government (Jason Schwartz, "High Tech Voting System Is Banned in California," *The New York Times*, May 1, 2004, Late Edition, A5). Diebold had installed new software on machines used by 17 counties—which had not been certified at the federal level, as HAVA and state law requires The software affected the optical scan machines in 13 counties and the DRE machines used by four additional counties.

[42] "State Decertification Looms for Diebold, Touchscreens," *Oakland Tribune*, April 20, 2004.

[43] Ian Hoffman, "Diebold Reports Multiple Problems; Registrar Wants Reason for E-Voting," *TriValley Herald*, April 13, 2004. Luis Monteagudo, Jr., and Helen Gao, "Some Votes Miscounted in Primary, Officials Say," *Union-Tribune*, April 8, 2004.

[44] California Secretary of State Kevin Shelly, "Secretary of State Kevin Shelly Bans Diebold TSx for Use in November 2004 general election; Also Decertifies All Touchscreen Systems in California until Security Measures Are Met," News Release KS04:030, April 30, 2004.

[45] The measures included printing a paper copy of every voter's ballot; providing the state with the source code for all software and firmware; ensuring there are no telephone, wireless, or internet connections into the unit; and prohibiting changes to the machines within 46 days of an election.

[46] In contrast with Alameda and San Diego, Kern and San Joaquin counties did not experience any problems with their Diebold machines.

[47] The requirement for VVPATs followed the recommendation of the state's Voting Systems and Procedures Panel. California Secretary of State Kevin Shelley, *op. cit.*, April 30, 2004.

[48] Michelle Dearmond and Michael Coronado, "State Bans E-Vote Screens; Inland Electronic Systems Can Return in November if Special Security Measures are Taken," *Press Enterprise*, May 1, 2004, A01.

Table 3. Type of Voting Machines Used by Counties, 2000–2008

	Prescored Punch Card	Other Punch Card	Optical Scan	Touch Screen
2000 General	9	21	27	1
2002 General	8	19	28	3
2003 Special	6	14	34	4
2004 Primary	0	13	31	14
2004 General	0	12	36	10
2005 Special	0	10	33	16
2006 Primary	0	0	51	37
2006 General	0	0	15	43
2008 Pres. Primary	0	0	56	2
2008 June Primary	0	0	57	1
2008 General	0	0	58	0

Notes: Rows do not total to 58 in the 2005 special election and 2006 primary election because counties reported using more than one type of machine. Except for 2000, data come from the California secretary of state's reports of voting systems used by counties (http://www.sos.ca.gov/elections/ vs_election.htm). The data for 2000 were made available by Brady, Buchler, Jarvis, and McNulty. The voting machines tabulated in this table are those machines used by voters at their polling places. By 2006, most counties were using optical scan machines for absentee voting. In addition, all counties were required to maintain at least one touch-screen machine for use by disabled voters in the 2006 and 2008 elections.

were 100 percent accurate . . . [a]nd then . . . he decertified them. . . . [He has] destabilized the entire election process in California and potentially nationwide."[49] Riverside County Registrar Mischelle Townsend was less sanguine, declaring the decertification order "totally unjustified. . . . Here you have Riverside County, which has conducted 29 successful elections over the past four years. There is nothing in our history to warrant this kind of overreaction."[50] Many registrars talked of suing the state to block enforcement of the decertification order; four ultimately did.[51] San Bernardino County said it would ignore the requirement to provide paper ballots.[52]

During June and July, the Office of the Secretary of State worked with the 10 counties not using Diebold machines to recertify their DREs in advance of the presidential election. The recertification process, however, did not proceed in a uniform fashion. Instead, the counties' machines were recertified on an ad hoc basis. Some counties had to meet stricter recertification criteria than others, increasing the tension between the county registrars and Secretary Shelley.

A Political Interlude

Already at odds with the local election officials, Secretary Shelley quickly came under scrutiny from a number of other sources. In August 2004, the *San Francisco Chronicle* published allegations

---

[49] Quoted in Katherine Q. Seelye, "He Pushed the Hot Button of Touch-Screen Voting," *The New York Times*, June 15, 2004, Late Edition, A16.

[50] Dearmond and Coronado, *op. cit.*

[51] Seelye, *op. cit.* The conflict over the use of VVPATs continued into 2005 when the California Association of Clerks and Elections Officials fought a bill, SB 1438, in the California state legislature that would require the use of the VVPAT for recounts and elections decided by less than one percent or less. Dan Seligson, "Use of Paper Trails Divides Advocates, Elections Officials," *Campaigns & Elections*, December 2005/January 2006, 56.

[52] Seelye, *op. cit.*

that Shelley received more than $100,000 in campaign contributions that were illegally diverted from a state grant.[53] The FBI, the Fair Political Practices Commission, and the California Attorney General soon began investigations into the source of these campaign funds.[54]

In December 2004, the California state auditor published a blistering report about the secretary's efforts to implement HAVA entitled, "Office of the Secretary of State: Clear and Appropriate Direction Is Lacking in Its Implementation of the Federal Help America Vote Act."[55] Shortly after the state auditor's report was released, the U.S. Election Assistance Commission contracted with the U.S. Interior Department's Office of Inspector General to perform an audit of the office's activities.[56] It also halted the release of $169 million in HAVA money to the state.

In January 2005, the State Personnel Board issued a report claiming that Secretary Shelley—who was prone to yelling at subordinates—had created a hostile working environment for state employees.[57] Moreover, the report found evidence that the secretary had used the civil service examination system to ensure favored candidates were appointed to jobs within his office.

Faced with mounting legal bills and the threat of testifying before the Joint Legislative Audit Committee investigating the use of HAVA funds, Kevin Shelley resigned on Friday, February 4, 2005.

Secretary Shelley's resignation left open two major questions about the state's HAVA implementation efforts. First, which voting machines could counties use to meet the January 2006 HAVA deadline? Although Shelley recertified DRE machines already purchased by counties for the 2004 presidential election, the April decertification order had effectively brought the process of replacing outdated voting technologies to a halt in the state, and little had been done to restart it. The Office of the

---

[53] Vanessa Hua and Christian Berthelsen, "Secretary of State Shelley Received Dubious Donations; S.F. Nonprofit That Got Big State Grant Brokered by Politician Is Linked to Sources Who Gave $100,000 to His Campaign," *San Francisco Chronicle*, August 8, 2004, Final Edition, A1.

[54] Christian Berthelsen, Vanessa Hua, and John Wildermuth, "Shelley Quits; Secretary of State says controversies over fund raising, use of federal money, and his volatile temper damaged his office's 'ability to function effectively,'" *San Francisco Chronicle*, February 5, 2005, Final Edition, A1.

A Shelley fundraiser, Julie Lee, would be convicted and sentenced to a year and a day in prison for channeling the money to Shelley's campaign. Nancy Vogel, "California Briefing/Sacramento; Fundraiser Gets 1 Year in Fraud Case," *Los Angeles Time*, September 24, 2008, Home Edition, B4.

[55] The report stated:

[T]he office's insufficient planning and poor management practices hampered its efforts to implement HAVA provisions in a timely way. Consequently, the office is at risk of failing to meet certain requirements by the January 1, 2006, HAVA implementation date. Additionally, the office's disregard for proper controls and its poor oversight of staff and consultants led to questionable uses of HAVA funds. As a result of these practices, the office runs the risk that the federal government may conduct an audit of the office's implementation of HAVA and its uses of federal funds and may require repayment of some, if not all, of the HAVA funds used to pay certain employees and consultants. . . . Finally, the office failed to disburse federal HAVA funds to counties for the replacement of outdated voting machines within the time frames outlined in its grants application package and county agreements.

Bureau of State Audits, California State Auditor, *Office of the Secretary of State: Clear and Appropriate Direction Is Lacking in Its Implementation of the Federal Help America Vote Act*, 2004–139, Dec. 2004, i.

The audit echoed criticisms repeatedly made by the California Legislative Analyst's Office (LAO) in its annual budget analyses. In the 2004–05 analysis, for example, the LAO noted, "Other than the proposed continuation of $1.7 million in administrative expenses, the budget does not propose or acknowledge the expected receipt of the more than $250 million in additional HAVA funds in the current and budget years combined. As such, there is no proposal for how the SOS plans to spend those dollars" (Californian Legislative Analyst's Office, *General Government, FY2004–05*, F58).

[56] California would ultimately be forced to repay about $3 million in federal HAVA funds.

[57] California State Personnel Board, *Secretary of State Final Personnel Audit*, January 2005.

Secretary of State had certified just one new machine for purchase by the remaining counties,[58] and the office had not issued guidelines for how counties were to meet the new requirement for VVPATs. Second, where did the development of the statewide voter registration database stand? As discussed below, almost nothing had been done by the secretary of state's office to meet this requirement at the time Shelley resigned.

Following Shelley's departure, the Office of the Secretary of State was effectively rudderless for two months. Governor Arnold Schwarzenegger's choice to replace Shelley, Bruce McPherson, was not confirmed by the state legislature until March 30. Given the contentious nature of the office's past actions, no one was willing to undertake new initiatives without a secretary in place.

Over the next year and a half, Secretary McPherson tried to return some measure of normalcy to the HAVA and Prop. 41 implementation process. Shortly after assuming office, McPherson flew to Washington, D.C., to meet with the Election Assistance Commission and reassure its members that California would not use its HAVA money improperly. Following the meeting, the EAC released the money it had held up following the audit of Secretary Shelley's decisions. McPherson also created a fresh process for certifying new voting machines for use in California elections. In October 2005, he announced the criteria for such certifications.[59]

Despite new processes and criteria, the Office of the Secretary of State was slow to review new machines for purchase by counties. Although the office had certified the ES&S Automark system in August 2005, the next (re)certifications—for Diebold's TSx and Optical Scan machines—did not occur until February 2006.[60] Though additional certifications quickly followed over the next two months,[61] at the time of the June 2006 primaries, seven counties—including Los Angeles County—were out of compliance with HAVA and state law.[62]

In November 2006, Secretary McPherson, a Republican, lost his bid for a full term as secretary of state to State Senator Debra Bowen, a Democrat.

The Top-to-Bottom Review

During the 2006 campaign, State Senator Debra Bowen had advocated a top-to-bottom review of the state's DRE machines to ensure their accuracy. Her criticisms fall neatly into the third election reform frame: How confident can voters be that the choices they enter into a machine are the ones that the machines tally? Draft plans for the top-to-bottom review were announced on March 22, 2007, and the formal announcement of the review quickly followed on May 9. In launching the top-to-bottom review, Secretary Bowen stated,

> California's voters are entitled to have their votes counted exactly as they were cast. This top-to-bottom review is designed with one goal in mind: to ensure that California's voters cast their ballots on voting systems that are secure, accurate, reliable, and accessible. . . . My goal is to get California to a

---

[58] California Secretary of State Kevin Shelley, "Secretary of State Shelley Certifies Voting System with Paper Audit Trail," News Release KS05:003, January 21, 2005.

[59] County of Los Angeles Registrar-Recorder/County Clerk, Letter to Honorable Debra Bowen, California Secretary of State, March 30, 2007, <http://www.sos.ca.gov/elections/voting_systems/ttbr/counties/los_angeles .pdf>.

[60] California Secretary of State, "Secretary of State Bruce McPherson Grants Certification with Conditions for Voting System," New Release BM06:021, February 17, 2006.

[61] The next certifications, for the Hart InterCivic eSlate and Sequoia AVC Eddge/Insight/Optech 400, came in March. In April, the ES&S InkaVote system was certified for use.

[62] County of Los Angeles Registrar-Recorder/County Clerk, *op. cit.*

place where voters, elections officials, candidates, and activists have confidence in the results of every election.[63]

As part of the review, every electronic voting machine used by California voters (DRE and optical scan) was to be subjected to three rounds of testing. First, each system would, for the first time, undergo a document and source code review to ensure there were no security lapses in its code. Second, a "red team" of computer scientists would try to hack into each machine to determine if they could alter its results. Third, each machine would be tested against a set of accessibility requirements to ensure that it complied with state and federal law in regard to use by voters with disabilities. The results of the tests would be made public for comment.

While DRE critics cheered the move, county elections officials were upset by the idea. To this point, counties had spent or set aside over $450 million in federal, state, and their own funds replacing their voting machines.[64] Contra Costa County Registrar Steven Weir stated, "That's giving notice of a process that's starting whose outcome could be between dire and draconian, depending if it's your neighbor or you."[65] Many and especially county registrars feared that the new secretary of state was predetermining the outcome. For example, Michael Shamos, a computer science professor at Carnegie Mellon University said, "The criteria are clearly designed to eliminate DRE voting in California. . . . An army of computer scientists will come forward to testify that computer programs cannot be verified to be secure against 'undetectable voter tampering' and therefore they all will have to be decertified."[66] The registrars and other critics also worried that the results of the top-to-bottom review would leave counties without machines cleared for use in the upcoming February 5, 2008, presidential primaries.

The timeline for the review was extremely constrained. The top-to-bottom review began on May 14, and California law required the secretary of state to announce which machines could be used in an election at least six months before the election took place. Given that California had moved its 2008 presidential primaries forward to February 5,[67] Secretary Bowen had less than three months—until August 5—by which to make decisions. Since the testing would take until late-July to be finished, there was little time for public comment before the secretary would be forced to announce her decision.

The results of the top-to-bottom review were largely as predicted. As the *San Francisco Chronicle* put it, "State-sanctioned teams of computer hackers were able to break through the security of virtually every model of California's voting machines and change the results or take control of the systems' electronic functions."[68] Based on these results, Secretary Bowen decertified all electronic vot-

---

[63] California Secretary of State, "Secretary of State Debora Bowen Unveils Details on Top-to-Bottom Review of California's Voting Systems Scheduled to Begin Next Week," News Release DB07:020, May 9, 2007.

[64] *Ibid.*

[65] Quoted in Ian Hoffman, "E-Voting Demise Could Be Near; Elections Chief Holds up New Standards That May Well Spell the Death of ATM-like Devices across California," *Contra Costa Times*, March 28, 2007, F4.

[66] Quoted in Hoffman, *op. cit.*

[67] All of California's primaries are normally held the first Tuesday in June. In order to increase the likelihood that California's votes would be decisive in determining the two major parties' nominees, the state legislature (like legislatures in many other states) moved its primaries to the first available date, February 5.

[68] John Wildermuth, "State Vote Machines Lost Test to Hackers," *San Francisco Chronicle*, July 28, 2007.

It is important to note, however, that the red teams' analysis did not account for any physical security measures that counties might have used to prevent someone from hacking into the machines, nor did they evaluate the likelihood that someone would be able hack into the systems under normal election circumstances. The teams also did not find any evidence of malicious source code in the machines that would cause votes cast for one candidate to be counted for another.

ing machines for use in California elections but then conditionally recertified some of the machines.[69] All of the DRE machines were decertified for general use. DREs manufactured by Diebold and Sequoia were recertified for early voting and to allow counties to have one device in each polling place to meet state and federal accessibility requirements for voters with disabilities.[70] All of the optical scan devices submitted for review were conditionally recertified provided the manufacturers and registrars incorporated additional security measures.

Given a 2001 district court order banning the use of prescored, punch-card machines and HAVA's requirement that all punch-card systems be out of service by January 1, 2006, the decertification order left counties with just one option for the replacement of precinct voting machines—optical scan devices. Thus the 23 counties using DRE machines as their primary voting method had to buy another set of voting machines quickly.[71]

Developing the Statewide Voter Database

Most of California's election reform efforts focused on HAVA's requirement to replace the PPC machines. As noted in Table 2, however, HAVA imposed other requirements on the state as well. First, the state had to develop a set of procedures for allowing individuals to cast provisional ballots. Second, the state had to enact and implement a set of identification requirements for new voters. Third, the state had to prepare and post on Election Day information for voters at each polling place. Finally, the state had to develop and implement a statewide voter registration database. The state easily met the first three of these requirements. However, as of this writing, California has yet to meet the fourth. This section describes the secretary of state's efforts in this regard.

Section 303 of HAVA requires each state to implement a uniform, centralized, interactive, computerized voter registration database that is defined, maintained, and administered at the state level. The story of California's attempt to develop its statewide voter registration database has fewer twists and turns than its efforts to replace the punch-card voting machines. Simply stated, California neglected to take any action until a deadline was at hand. The initial state HAVA plan offered a vague outline for state compliance: "the Secretary of State . . . will . . . as soon as is reasonably possible, either modify California's current statewide database (Calvoter) so that it complies with HAVA or establish a new statewide database that complies with HAVA."[72] Thereafter, California requested and received a waiver from the U.S. Election Assistance Commission to delay its implementation of this HAVA requirement from January 2004 to January 2006.

---

[69] Secretary of State Deborah Bowen, "Secretary of State Moves to Strengthen Voter Confidence in Election Security Following Top-to-Bottom Review of Voting Systems," California Secretary of State News Release DB07:042, August 3, 2007.

[70] All of the machines were subjected to additional security requirements and 100 percent manual counts of the VVPATs were required for the DREs. Election Systems and Software (ES&S) chose not to submit one of its machines (AutoMARK 1.0) to the review and submitted the materials for another—InkaVote Plus, used by Los Angeles County for HAVA compliance—too late to be part of the top-to-bottom review. As a consequence, all ES&S machines were initially decertified (State of California, Secretary of State, "Rescission and Withdrawal of Approval of the Election Systems and Software Inkavote Plus Precinct Ballot Counting System, Version 2.1, as Approved on April 21, 2006," August 3, 2007). The Office of the Secretary of State worked to recertify Los Angeles County's system before the February primaries.

[71] Table 3 shows 28 counties using DREs. Many of the counties, however, used two types of machines—DRE and optical scan. According to the secretary of state's office, at the time of the August decertification/recertification order 35 counties relied primarily on optical scan systems (California Secretary of State, "Frequently Asked Questions about Secretary of State Debra Bowen's Top-to-Bottom Review of California's Voting Systems," News Release, August 15, 2007.

[72] *My Vote Counts, op. cit.*, 13.

In January 2005, shortly before he resigned from office, Secretary Shelley wrote to the U.S. Justice Department for guidance on his proposal to make minor modifications to the existing, highly decentralized, CalVoter system. He hoped that such modifications would allow the system to meet the HAVA requirements. Shelley's letter appears to have been California's first official effort to address this HAVA requirement. The Justice Department quickly notified the secretary that such modifications were not sufficient to meet the federal requirements.

Throughout the circus that followed Secretary Shelley's resignation, the Office of the Secretary of State continued to negotiate with the Justice Department to avoid becoming out of compliance and forfeiting the state's HAVA funds. In November 2005, the two offices signed a seven-page memorandum of agreement outlining the steps California would take to develop a statewide database. Part of the agreement was that the secretary of state would notify the Justice Department in writing updating its status in regard to implementing the agreement *each week* until the project—now known as VoteCal—was completed.

The Office of the Secretary of State began issuing requests for proposals (RFPs) for the different elements of the VoteCal project in October 2006, and the project was to be completed by December 2009—three years after the statutory deadline. The state's initial plan estimated the cost for the system at between $8 million and $40 million. The most recent estimate, according to the LAO's analysis of the 2007–08 budget, is that the program will cost at least $60 million when fully implemented, with ongoing operating costs of $10 million per year.[73]

Conclusion

By 2008, eight years after the contested 2000 presidential election, California had succeeded in changing how its counties conducted elections. The state ultimately responded to all three policy frames developed as part of the national conversation concerning the administration of elections. By no means was the process of reform smooth. After mismanagement in the Office of the Secretary of State, diverse responses by county registrars of voters, multiple special elections, three different secretaries, and wide-ranging interest group participation, California ended up in a very different place in 2008 than most had envisioned in 2000. What began as a generalized and consensual effort to ensure voting rights, increase participation, and smooth the operation of California elections became a narrowly focused and heated battle over how voters would cast their ballots. Counties anticipated new, DRE touch-screen machines in 2000, but were limited to optical scan devices by 2008. Instead of spending just $46 million of the state's HAVA funds to supplement Prop. 41's combined $300 million, the state spent nearly $200 million (about 57 percent) of its HAVA funds helping counties buy multiple types of machines. Between 2000 and 2008, the average county used three different types of voting machines.[74] Some counties used as many as five different voting systems over the period. Planned voter-education and poll-worker education efforts largely—though not completely, as detailed in the following chapters—fell by the wayside as the fights over the use of DRE machines took center stage. To date, the holy grail of a technological fix to California's election system continues to be out of reach, and improvements to the election system based on education as yet not fully tried.

---

[73] Californian Legislative Analyst's Office, General Government, FY2004–05, F-47.

[74] Data come from the California secretary of state's reports of voting systems used by counties, <http://www.sos. ca.gov/elections/vs_election.htm>.

Part II: Communication Problems and Strategies in Voter Education

The Local Political Economy of Elections: Information Delivery, Voter Education, and the Rationality of Voting Behavior

Paul Turpin[1]

Overview

The fairness and legitimacy of elections is a recurring feature of the American political landscape. Reforms to make the processes of voting clearer and easier, while legitimately cast in terms of strengthening democratic ideals of participation, nevertheless engender considerable conflict given the nature of locally administered elections. This essay extends Anthony Downs's concept of information costs[2] to a voter's decision-making by theorizing rhetoric as an economics of attention. A focus on the dynamics of attention expands the scope of information costs from Downs's issue-oriented, consumer-choice transactional model toward a rhetorical model of interactive communications that include the costs of information processing within the electoral process itself. The communicative interaction of voters, election officials, and their commercial vendors comprise a local political economy for the electoral process, one in which there is competition over which parties should bear what costs.

To illustrate how information costs compete with financial and organizational costs, this essay examines official election communication in the 2008 election cycle in San Joaquin County, California. The conclusions drawn by the study indicate that easing the information-processing costs to voters is possible by using appropriate graphic design principles, but changing practices to implement such principles face the obstacles of increased financial costs to officials and institutional and organizational dispositions. The use of vote by mail (VBM), however, promises reduced financial costs that could help offset costs of better design. Understanding the competition over relevant costs between the parties in the local political economy of elections is an essential prerequisite for comprehensive reform.

The dictum "all politics is local" is nowhere more evident than in election administration in the United States. Whatever the structure of the local county Registrar of Voters Office, whether elected or appointed or combined with other duties, local election administration is where democratic practice

---

[1] Department of Communication, University of the Pacific.
[2] Anthony Downs, *An Economic Theory of Democracy* (New York: Harper Collins, 1957).

reaches its culmination in the electoral process. The argument of this essay is that local election practices should best be understood not simply as the practical conduct of politics, but as a form of political economy. That is, they should be appreciated not simply for their role in tallying the expression of voter preferences about governance but also for the roles they play in a mix of authoritative and market structures, each revealing its own institutional and organizational frameworks and interests in competition with others. Such competition arises because of the costs borne by different participants in the electoral process.

The key participants are three: voters, county registrars and their staffs, and the commercial vendors that produce the election materials themselves—voter information booklets, ballots, and so on. The ideal balance is one where clear election information is produced and distributed as cheaply and efficiently as possible. Where this balance is achieved, voters are not burdened with confusion; election officials can be reasonably parsimonious with public funds, and commercial vendors make a profit. What sounds simple in theory, however, can be very difficult in practice. Reducing the information costs to voters can raise other costs for election officials and their vendors. Understanding how this can happen provides needed context for any attempts to lower voters' information costs.

Reducing information-processing costs to voters (attention, cognitive demands, etc.) can increase costs of design and production of information borne by a registrar of voters. Some of the registrar's costs are financial (increased vendor costs) and some are organizational in nature (customary practices, vendor practices). A case study of San Joaquin County illustrates how these costs are manifested even in the production of the official election communication sent to each voter's address: the sample ballot booklet. Of particular interest here will be an initiative to solicit new vote by mail (VBM) voters through an advance postcard mailing limited to that purpose. In comparison to those who just receive the customary signup postcard in the sample ballot booklet, voters who receive the single-purpose postcard sign up in dramatically greater numbers for VBM, and their turnout has been higher. Such successes associated with the advance VBM postcard strongly suggest that information overload of both quantity and quality adds significantly to voters' information costs.

To examine the conflicting problems of cost among the key participants, this essay will apply Anthony Downs's economic metaphor of information costs to a description of voters' reasoning. Then, taking up Richard Lanham's view of rhetoric[3] as an economics of attention, the essay enlarges Downs's economic metaphor to include the costs of attention and information processing. Applying a rhetorical sensibility to the economic metaphor helps demonstrate how the concept of cost may be enlarged to encompass constraints of different types. In considering how the implementation of good graphic design principles aids in attention and information processing, the essay shines a light on the methods of production and distribution of voter education materials. Taking the perspective of political economy, the factors of production and distribution can be understood as generating differing institutional imperatives and organizational frameworks which themselves function as constraints. From those constraints come the financial, institutional, and organizational costs that undercut the implementation of good design principles.

From the Rationality of Voting to the Political Economy of Elections

A core insight of Anthony Downs's *An Economic Theory of Democracy* (1957) is that voting is a costly behavior, and because it is costly, voters will have varying degrees of motivation about voting, including whether to vote at all in a given election. Downs's argument has been a staple of rational choice theory as applied to political behavior, and it is primarily focused on the cost of the information necessary for making rational decisions about issues and candidates. According to Downs's application of the economic principle of utility to rational decision making, voters weigh the costs of

---

[3] R. A. Lanham. *The Electronic Word: Democracy, Technology, and the Arts* (Chicago: The University of Chicago Press, 1993).

gathering information about candidates and issues against the probability of receiving a return on their efforts. The decision to participate at all, however, is prior to questions of issue selection and candidates, and it also has costs that need to be taken into account.

Including information processing as a cost factor expands Downs's original idea that voters navigate among costs in their rational decision making. Voters not only face costs in their individual decisions, they also face the collective costs of the electoral processes. Elections have costs, and information about the electoral processes is part of those costs. Understanding the full range of cost factors reveals that electoral processes creates a local political economy of costs that affects all the participants in the process. This includes not only voters' strategies in dealing with the cost of information, including the matter of participation itself, but also the costs of information production and communication that range across the institutional electoral structures of county registrars and their interaction with the commercial vendors that produce communication media. The costs faced by these participants include time, attention, financial resources, institutional and organizational structures, and political sensitivities. Any effort to strengthen our electoral processes should take into account the entire web of relationships and interactions that make up the political economy of voting.

Rhetoric and the Economics of Attention

Rhetoric has long been associated with politics, but there is a strong tendency to view rhetoric too narrowly as being mainly about deliberative matters—or worse, as being about deceptiveness in deliberation, or *spin*. The early history of the communication discipline in the twentieth century was dominated by the idea that its proper subject matter was political oratory.[4] While political oratory is certainly an essential dimension of political practice and a worthy field of study, restricting the field to oratory alone underestimates the range of rhetoric's architectonic principles.[5] The purposes of rhetoric articulated by Cicero, for example, were to instruct, to delight, and to move (*docere, delectare, et movere*),[6] and each of these purposes had its own stylistic markers. While Cicero's primary concern was with political oratory's ability to move its hearers, working as he did in the dying throes of the Roman Republic, he understood that for instructional purposes, clarity and simplicity were best.

Richard Lanham in 1993 made the case for the relevance of rhetorical thinking in the information age by describing rhetoric as being the "economics of human attention-structures".[7] A recurring theme in his argument is that aesthetics is fundamental to communication because of its role in focusing attention. This is a contemporary version of Cicero's understanding of the link between aesthetic

---

[4] H. A. Wichelns, "The Literary Criticism of Oratory," in *Studies in Rhetoric and Public Speaking in Honor of James Albert Winans,* ed. A. M. Drummond (New York: The Century Co., 1925). Wichelns's distinction between the timeless features of literary art and the time-bound practices of political oratory became a central touchstone in the development of the speech communication discipline. To illustrate, a search of author-supplied keywords "public address" or "oratory" yielded 1,783 journal hits in the Communication and Mass Media Complete database.

[5] Arguments about the relation of reasoning and language/rhetoric have appeared in the pages of this journal before. F. A. Beer, "Words of Reason," *Political Communication* 11, no. 2 (1994): 185–201; D. A. Graber, "Why Voters Fail Information Tests: Can the Hurdles Be Overcome?" *Political Communication* 11, no. 4 (1994): 337–46; R. Hart, "Communication, Politics, and the Notions of Martin Spencer," *Political Communication* 23, no. 3 (2006): 255–62. They, as scholars in speech communication tended, investigated issue-oriented questions. My aim is not to displace them, but to add questions about electoral processes and to draw attention to rhetoric's place outside of words.

[6] For an extended discussion of the offices (duties) of rhetoric and Cicero's place in the peripatetic tradition of Aristotle, see L. C. Montefusco, "Aristotle and Cicero on the '*officia oratoris*'" in *Peripatetic Rhetoric after Aristotle*, ed. W. W. Fortenbaugh and D. C. Mirhady (New Brunswick, N.J.: Transaction Publishers, 1994), 66–94. Attention as a fundamental aspect of rhetoric was already long established by Cicero's day.

[7] Lanham, *op. cit.,* 227.

style and rhetorical purpose, and one shared among a wide range of rhetoricians today. Lanham's argument is important because it reminds us of an important facet of modern life: "It is in the nature of human life that attention should be in short supply, but in an information economy it becomes the crucial scarce commodity."[8] The conditions of modern life, unlike in Cicero's era, are prone to create information overload, generating cognitive obstacles where clarity may be needed.

The cost of cognitive obstacles points to a consonance between Downs's concept of information costs in rational decision making and Lanham's concept of rhetoric as an economics of attention that has applicability to instructional communication as well as the more obvious cases of political persuasion about issues and candidates. Information overload is sometimes characterized as a problem of quantity, as in the metaphor of trying to drink from a fire hose. Some economists are now exploring how the proliferation of choices can itself become a problem, including Schwartz in 2004.[9]

But information-processing problems can be qualitative as well, as illustrated by the cultural jokes about product instructions written by nonnative language speakers. Cognitive obstacles can be about sense making as well as sheer overload, so anything that makes sense making harder worsens the problem. At a simple level, this is why misspelled words and poor syntax are a problem; they make the reader work too hard and guess too much. At a higher level, organizational coherence and stylistic appropriateness can also advance or hinder sense making, as can sheer density or volume of information.

While Downs focuses primarily on economic principles like scarcity of time and information to ground his concept of cost, he does not offer a theory of communication with which to assess types or degrees of information costs; it is enough for his purposes to recognize that costs lead voters to a variety of cost-saving strategies in their search for adequate information to make rational decisions. It is important to keep in mind, however, that one of those strategies is *not* to vote; one of Downs's purposes in his analysis was to demonstrate that abstaining from voting could be a rational response to information costs. Yet democratic legitimacy, another of Downs's key themes, is not well served by electoral policies that function to promote abstention. If our purpose is to make voting more accessible, as the Help America Vote Act (HAVA) mandates, understanding information costs can help us.

Lanham's idea of rhetoric as an economics of attention expands the understanding of communicative interaction beyond the sender-message-receiver theory of communication. His is a rhetorical theory of communication not only in its appreciation for the significance of style, but also because of rhetoric's broader principle of contextualized communication with audiences. Rhetoric always implies an audience—and often more than a single audience. A rhetorical understanding of audience is one that should be alive to the audience's situation, which includes both its needs and its constraints. Communication, in an expanded rhetorical view, always occurs in a situation of interacting influences. It is not just a one-to-one or even one-to-many model of communication, but a situation where there are multiple cross-influences among participants. Rhetoric, we might say, understands communication not just as a transaction, but also as a marketplace of competing possibilities. To the extent that markets and audiences share similarities, the costs that are central to markets are mirrored by the constraints that audiences will inevitably have. The political economy of elections encompasses a competitive interaction not simply among potential vendors to government, but also in the competing imperatives of voter needs, institutional purposes, and organizational capacities.

The interaction of conflicting purposes creates the situation of conflicting costs that I have called a political economy of election costs. Some of those significant costs also find their sources in the basic principles of scarcity of time and resources that Downs relied on, but they have institutional and organizational dimensions that structure their financial dimensions.

[8] *Ibid.*
[9] B. Schwartz, *The Paradox of Choice: Why More Is Less* (New York: HarperCollins, 2004).

Political Economy: Institutional and Organizational Factors
of Information Production

Political economy has a wide history of differing meanings.[10] The term here is used primarily in a functional sense to indicate the intersection of authoritative and market-based activity. The first and simplest sense of the term political economy stems from the etymology of economics: from the Greek *oikonomos*, or household management. Political economy in this sense refers to the household management of the *polis*, or state. The process of staging elections certainly fits this description. A second and more modern sense of the term is the establishment and conduct of a market system under a particular set of authoritative rules. Election processes fit this model as well insofar as some of the work necessary to conduct elections occurs under market conditions through the use of commercial vendors, as well as through the agents of government directly. This is especially the case in information production and distribution.

The distinction between authoritative and market-based imperatives is cross cut by a distinction between institutional and organizational dynamics. Institution here refers generally to a group's understanding of itself and its goals and purposes in light of its authoritative or market warrant, while the term organization refers to a formal structure of relationships in a division of labor. This means county registrars and commercial vendors are different types of institutions; that is, they are motivated by different warrants for their actions. This quality is distinct from whatever their organizational structures may be. Commercial vendors as institutions are businesses—that is, market-based enterprises that offer goods or services for a remuneration that pays the expenses of the enterprises and makes their owners a profit. The economics of staging elections pretty much demands an interaction of government institutions and business institutions. Because elections are periodic in nature rather than ongoing, it is not cost-effective for government itself to produce all of the work needed for an election. Contracting with businesses that offer relevant services is cheaper and more efficient.

In contrast, in the U.S., all governments as institutions are strongly oriented to public rather than private values. Exactly what those public values are may differ across different locales and regions. To some degree they are defined by statute, and they definitely undergo historical change, again through statutory as well as customary shifts. This is an empirical rather than normative claim, by which is meant that public values, however articulated, are the public face of government administration. If the articulated public values are poll taxes and literacy tests, then counties work to enforce them.

The very history of poll taxes and other means of limiting the franchise, of course, points to how normative resistance has changed the face of government administration. The result today is a strong electoral culture committed to being even-handed. This takes formal shape in an avowed commitment to nonpartisanship, but partisan neutrality is reinforced by the appearance of showing no favoritism on any other grounds as well.[11] Because of the sense in which elections are part of the "household

---

[10] For overviews of conceptual and historical views of political economy, see J. A. Caporaso and D. P. Levine, *Theories of Political Economy* (Cambridge: Cambridge UP, 1992); and B. Clark, *Political Economy: A Comparative Approach,* 2d ed. (Westport, Connecticut: Praeger, 1998). The term political economy is sometimes interpreted as invoking a specifically Marxist analysis, so-called because of Marx's critique of the classical political economists (Adam Smith, Ricardo, et al.); such contemporary analyses often use the language of production and consumption to identify their objects of study. While the terms production and distribution are used in this analysis, they are not intended to invoke the Marxist tradition of analysis that continues today in cultural studies, but rather are meant as generally descriptive terms for economic processes.

[11] Questions about the legitimacy of a public value continue to reverberate even after formal acceptance of the value. Extending the franchise to the previously unenfranchised (pick your group) creates historical ripples that can take generations to die out. The requirement to print election materials in languages other than English continues to draw derision from those who identify citizenship with a particular ethnic identification and language.

management" of the state, the public value of showing no favoritism helps mitigate against opportunities for cronyism and corruption.

The differences between institutional purposes of businesses and local governments are important for more than merely organizational structure. Government has a type of fiduciary duty to its citizens that influences its organizational processes; again, some of this duty is rule-bound by statute (federal and state election law, rulings from state election agencies, etc.), some is customary (tradition, best practice discussions among registrars, etc.), and some is regulated by local political pressures (through county supervisors, for instance, in California). These factors make government practice less nimble than business practice, and though government is often mocked for bureaucratic inflexibility or inefficiency, the problem is less the organizational factor of bureaucratic structure and more the institutional factor of its fiduciary values. Government must (in the sense of having an obligation) be available to everyone eligible to participate. Business, on the other hand, is free to limit its focus to those who can pay for goods or services.

With government being a buyer of commercial services, the second sense of the term political economy becomes manifest—the more general sense of a market that occurs within a framework established by a political authority. But government is not simply a buyer, or rather not a *simple* buyer, because of its fiduciary values. On the one hand, government must represent itself as showing no favoritism, and especially no cronyism or corruption; it does this by requiring competitive bidding among its vendors. The actual competitiveness of the bidding may be limited by the nature of the work; the scale of the work required may make it difficult for smaller businesses to compete, for example, or the need to carefully observe statutory requirements may require more specialization than businesses care to develop. This can create a theoretically open market that, in reality, consists of a small number of players.

To observe these differences between government and businesses when they contract is not to make a judgment that one institutional purpose or organizational framework is superior to the other. It is rather to be clear about the constraints that guide decision making among the different participants in the political economy of elections. The effort to introduce changes into a set of ongoing practices unsurprisingly runs up against both institutional and organizational resistance to change, because change—*any* change—will cost someone something.

Information Design for Better Information Processing

When it comes to understanding the practical problem of information overload for voters, graphic designers are well aware of the problem. The American Institute of Graphic Artists (AIGA, 2009) has been engaged in an ongoing Design for Democracy project since 1998, and Marcia Lausen's 2007 *Design for Democracy: Ballot and Election Design* provides a good overview of that work.[12] Similar advice is available at the U.S. Election Assistance Commission (EAC) web site.[13] From a design perspective, one overarching principle stands out: clear instructional information needs "white space" (i.e., blank background) in order to stand out. This principle is necessary to reduce information density (quantity) and create a background for clear structure. Instructional information booklets for voters, however, have tended to be printed like newspaper text: relatively small fonts with a high text density. Newspapers themselves typically only have white space within advertisements. The reason: blank space on the page costs money.

---

[12] See T. Anstey, "The Dangers of Decorum," *Architectural Research Quarterly* 10, no. 1 (2006): 131–39, for a discussion of the common themes connecting design with rhetoric. Anstey's subject is the emergence of the figure of the architect in Renaissance Italy, and he draws parallels between the practice of architecture as persuasion—of client by architect—and the practice of architecture as design, in tracing the architectural meaning of *décor* from its basis in *decorum*, or fittingness.

[13] <http://www.eac.gov> (2009).

Here is an initial level of conflict: better graphic design will lower information-processing costs for voters, in theory leading to fewer errors and more effective participation. Better design that uses more white space, however, generates higher financial costs because of using more paper and print services. Hence, in becoming easier to process, information can become financially more costly, which can generate political resistance to the expense. Because these costs tend to be very local in nature, any changes become topics of conversation in short order, and resistance is easily organized. Political resistance is readily mobilized against the additional public cost; vendor resistance can develop in face of pressure for the vendor to absorb extra costs.

While financial costs were crucial obstacles in attempting to put design principles like those AIGA advises into practice in San Joaquin County, the immediate objections during the production process arose around the working patterns and operational methods of the registrar and the vendors. To be sure, changes would mean more pages and hence higher costs, but even more importantly the changes would mean registrar workers and/or vendors would have to change their practices or routines. The combination of forces proved difficult to overcome.

The Case: Voter Education in San Joaquin County in 2008

In 2008, the San Joaquin County's Registrar of Voters office entered into an agreement with a team of faculty from the University of Pacific under the auspices of the federal Help America Vote Act (HAVA). The project had three main purposes: (1) to inform voters about the return to using paper ballots;[14] (2) to reduce the incidence of errors in filling out the ballots through both voter education and poll-worker training; and (3) to encourage the use of vote by mail (VBM, formerly absentee balloting).[15] The project covered three 2008 elections: the presidential primary in February 2008, the California state primary in June 2008, and the general election in November 2008. San Joaquin County is just south of Sacramento County in California's central valley and is a mid-size county at approximately 250,000 voters.

The tasks set for the university research team by the registrar combined elements of a consulting project and a research study. The consulting dimension called for the research team to produce persuasive educational content for dissemination to the voting public; the research study called for investigation into the behaviors of potential voters.[16] These two imperatives generated a certain degree of unavoidable tension insofar as the consulting aspect of the project was production oriented, in the sense of its goal being to produce a set of media messages and artifacts, without necessarily being able to stage them appropriately for social-scientific study.

The staples of election information are the official mailings of print communication from registrar to voters. The primary official election communication from a registrar in California is the sample ballot and voter information pamphlet, informally referred to as the sample ballot. In the process of suggesting design changes in the sample ballot, the university team interacted with the registrar's staff, the vendor whose software created all the preproduction layout work for the printer, the sample ballot printer, and the vendor whose software produced the actual ballot design. The software required dictated both the design for paper ballots, and for the sample ballot booklet.

This list of participants is not intended to be exhaustive in its description; the ordinary business of running elections is much more detailed and complex than can be recounted here. Rather, this account is intended to suggest the dynamics at work that introduce friction and resistance in efforts to make

---

[14] California returned to using paper ballots after its electronic voting machines were decertified by its secretary of state; see D. Bowen, "Elections and Voter Information: Top to Bottom Review," retrieved from <http://www.sos.ca.gov/elections/elections_vsr.htm> (2007).

[15] See Appendix A for more details on the scope of work.

[16] The members of the research team included faculty from Theater Arts, Communication, Visual Arts, and Political Science.

changes. A crucial dimension of this caveat is that the friction and resistance were not the result of personality differences, inadequate performance, or operational issues. On the contrary, the university team found all participants to be committed to their work and reasonably professional in their behavior. The friction and resistance, in other words, occurred even when the social interactions were positively conducted. Understanding why conflicts still surfaced is the goal of this essay. The underlying causes of friction in this case, therefore, appeared to be systemic.

The time crunch of an election cycle cannot be understated. Elections generate long and complex workflow charts and extensive punch lists of necessary tasks. Dates are talked about in terms of their distance from the election; for instance E-90 is 90 days before Election Day. Two major functions of the registrar's office are to maintain accurate voter registration rolls, which may be in greater flux than usual if a significant election is nearing, and to prepare the official ballot information. Filing deadlines for candidates and ballot measures mean a relatively narrow window of time between finalizing ballot information and formatting the information for the sample ballot. While the registrar's staff handle all the official business of vetting and producing the text that appears on ballots, they use templates provided by commercial vendors for the preproduction processing of the page layout needed to produce the finished files for the printers. The registrar's staff has to be in close touch with the page layout vendors while this process goes on.

The task is complicated by the fact that, while elections are organized and administered at the county level, any given election date may include contests targeted to as many as several hundred smaller jurisdictions within the county. In addition to different federal, state, and municipal ballot items, there may also be ballot items for school districts, water districts, sewage districts, and the like. California has more special districts than any other state. Each of these election jurisdictions requires its unique ballot and its unique sample ballot. For the June 2008 primary, San Joaquin County produced over 200 different ballots and sample ballots (not counting ballots in languages other than English) of varying lengths.

The time-pressure, scope, and complexity of assembling the ballots and sample ballots were surprises for the university consulting team. The consulting mission with respect to the sample ballot booklet was to offer suggestions for changes to the covers, changes to the instructional pages—called "filler pages" to distinguish them from the candidate and proposition information—and changes to the vote by mail registration instructions on the back cover. The consulting team's suggestions addressed problems of voter errors (the instructional "filler pages") and both promoted and explained vote by mail registration.[17]

The redesigns of instructional filler pages and the efforts to find places in the production for their inclusion were often opposed by staff who were accustomed to doing things the way they always had done. The university's intervention represented a cost to both registrar and vendor staff, a cost that resulted from the interruption of a familiar and hurried routine. Both registrar and vendor staff were intent on keeping the sample ballots as compact as possible to keep costs low either to save money or to maximize profit.

The clearest instance of resistance occurred in a session with the ballot designer, Registrar Austin Erdman, and a university representative. The official ballot format had been constructed by a specialized vendor using proprietary software. Once finalized, the ballot design was sent on two paths: one to print the actual ballots used on Election Day, and the other to be incorporated into the sample ballot booklet. As with the sample ballot booklet production, the ballot design pace is fast, not least because the vendor's representative worked across half a dozen western states. During election season, this means an intensive travel and work schedule for the vendor. The decisions about ballot design were made in the course of a single afternoon; by comparison, the sample ballot booklets layout was done over the course of a few weeks.

---

[17] The university team also participated in composing a letter to voters from the registrar explaining the changeover from voting electronically to voting with paper ballots. For more details on our mission directives, see Appendix A.

The university research team focused especially on ballot design issues that could reduce mismarking errors, especially the problem of overvoting.[18] There was some concern that the separate races were not adequately distinct from each other, possibly leading to confusion about which lists of candidates went with which office.[19] During the course of the afternoon, the university team suggested a small change in formatting to incorporate some of the design principles they favored

The customary practice up until that point was to align the text centered in each of three columns. One of the top AIGA guidelines is to align text to the left, not centered, because the eye returns to the left margin at the end of a line of text. Therefore, the university team asked if they could align the text to the left.[20] The initial default response was to resist. While the registrar went to check the election code to see if alignments were specified, the vendor asked with some impatience who the university team members were to be slowing them down. The team explained again why it was there and what it was trying to do. The vendor was not impressed and cited her own experience of approximately a decade of producing ballots across the western U.S.

It turned out the code did not mention alignment, leaving it unspecified, so the university team again asked if the vendor could produce a left-aligned sample to compare with the usual center-aligned sample. This proved possible, and all participants in the meeting looked at both samples. Both the vendor and registrar's staff said the center-aligned text looked better, so they voted to continue with that formatting, overruling the university team suggestion with no further discussion.

The university team realized the two other groups were almost certainly viewing the body of text as a sort of gestalt graphic object, and not as something that needed to be *read*. As a purely graphic object, the bilateral symmetry of the columns of text did have an aesthetic appeal, but one different from what was needed to process information from the words. The experience paralleled Kenneth Burke's (1954) reading of John Dewey's "occupational psychosis [as] . . . a *pronounced character* of the mind" (original emphasis).[21] The difference between graphic appeal and readability can blur when the primary impetus is production. Keeping the audience's needs uppermost is a critical counterweight. The experience of resistance did not appear to be a matter of personal stubbornness or advantage seeking on the part of a special interest, beyond the habitual inclinations that longstanding usage imparts. The vendor's impatience was understandable; the university team was slowing things down. The instance points up, however, the difficulty of introducing changes into a fast-paced process.

Vote by Mail Economies

One of the primary directives of the HAVA project was to increase the use of permanent vote-by-mail (VBM) status. The impetus to promote VBM stems from several problems of relating to cost. There are costs of time and convenience for voters to go to the polls on Election Day. It has become a commonplace of elections that bad weather, for instance, leads to lower turnouts. There is also evidence that VBM programs lead to higher turnout rates, as in the Oregon case.[22] At the same time, the VBM

---

[18] One type of overvoting occurred when a voter would mark the bubble at a candidate's name and then also fill in the candidate's name on the line for "write-in candidate." At first glance, this looks like the voter's fault. The language "write-in candidate," however, is ambiguous as to whether it is a verb being used as an adjective (a particular type of candidate not listed on the ballot) or the imperative form ("write the candidate's name here"). While "write-in candidate" in the first sense may be customary usage for those who work on elections, it is nevertheless ambiguous and a point of possible confusion to voters.

[19] See M. Lausen, *Design for Democracy: Ballot and Election Design* (Chicago: The University of Chicago Press, 2001), for the example of Cook County judicial races where a similar problem occurred (14–21).

[20] See *Ibid.*, 30–31 for a clear exposition of left-align vs. center-align readability.

[21] See Kenneth Burke, *Permanence and Change: An Anatomy of Purpose* (Berkeley: UC Press, 1954), 49.

[22] A. J. Berinsky, N. Burns, and M. W. Traugott, "Who Votes by Mail? A Dynamic Model of the Individual-Level Consequences of Voting-by-Mail Systems," *Public Opinion Quarterly* 65, no. 2 (2001): 178–97.

initiative may reduce election administration costs by providing more time for processing those ballots. VBM balloting eases time pressures and therefore labor costs on the registrar by spreading the work of processing the ballots over a larger window of time than where polling place balloting predominates. VBM ballots are not actually counted ahead of time, but preparation work such as verifying signatures and readying the ballots can be done so that they are prepared to be tallied on Election Day.

In addition to redesigning the sample ballot booklet's VBM postcard application, which has customarily been part of the back cover, the university team also initiated a strategy used in Sonoma County to advertise VBM directly to voters ahead of receiving their sample ballot booklets. The team adapted a postcard application form from Sonoma County, California.[23] Mailing a postcard application in advance of the sample ballot booklet reveals yet another economy: California law prohibits registrars of voters from doing mailings for the sole purpose of "cleaning their files," the expression used by registrars to indicate gathering information about voters who have moved from their registered addresses. Having the purpose of soliciting signups for VBM enables registrars to use return service on the postcards to update their files—that is, to purge addresses that are no longer valid.[24]

Having more-accurate voter records prior to the printing of the sample ballot booklets, by itself, can generate significant savings. One of the election consultants the university team met during the project estimated that 10 to 15 percent of voter rolls in California counties were "deadweight"—that is, addresses that were no longer valid because of people moving between elections.[25] The advance-mailing postcard for VBM registration for the June 2009 election was sent to 116,000 voters, with 15,000 returned as undeliverable, about 13 percent deadweight. Even a conservative estimate shows the potential cost savings: with 250,000 voters showing on the rolls, 10 percent would mean 25,000 fewer sample ballot booklets to print and mail, at somewhere between three and four dollars each.

While this potential savings alone would suggest an efficiency rationale for advance VBM postcard mailings in and of itself, especially in an increasingly mobile society, the university team also had striking findings on the efficacy of the VBM postcard signup on both frequency of registration and turnoutThe team randomly selected San Joaquin County precincts that represented a little under half of the voter population to receive the postcard for the June 2008 primary.[26] This gave the team a clear comparison of both signup (Table 1) and turnout rates (Table 2) for the different voter populations. Voters receiving the postcard mailing signed up at higher rates than other voters, and they also voted at higher rates.[27]

The successful outcomes of the postcard mailing can also be seen as a confirmation of the hypothesis stated earlier in relationship to information overload and information processing—the economics of attention. The large increase in VBM postcard signup responses occurred soon after receipt of the postcards, before the sample ballot booklets were mailed. This is strong evidence that the post

---

[23] Sonoma County's registrar, Janice Atkinson, was very helpful in the process.

[24] At the time of this study, return service was a return-to-sender feature of postal mail through which a registrar could identify addresses that are no longer viable. Recently this procedure has been modified so that such voters are not purged, but are instead moved to an inactive status.

[25] Jess Cervantes of Leading Edge Data Services in Stockton, California, prepared reports from the registrar's election data. From June to November 2008, the problem of voters leaving their registered addresses became aggravated by Stockton's status as the leading mortgage-default city in the nation. Postal service representatives at registrar planning meetings told of delivery routes being redrawn because so many people had walked away from their houses without filing a change of address. During the housing boom of the last decade, San Joaquin County as a whole had become a bedroom community for the San Francisco Bay Area, about an hour's drive to the west. The mortgage and financial crisis heightened the flux of an already mobile population, making the problem of cleaning the voter files that much more pressing.

[26] The equality-of-treatment principle was satisfied by the registrar's decision that the November election would suffice for sending the postcard to the rest of the voters, both other precincts and newly registered.

[27] Source for figures. San Joaquin County election data for the June 2008 primary. Report compiled for the registrar by Jess Cervantes of Leading Edge Data Services.

Table 1. Voters Converted to VBM through Advance Postcard

VBM Registration	Received postcard	No postcard (control)
Treatment populations	101,553	82,903
New VBM registrations	20,400 (20%)	8,151 (10%)

Table 2. Turnout among Postcard VBM and other New VBM

New & old VBM	Registered	Turnout	%
New VBM - postcard	20,400	9,974	49%
New VBM - other	8,151	3,091	38%

Note: "New VBM—other" includes all other methods of registering for VBM, including the sample ballot's postcard, the registrar's web site, and walk-in visitors to the Office of the Registrar.

cards worked well precisely because they had a simple, focused message. If the communication principle had been, say, repetition, then one could have arguably expected a greater response after the sample ballot booklet had been received, since that would have been the second exposure to VBM signup. That was not the case, however; signups from sample ballot booklet VBM applications were within the usual range.

Conclusions

The university's consulting and research project with the San Joaquin County Registrar of Voters was, broadly speaking, a success. Some of that success took the form of feedback to the registrar about election information. The VBM postcard produced positive results. The sample ballot booklets incorporated design changes, but somewhat haphazardly. The experience also had valuable lessons for the research team about on-the-ground processes of democracy, leading to the following observations:

1. Accuracy enables true access to the polls. Votes that are not counted are in some ways worse than votes never cast at all, especially because their absence from an election can be more subtle and less felt at first. That makes any subsequent discovery of disenfranchisement more fraught with implications of deception.[28]

2. Changes in the guidelines for graphic design and information presentation as recommended by the AIGA are essential for both improved access and improved accuracy because both access and accuracy are affected by the cost to voters of processing information. The aesthetics and functionality of information presentation matters; text and image need to be treated differently.

3. Such changes are difficult to institute during elections at the local level because of the inertia of institutional and organizational factors. Standard practice tends to prevail, even when standard practice is not best practice. Such inertia is a systemic problem of countervailing institutional and organizational habits, pressures, and costs rather than simply problems of obstinacy or poor performance. Local change badly needs direction from higher sources such as state and federal election regulations in order to provide clear specifications for registrar staff and commercial vendors to work with.

---

[28] The question of significance will always matter in elections. An error rate of one percent will not decide the outcome in an election decided by a four percent difference, although even small rates of discounted votes can fuel worries about legitimacy.

4. At the same time, the historical rooting of elections in local practice may make more centralized directives about staging elections legislatively difficult. In addition, the centralized funding necessary to assist poorer communities who wish to increase the flow of information to voters may be contentious because it may be perceived by state legislators as benefiting one party or locale more than another.

5. Vote-by-mail strategies can substantially lower local election costs in two ways. First, during the election itself, VBM ballots can be processed over a larger window of time, easing labor costs to the registrar and increasing the accuracy of the count. Second and less obvious, VBM postcard communication enables registrars to update their voter files, removing voters who have moved, and thereby can substantially reduce the overproduction of sample ballots with a related cost savings.[29] This is a genuine administrative efficiency that brings government record keeping closer to real-time election conditions, and as such, prevents waste of resources. In an increasingly mobile society, enabling registrars to track their voting populations as accurately as possible is a major opportunity for more efficient election administration.

6. The success of San Joaquin County's advance VBM postcard mailing strongly reinforces the hypothesis that reducing information density, and thereby reducing information costliness, increases access in terms of both VBM signups and election turnout. This is more support for reducing information costs to voters, and with the savings from reduced waste from updated voter files, suggests that increased costs in information design may be traded off against efficiency savings in administration.

7. San Joaquin County's VBM campaign, however, does not conclusively demonstrate increased participation overall in the sense of demonstrably attracting new voters to the process. The possibility remains that VBM, at least as practiced in San Joaquin County, mainly moved already-active voters from poll-going to voting from home, without a net gain in participation. The experience of other vote-by-mail programs, like Sonoma County's in California and Oregon's statewide program, while not contradicted by the San Joaquin County experience, offer better support for the connection between voting by mail and both higher registration and election turnout.

8. Finally, a grounding in rhetorical understanding helps expand Downs's theory of information costs into new territory by outlining a theory of communication that conceptualizes the costs of information processing and connects its production to real-world practices. A rhetorical sensibility lets us see that the economic metaphor of scarcity in rational decision making upon which Downs relied can be extended to understanding the processes of election administration as a type of local political economy that produces the information necessary for elections to happen. This information must be produced rhetorically—that is, with an eye toward its effective distribution and consumption by the audience who needs it, citizens in their capacity as voters.

As the AIGA guidelines put it, ballot design and election administration should be driven by the needs of the voters rather than the desires of the vendors or administrators; the question now is how to achieve that end.

---

[29] The savings would be offset by the cost of the postcard's mailing. A question worth more study is whether a regular postcard mailing would continue to clean substantial numbers from voter rolls.

Appendix A

EXHIBIT A Page 1 of 4 VoteSmart Voting Systems Program

(A component of HAVA Section 301 for San Joaquin County)

Scope of Work

Purpose of the Agreement

1. Educate voters of the consequences of "overvotes" (the voter selects more candidates than permitted before a ballot is cast) or other voter errors that would result in the disqualification of a vote cast for a given race or measure through a voter education program.

2. Educate voters of the availability of absentee ballots and permanent absentee voting and the advantages of using these alternatives through a voter-education program.

3. Educate voters about the switch from electronic voting to paper ballot voting.

4. Train poll workers in regard to appropriate responses to occurrences of "overvotes" and other voter errors that could result in the disqualification of a vote cast for a given race or measure, and in regard to the submission of absentee ballots at polling places.

5. Engage in these educational and training initiatives for poll workers and voters in elections to be held in February, June, and November 2008.

6. Provide an analysis of voter-education program effectiveness in lowering the number of ballots disqualified because of voter error and in raising the number of voters who vote absentee.

Chapter 5

Voter Education: The Message through the Media

Lisa Tromovitch, Brett DeBoer, and Alan Ray[1]

I. Introduction

The mission of the Help America Vote Act (HAVA) was to increase successful voter participation overall, not just in a specific group of voters, for example, younger voters. The desired result is for all voters to envision themselves as successful participants, who can deposit their ballots, have them received appropriately and thereafter have them counted equally.

Thus, when a public agency is doing outreach to the general public regarding voting, every effort should be made to reach all sectors of the community, and not to inadvertently favor one group over another. Such outreach is complicated where television and print images are used because they project a visual element that is open to multiple interpretations. In a radio ad campaign a voice may not be readily identified as belonging to a person of a particular age or ethnicity, whereas in a television educational spot, the age, ethnicity and, based on clothing, the economic status of the person can be readily read by the viewer.

California is noted for the diversity of its population. Therefore in California the challenge of presenting visually based information to educate voters is to reflect this diversity by employing a variety of ages, ethnicities, implied socio-economic status, and gender roles, while at the same time not projecting favoritism. Of course this must all be done within a manageable budget.

The style of presentation as well as the information communicated may affect who is reached. An ad that is "hip" may be appealing to young voters, but appear "liberal" to older or traditionally conservative voters. An ad done in a 1950s style might appeal to older voters, but be completely ignored as "boring" and irrelevant by younger voters, who walk away before getting the educational message.

In sum, getting messages, particularly visual ones, out to the public about exercising their right to vote requires the intelligent use of the media. In today's world, that involves more venues than ever before. Whereas in the past, direct mail and newspapers were the principle media employed to disseminate messages about voting, the modern election now requires in addition to those channels, the

---

[1] Lisa Tromovitch is in the Department of Theatre Arts at the University of the Pacific; Brett DeBoer is in the Department of Visual Arts at the University of the Pacific; and Alan Ray is in the Department of Communication at the University of the Pacific.

use of radio, television, new media (Internet) and nontraditional venues such as billboards and ad specialties (e.g., buttons, key chains, etc.).

The Vote Smart project approached voter education as a media marketing campaign and assumed the following four axioms about politically oriented media:

1. The public has experienced the quick dissemination of information and issue "branding" and therefore anticipates the use of media during a political campaign.
2. Media is a powerful tool that can and does influence public perception, and perhaps behavior.
3. The design of a media campaign involves an understanding of the several phases of media marketing including:
    a. Background
    b. Objectives
    c. Audience Characteristics
    d. Media Properties
    e. Methods
    f. Implementation
    g. Results
4. Media uses and gratifications by audiences are complex and difficult to ascertain, as testified by theories of communication.

These axioms influenced the Vote Smart team's pursuit of following overall project goals:

*   To increase voting by mail (voting at home, absentee voting).
*   To reduce voter error.
*   To ensure that all messages created would reach as many voters as possible.
*   To inspire more and better poll-worker involvement on Election Day.

One way to summarize these goals would be that the project hoped to increase *access* to the voting process and *accuracy* in the process itself. Thus the media strategies adopted could be organized under these two summary objectives.[2] However, the project was implemented using three distinct initiatives: a coordinated print and radio strategy, a television strategy, and a branding and signage strat-

---

[2] The following offers an alternative way to conceptualize these initiatives:

I. ***Access*** to the Voting Process was promoted by:
    A. BROADCAST MEDIA
        1. Televised media utilizing a diversity of styles of presentation
        2. Radio ads focusing on vote by mail
        3. Internet advertising
    B. PRINT APPLICATIONS
        1. Bilingual signage
        2. Vote-by-mail promotional material
        3. Redesigned voter education pamphlet
        4. Newspaper ads explaining the benefits of voting from home

II. ***Accuracy*** of the Voting Process was promoted by:
    A. BROADCAST MEDIA
        1. Encouraging personal identification with the message
        2. Featuring actors with a range of ethnicities and ages
        3. Use of rhythm and repetition to assist recall of the message
        4. Costuming across a range of socio-economic classes
    B. PRINT APPLICATIONS
        1. Clarity of information
        2. Organization of information
        3. Typographic variables
        4. Grouping and hierarchy of information
        5. Method of delivery
        6. Sequence and frequency of information
        7. Focus on the actual filling out a ballot correctly in newspaper and other print media

egy for official voting communications. Thus, it may be more useful to use these categories to organize a review. Though each initiative was developed in coordination with the others, each initiative employed different techniques, personnel, and pacing.

II. Coordinated Print and Radio Campaign

A. Theoretical Concerns and Assumptions

The voting public in San Joaquin County, California, is diverse. Different age groups, economic classifications, and ethnic backgrounds make it difficult to reach all people with a media campaign. One characteristic that might cut across much of this diversity and provide a unique opportunity to reach most of the electorate is motorized transportation along public streets and highways. A large percentage of the voting public is on the road to work daily. Many drop children off and pick them up from schools and activities regardless of background. While lifestyles or "psychographics" may differ, mobility by automobile or public transportation in and around the county is a common thread.

Having decided to target people in their cars or on buses as the most effective and efficient way of disseminating a vote smart message, radio and outdoor advertising were assumed the most significant venues for advertised messages. To supplement these channels, it was decided to also use newspapers and the Internet for two reasons. First, it was concluded car owners were particularly likely to have access to the Internet at home and at work. Second, the readership of the major newspapers in San Joaquin County, *The Record*, is high for the market, especially among older car owners.[3]

The influence of the media on partisanship in political campaigns has been widely acknowledged, but the challenge for voter education is to influence behavior without engaging in partisanship. The team decided to limit the campaign to a month immediately prior to the election to limit confusion with messages sent by candidates and parties.

Congress has charged the Federal Communications Commission with regulating campaign advertising on local radio and local television stations. That regulation includes the encouragement of political information on the airwaves. As a result, radio and TV stations offer discounted rates for voter education. Stations are not to edit the content of such ads. Thus, over the years, political ads have become a common tool for dissemination of political messages.

The six advertising venues for political messages—television, newspaper, radio, outdoor, ad specialties, and the Internet—have different advantages and disadvantages. The primary advertising medium for major political campaigns has been television. Its presence in the American living room has helped shape political discussion since the 1950s.[4] The advantages of advertising on TV are its believability among audiences and its instant access to homes. The biggest disadvantage of advertising on television is the cost, even with discounted rates for political messages. The growth of cable advertising, however, has lessened the expense, especially in local races among county and city politicians and issues. Cable advertising rates are cheaper because the audiences for its channels are substantially smaller than broadcast stations.

Newspapers have also been a traditional medium of the political ads. Political campaigns have long believed that the concrete nature of the printed page was advantageous to driving home talking points. However, the shrinking readership of newspapers, especially among younger voters, is a growing drawback for those looking for places to put effective ads.

Radio has been used aggressively by political campaigns since the 1920s. The radio is inexpensive and it promotes the illusion of a one-on-one relationship with the audience and a campaign. The lack of visual contact is radio's biggest drawback.

---

[3] Audit Bureau of Circulation Data, Spring, 2009.

[4] See Erik Barnouw, *Tube of Plenty: The Evolution of American Television,* 2d ed. (New York: Oxford, 1990).

Outdoor advertising has traditionally been used in campaigns to brand a politician's name, a proposition's name, or short slogan in the public mind. Outdoor and specialty advertising includes billboards, placards, bumper stickers, and all sorts of "give away" items. The advantage of a billboard is size. The disadvantage is the environmental clutter. The smaller types of outdoor advertising are inexpensive, yet are hard to read. Advertising specialties, including hats, shirts, key chains, and pens and pencils help brand a candidate's name, yet can be quite expensive to produce and deliver.

Finally, Internet advertising is fast becoming a popular venue for communicating a political message. The placement of "tile ads" on an existing website is inexpensive. Further, a political campaign can create its own website to place messages. However, the measuring of website response to ads is inexact and an obstacle for those who want to determine effectiveness.

B. Developing a Print and Radio Campaign

With the theoretical assumption noted above in mind, a graduate seminar in the Department of Communication at the University of the Pacific assisted the Vote Smart team in developing a communication strategy focused on print and radio communication for San Joaquin County. The class subdivided itself into the four divisions of an advertising agency—message design, ad sales, placement, and research. The message design subsection focused on a specific theme for the campaign. The sales subsection invited area media representatives to present their best case for buying a specific media. The placement subsection developed a strategy for buying media time and space. Finally, the research subsection designed a postcampaign evaluation method to test the effectiveness of this particular media campaign.

Subsection One: Message Design

The message design subsection decided to focus on the themes "Vote from Home" and "Vote by Mail." Because cable television ads were already stressing the elimination of voter error and poll-worker participation, it was determined that the issue most in need of attention was use of the absentee ballot. The subsection created a mixed visual campaign using billboards, Internet ads, and newspaper ads. One ad featured a drawing of a colonial style home with an American flag and a sign over the door with the words "Home Sweet Home." The caption read, "Your New Polling Place, Vote from Home." Another ad showed a mailbox with the caption, "Your New Voting Booth, Vote from Home, Vote by Mail." The radio ads contained the basic "talking points" for the vote from home/vote by mail campaign: "life is stressful enough, no one has enough hours in the day, take the time to vote at home, and drop your ballot in the mailbox."

Subsection Two: Ad Sales

The second graduate seminar subsection heard presentations from the radio advertising representatives of six radio stations, a newspaper-advertising representative, and a billboard-advertising representative. Both the newspaper and the six radio stations also sold Internet "tile ads" on their websites. The representatives made presentations, covering the range of channels appropriate for political advertising. All presentations contained audience demographic breakdowns as well as the frequency of exposure to advertised messages.

Based on this information, the subsection determined that four radio stations and their websites were the most effective media in reaching San Joaquin car owners, the target of the campaign. They also decided that the regional newspaper and its website were useful because of its unusually strong readership in both English- and Spanish-speaking communities. Finally, it seemed prudent to contract a limited number of billboards on the major freeways given the emphasis of the campaign on reaching those with access to cars and buses.

Subsection Three: Placement

The placement subsection worked with each media representative to check availability of ad inventory in specific sections of the newspaper, of specific "dayparts" for the radio stations, and of locations on freeways for billboards. The subsection suggested newspaper ads be run in the "local" section of the newspaper because of its attention to weather and road conditions. The students recommended "drive times" for radio advertising, 6–9 a.m. in the morning, and 3–7 p.m. in the afternoons. And the group urged the purchase of billboards on the east-west highway corridors that connect San Joaquin County to the San Francisco-Oakland-San Jose metropolitan areas.

Subsection Four: Research

The research subsection formulated a post-test to measure the effectiveness of the media marketing campaign. A brief, postcard-size questionnaire was created asking respondents to identify if and where they heard the message of the campaign. It was suggested the questionnaire be mailed to the homes of absentee ballot voters and be made available at a random sample of polling places on Election Day. These strategies were selected to help capture the opinions of voters who were actually exposed to one or more of the ads.

Proposal to the Registrar of Voters

The strategy developed by the graduate seminar, once complete, was proposed to the San Joaquin Registrar of Voters. It suggested that the "Vote from Home/Vote by Mail" campaign be run over the four weeks preceding the June 6, 2008 California primary. It also recommended that radio, newspaper, billboards, and the Internet be the media in which to advertise. It argued that a post-test survey of the campaign's effectiveness be implemented on Election Day and after the election. Finally, it proposed a total budget of $56,500 to fund this month-long campaign. The registrar of voters praised the overall thrust of the campaign, but was forced to limit funding to $21,000.

Billboard advertising was subsequently cut from the campaign, as were two of the radio stations with smaller audiences among car owners. The newspaper ads were limited to running two rather than four days a week. Budget constraints also prevented an independent assessment of the effort, though some of its effects were captured by a survey conducted by other members of the Vote Smart team.[5]

Implementation

The altered media marketing campaign was implemented in May 2008. Ads were placed in the regional newspaper and two radio stations. Ads also ran on the websites owned by these outlets as tile ads with links to the San Joaquin County Registrar of Voters' website. The newspaper ads ran on Wednesdays and Sundays, the two heaviest readership days for the newspaper. The radio ads ran Monday-Friday in the mornings, between 6 and 9 a.m. and in the afternoons between 3 and 7 p.m. Additionally, a press release was generated to announce the implementation of the campaign to gain free publicity from the media regarding this unique activity and the role played in its design by a graduate seminar at the University of the Pacific.

III. Television Spots

A. Theoretical Concerns and Assumptions

The HAVA grant specifically targeted voters to encourage vote-by-mail (VBM) options and to educate voters to reduce errors. The Vote Smart team's research revealed that several issues needed to

---

[5] Nathan Monroe and Dari Sylvester.

be addressed in order to stimulate vote by mail and to reduce voting errors. In what follows, one can see how television spots addressed specific concerns and how diversity of age, gender, ethnicity, and socio-economic status were included to create opportunities for identification across a broad range of voters. Six voter education television spots and three poll-worker education spots were created.

With the above concerns in mind, the spots were conceived and written utilizing a variety of styles and featuring a diversity of actors. Attention was paid to costuming and to utilizing a myriad of locations. No one spot can cater to all of a voting age public, but across the series a conscious effort was made to create an opportunity for every voter to feel invited into the conversation about effective voting.

The ad process works through identification: individuals see themselves as the characters in the television spots and then make the imaginative leap to wanting to do the things that the characters are doing. If voters do not identify with the character on the screen, they are less likely to take the information to heart. If voters identify with the character portrayed, they are more likely to emulate the character's actions. For example, if the character identified with is voting from home, and taking special care to fill in the ovals correctly, the viewer will want to do the same thing. This is the premise of most television marketing.

Many a car commercial aimed at an adult male consumer will feature a normal looking guy standing next to a gorgeous model. Subconsciously, the potential customer ("normal guy") equates buying that particular car with being attractive to beautiful women. In a similar fashion, education spots can be created that allow voters to see themselves in the voting situation and carrying out the actions that make their vote count.

B. Television Ad Strategies and Implementation

1. Vote by Mail and Voter Error Ads

The best way to understand how these concerns were incorporated into the television ad is to examine scripts. Here are summaries of the scripts to increase vote by mail and reduce voter error:

"THE CHEER"

3 Actors: 1—female, Latina, early 20s (college student)
                  2—female, Asian, middle 30s
                  3—male, Caucasian, early 40s

Costuming: "California leisure" in red, white, and blue—aimed at middle-class tastes

Location: The set included the American and California flags draped in front of a red brick background. The setting would not offend anyone, but also not be of particular interest to younger voters, appealing instead to those with a more conservative taste.

Style: This is "used-car commercial" style. The use of a chant, bright colors, and a straightforward approach is aimed at a public of a lower- to middle-class background. Both educated and uneducated voters should feel comfortable with the presentation, even if they consider it a bit "cheesy." The choices tie into the presentational style of the cheerleading squads at high school and college athletic events, which are widely popular in the United States, making the presentation familiar and non-confrontational to the viewer. The energetic activity of cheering creates a sense of urgency. The repetitive nature of a chant is designed to help the listener retain the information. It is widely accepted that putting information to a melody enhances retention, hence children being taught grammar with songs and rhymes.

Problem to Solve: Voters risk their vote not being counted when it is miss-marked. Such problems occur when ovals are not properly filled in, and where ballots are disqualified or "spoiled" by initials or other markings. Therefore it is a significant goal to reduce these errors.

While the first set of television education spots focused on these errors were being produced, the Vote Smart team was concurrently working on a study that numerically confirms and expands the types of voter error; this data also indicates that there may be some impact on error rates related to voter education.[6]

Message: Fill in the ovals correctly in order to "make your vote count." Leave "no stray marks."

"THE COUPLE"

2 Actors: 1— female, Asian, 30s
2— male, Caucasian, early 40s

---

[6] Qingwen Dong and Erin O'Harra, Chapter 7 in this book.

Costuming: "California casual" is aimed at the upwardly mobile Californian.

Location: The look is of a loft apartment or condominium with brick wall, sofa and coffee table, indoor plants, and jazz music playing in the background.

Style: The spot is a 30-second play. It relates the story of a young, upwardly mobile couple, good-looking people in their 30s who have busy, fulfilling lives, who attend theater, are technologically savvy, and keep their joint schedules on their laptop. They are happy; they are in love; and they vote. They have what he thinks is a little "marital spat," only to find that his charming wife is teasing him, and has found a way for them to spend more time together, alone, in their lovely condo. The reach is to those who are, *or aspire to be*, among the young upwardly mobile middle class, successfully balancing work, marriage, and patriotic commitments.

Regardless of how we really look or behave, most Americans identify with actors in television series. Such actors appeal to the natural human desire to be considered successful, happy, and sexy and bring the potential voter into their story. Once they have identified with the character, viewers will naturally want to do as the character is doing, in this case vote by mail, and use dark pens to fill in the ovals.

Problem to Solve: San Joaquin County hopes to increase vote by mail. Improperly filled in ovals cause ballots to be marked as "spoiled."

Message: Voting by mail will ensure your vote gets in, is not edged out by other commitments, and ensures you and your sexy spouse will have more time together. Using those black pens will make one a successful voter.

"PINK ENVELOPE"

4 Voices: Characters are animated envelopes. The actors hired for the voice-over work include one African-American female, two Caucasian females, and one Caucasian male.

Costuming: The talking envelopes are all modeled on the actual pink envelope used by San Joaquin County for provisional ballots. Animation of eyelashes and lips, as well as the use of four voices with different accents implies both genders, and an open interpretation of ages, ethnicities, and socio-economic backgrounds. Picturing the envelopes was intended to familiarize the voters with the look of the envelopes, in part so that the appearance of the bright pink envelope would be less alarming at the polls.

Location: Neutral: the inside of a ballot box

Style: The choice of animation was specifically aimed at attracting the attention of a younger voter. While animation and CGI (computer generated images) are in wide usage in popular television and film and likely to be accepted by a wide variety of voters, the team felt it important to chose a style of presentation that would be of interest to younger voters. The concept of talking envelopes also reminds the viewer of cartoons, bringing to mind a nonthreatening way of receiving information. The hope is to relate voting to something anyone can do successfully, in order to combat any fear voters might have in making a mistake that costs them their vote.

Problem to Solve: The registrar of voters office staff was concerned that voters might be discouraged from voting when presented with a provisional envelope at the polls. They asked that the team familiarize the voter with the envelope and its uses in advance of Election Day. The hope was that voters who may be new to the area, had lost their vote-by-mail ballot, or for some other reason were not properly entered on the rolls, might still be encouraged to vote, thereby increasing overall voter turnout.

Message: Submit your ballot for consideration by the registrar of voters—do not be discouraged if your ballot needs to be submitted provisionally. Vote!

"VOTE SMART"

4 actors: 1—Caucasian male teacher
2—Caucasian female student
3—Latina student
4—African-American male student

20 student extras: a wide variety including Asian, Caucasian, Latino, and Pacific Islander

Costuming: The costumes are contemporary. The teacher is attired in casual suit and tie. The students are dressed the way they attended class that day in 2008.

Location: The scene was shot in the Drama 1 classroom of University of the Pacific using students from the Introduction to Theater and Advanced Acting classes.

Style: Here a question-and-answer style is used. The teacher asks questions that betray myths surrounding vote by mail, such as "True or False? Only people who are disabled or out of the country can vote by mail." The students correctly answer the questions thereby getting the proper information to the public. The spot ends with a positive encouragement, "Smart Class!" in order to leave the voter with the sense that they too can be "smart" if voting by mail.

Problem to Solve: There are a variety of urban myths surrounding vote-by-mail rules. Some voters believe they do not qualify for vote-by-mail ballots. The federal government began re-education attempts by renaming absentee ballots "vote-by-mail" ballots in order to dispel the myth that only citizens who are out of the country may use the service. The Vote Smart team discussed the potential benefits of altering the phrase again to "vote-from-home" in order to encourage a sense of comfort and safety around voting and in order to disassociate the voting process from a distrust of the postal service. The team discussed the potential benefit this might have for older, bilingual, or disabled voters who might utilize the assistance of family members in filling out their ballot.

However, the suggestion to use the "vote-from-home" phrase could not be implemented given the current wording adopted by the federal government. The team continues to think such reconsideration might have merit and should be raised in the future.

Message: Any voter may vote by mail, and it may be easier and more convenient.

"ANIMÉ ANNIMATIONS"

3 Voices: Animated Characters—animé-style

Costuming: The animation was done in the style of animé, lending itself to a sophisticated, young, Asian feel. Similar to all the media spots, these animations were delivered to both English-speaking as well as Spanish-speaking audiences.

Location: Due to the visual style, backgrounds were artistically rendered, utilizing color and line to lend visual interest and excitement to the story. Backgrounds change frequently, are abstract at times, specific at others, creating a sense of fun and excitement.

Style: The animé style was specifically chosen to attract the younger voter. These two spots were the last ones produced in the series of voter-education spots. The previously produced spots were executed adopting a more a conservative perspective. It was agreed that an outreach to younger voters was necessary to balance previous outreach attempts with an equal effort to encourage youth to become a part of the process. On the other hand, the current popularity of animé films made it possible that there would be a wide interest in the style across age groups. The use of bright colors, young sophisticated characters, and abstract backgrounds are meant to attract and hold the attention of the younger voter, those used to quick visual changes on their computer screens. The return to the repetitive chant-style of the first education spot, "The Cheer," combined with the use of rhyme and near rhyme creates a sense of urgency and an easy prompt for the message.

Problems to Solve: It was assumed that the number of spoiled ballots could be reduced with increased education efforts. In the 2008 San Joaquin early primary election, 2,216 votes were spoiled due to failure of the voters to fill in the ovals clearly or completely, representing 62.6% of the spoiled ballots. In addition, 204 ballots had signature problems in the same election.[7]

Message: The messages from these two television spots were: Voting is easy—don't be afraid. Don't worry if you make a mistake; you can ask for up to three ballots. Fill in the ovals completely. And sign only once; whether voting by mail or at the polls—don't mark or initial your ballot.

2. Poll Worker Television Ads

In addition to spots meant to increase vote by mail and reduce voter error, the registrar of voters commissioned a triptych of spots to encourage a variety of people to sign up as poll workers. While not directly related to reducing voter error, these outreach tools also attempted to increase the interest

---

[7] See Appendix A, Tables 3a and 4a, 111–114.

of potential voters in the voting process across ages, ethnicities, gender, and socio-economic backgrounds. The following summarize the resulting spots:

- *"**Store Owner**"* introduces an Asian-American female (in the English version) or a Latina (in the Spanish version); this restaurant owner suggests that the retired customer (male Caucasian, early 70s) consider being a poll worker, like she is.

- In *"**Professor and Student**"* the retired customer reappears with a former student (Latina) and suggests she consider being a poll worker, as he is.

- In *"**The Graduate**"* it is revealed that the student has indeed become a poll worker, and her father is proud of her. She suggests that her fellow student, a male Pacific Islander, consider doing poll work as well.

The three spots work together to create the image of an entire community, with representatives of all ages, work status, gender, and ethnicity, volunteering to help with the voting process.

3. Outreach in Multiple Languages

Since there are a high percentage of Spanish speakers in San Joaquin County, all television spots were presented in English and Spanish. According to the United States Census Bureau, San Joaquin County includes 37 percent people who self-identify as of Hispanic or Latino origin, and 33.7 percent indicate that a "language other than English" is spoken at home.

Comcast disseminated the spots across a range of times of day, on both English and Spanish stations, and in association with a variety of programming in a concerted effort to reach different groups of voters. Comcast Spotlight provides detailed demographic information on their viewers that they presented to the registrar.[8] Using this data, the registrar was able to purchase air-time that carefully balanced the gender, ethnicity, and socio-economic status of the viewer in an effort to reach all voters that might watch television.

When working with translations of any sort, there are additional considerations. One issue with English-to-Spanish translations is length: an idea that can be expressed in one word in English may require a phrase in Spanish. This puts the onus on the actors, director, and editor to keep the message exactly the same, and yet keep each of the spots within the 30-second time limit. Learning to write the English version short and padding the end with the Registrar of Voters emblem and web site, bought a much-needed second for the Spanish version. Both versions have access to the emblem and web site, but the need for more time with the spoken message was accommodated in this way. Sometimes, asking the actors to simply talk quickly in Spanish solved the problem. Regardless, sensitivity to the issues of translation is needed when working with diversity in voter-education materials, whether they are print, vocal, or visual materials.

IV. Branding of Official Voting Materials and Signage

A. Vote at Home/By Mail Campaign Literature

Responding to needs articulated by the San Joaquin County Registrar involved creating a recognizable visual symbol to brand the vote-by-mail campaign. This particular phase of the project had a very short time horizon for the generation of the symbol as well as the creation of an animated symbol for use on televised information spots. During the process, the name of the project shifted from Absentee Vote to Vote at Home and subsequently to Vote by Mail. The revisions occasioned by the last name change are not incorporated here.

In developing this logo, it was necessary to take into account one of several mistakes that voters make in marking their choice with a check mark rather than completely filling in the oval provided. Other common mistakes include marking with an X or by using a pencil. Below are some of the initial attempts at a logo:

---

8 Dave Wilcox, "Cable TV Advertising Proposal for San Joaquin County Registrar of Voters Air dates: July 1 to November 2, 2008" Comcast, Stockton, Calif.

The symbol finally evolved to fully incorporate the actual voting action, which could be accomplished from one's own home.

The animated version for inclusion in the televised sports included expanded imagery meant to provide further cues to restrict voter error.

B. Information Signage outside Polling Places

Information signage was developed for placement outside polling places during the primary election to serve two main purposes.
- To address main mistakes made by the voter on the ballot itself
- To remind voters they could complete the process from home next time

This signage information was presented all under the heading "*You Can* Make *Your* Vote Count." All information was presented in both English and Spanish and specifically reminded voters that they would be voting by using paper ballots. They were also reminded not to spoil their ballots by signing or making any other stray marks on their ballot and to completely fill in the oval with pen, no Xs, check marks, or pencil.

This signage, as originally designed, was to be presented on freestanding, three-sided pylons lining the approach to the polling place. On one side the information was presented in English, the adjoining side in Spanish, and on the back side (meant to be seen when leaving the polling place) a reminder to vote from home next time in both languages.

A modification of the pylon used to present this information was subsequently made. The structure was modified from three-sided to one sided with a pole anchored into a traffic cone base as a means for displaying the laminated posters. As this modification was not thoroughly pretested, it presented several problems. The most damaging of these problems was that installation of the signs in this format required more time and the active involvement of the poll workers to set up correctly and to be effective at each polling place.

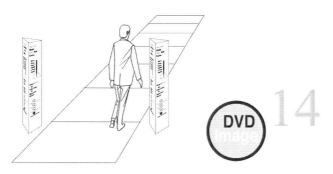

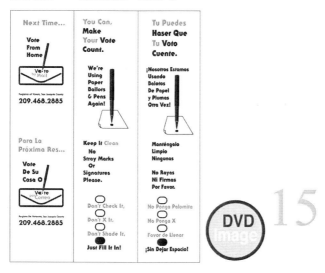

In spite of hands-on installation practice and a handout of instructions given to workers who delivered the signage to polling sites, not one sign was installed correctly and the vast majority was not set up at all. This disappointing result can be attributed to several mitigating factors.

1. The decision to switch the structure from the pylon to the pole design creating several additional steps in the installation process.
2. The reliance on the abilities of volunteer workers to assure success.
3. The absence of a quality control person to check polling place signage.

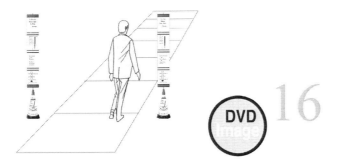

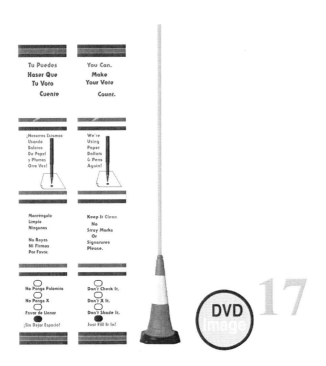

C. Information Signage inside Polling Booth

Polling booth signage was developed to hang inside the actual booth where voting takes place. This sign was a graphic instruction sheet highlighting the most common mistakes made by voters in the act of voting and how to avoid or correct them. These signs were placed in the polling booths before they were transported to each individual site. This assured proper placement and 100% installation of this information.

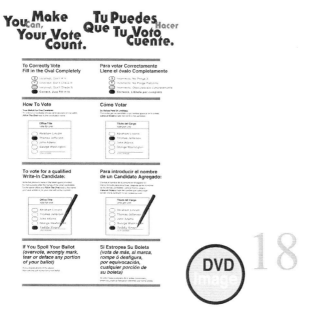

D. Sample Ballot Booklet Redesign

The redesign of the sample ballot booklet included the following five elements:
- cover, front, back, and inside
- "filler pages," several pages specific to individual voting topics
- instructions to voters, how to vote correctly
- vote from home instructions
- sample ballot

Each of the print pieces focused on delivering the information in as clear and understandable a way as possible. New information included revisions to the vote-from-home/vote-by-mail application and a discussion of major errors committed by voters in previous elections and how to correct them. An attempt was made to improve the clarity of information presented within the booklet by:
- visual organization
- grouping of similar information
- clear hierarchy of information
- typography

OLD Back Cover

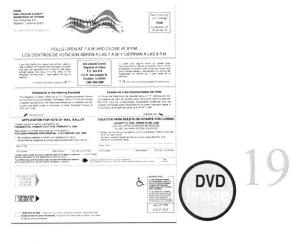

OLD Front Cover

NEW Back Cover

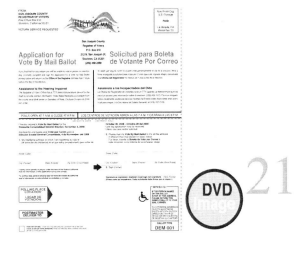

NEW Front Cover

Sample page "filler"

How To Vote

To Vote, use ballpoint pen with dark ink to fill in the oval completely like this: ●

| To Correctly Vote |
| Fill in the Oval Completely |
| Incorrect, Don't X It |
| Incorrect, Don't Check It |
| Incorrect, Don't Shade It |
| Correct, Just Fill It In |

Your Ballot For One Candidate
To vote for a candidate whose name appears on the ballot, *Fill In The Oval* next to the candidate's name.

| Office Title |
| vote for one |
| Abraham Lincoln |
| Thomas Jefferson |
| John Adams |
| George Washington |
| other candidate |

Vote By Mail Voters:
(Application for Vote By Mail Ballot is located on back cover)
Separate from the rest of the Pamphlet along the dashed line.

Back Cover

Where Two or More Candidates Are To Be Elected
Fill in The Oval next to the names of all candidates for the office for whom you desire to vote.
Do Not Exceed the Number of Candidates To Be Elected.

| Office Title |
| vote for two |
| Abraham Lincoln |
| Thomas Jefferson |
| John Adams |
| George Washington |
| other candidate |

To Vote for a Qualified *Write-In* Candidate
Write the person's name in the blank space provided for that purpose after the names of the other candidates for the same office and *Fill In The Oval* next to the name you have written in, or your vote will not be counted.

| Office Title |
| vote for one |
| Abraham Lincoln |
| Thomas Jefferson |
| John Adams |
| George Washing |
| Teddy Kowa | other candidate |

To Vote on Any Measure
Fill in The Oval next to the word "Yes" or the word "No". All distinguishing marks or erasures are forbidden and will make the ballot void.

| Proposition 3 |
| Yes |
| No |

If You Spoil Your Ballot
(overvote, wrongly mark, tear or deface any portion of your ballot)
If you should do any of the above then contact the Registrar of Voter's office at: (209)468-2890.

Returning Your Ballot
After you have finished voting, seal your ballot in the return envelope. Be sure to sign and complete the information on the reverse side of the envelope. You may mail or hand deliver your ballot to the Elections Office, or hand deliver it to any polling place on Election Day.

If for this election there were no qualified candidates for partisan offices in your district for the **American Independent Party, Green Party, Libertarian Party, or Peace and Freedom Party.** Nevertheless, voters affiliated with these parties will be able to vote for all measures and candidates for nonpartisan offices on a nonpartisan ballot that will be available either at the polls or through the mail. If you have any questions please call (209)468-2898.

Helpful Hints
To Make Election Day Easier

Precinct officers are citizens like you. They sincerely want to make voting easy while protecting against voter fraud. Here are some ideas for you to make Election Day easier for all.

- Polling Place locations may change at each Election.
  Your polling place is listed on the back cover of this Sample Ballot booklet.

- If you are not planning on a Vote By Mail ballot, check to make sure you know where your polling place is located. If you are not sure how to find your polling place, check a map or call (209) 468-2890 before Election Day.

- Take this Sample Ballot booklet with you to the polls to help your precinct officer quickly locate your name and address on the voter roster.

- Go to the polls prepared. Read and mark your Sample Ballot prior to Election Day and take it with you to refer to while you are in the voting booth. This is especially helpful with a lengthy ballot.

- If you are a first time voter, be prepared to show identification

Save Time

- Mark your choices in this Sample booklet and take it to your polling place for reference.

- Your polling place location is shown on the back cover.

- If possible, vote in the mid-morning or mid-afternoon hours. This will help shorten lines during the evening rush.

Polls are open from 7 a.m. to 8 p.m.

V. IMPACT

A. Coordinated Print and Radio Campaign

Budget limitations prevented the full implementation of the post-test of the print and radio media campaign. However, the impact of the campaign was assessed by an analysis of caller responses to the radio stations, to the newspaper, and to the registrar of voters' website.
Four specific conclusions can be drawn from this evidence:

1. A surprising number of "hits" were recorded on the registrar of voters' website following the Internet ads on the radio stations. It will be recalled that the tile ads linked the radio station sites to the registrar of voters.
2. The radio station ads generated calls to the stations for more information. Even though the ad mentioned the registrar of voters' phone number, the listeners instead chose to call the radio station. This may signal the lack of clarity in the ad and/or the limited amount of attention paid to the ad by the listener.
3. The newspaper ads did generate a few calls to the registrar of voters. Callers asked questions about the absentee ballot procedures. Newspaper readers' inquiries tended to be more serious and specific about the voting process.
4. An unintended result of the campaign was the "front page" news it generated in the regional newspaper. A feature article on the Vote Smart Project's media campaign appeared as a consequence of allowing students to participate in a countywide project. News editors considered this unique activity newsworthy. Such coverage, of course, raises the question of "when should an advertiser become news content."

B. Television Spots

Anecdotal evidence suggests that the television media campaign was successful and contributed to what was deemed "the most successful election ever" by Registrar of Voters Austin Erdman. Making the effort to address specific voter errors that had, in the past, resulted in voters' ballots being marked "spoiled" helped to reduce those specific errors. While there were larger issues at stake in the 2008 presidential election, voter turnout was high, and encouraging all San Joaquin voters to participate successfully reflected well on the Office of the Registrar of Voters and helped to garner them compliments and thanks from their constituency.

C. The Branding of Official Voting Materials and Signage

This application of basic design principles can help to reduce errors in the balloting process by aiding in the reevaluation and presentation of information. It can also introduce a more systematic method for presentation of information in a clearly recognizable and familiar format, a brand identity. Design makes use of visual principles to aid in this communication by creating a sense of visual order, grouping, and hierarchy. *Form* is defined as the material, medium, or method that is used to deliver the message. *Content* is defined as the information or message itself. It may be factual or persuasive in nature. The primary purpose of good design is not aesthetic (although aesthetics are certainly a major influence on the efficacy of delivering the message). It is instead, the clear communication of information. It emphasizes how *Content* may be more easily understood because of the *Form* it is presented in.
Resistance to new design directions is driven by several main factors.
1. Comfort level with what is known or established
2. Long-established practices and work-flow habits

3.   Suspicion of "outsider" suggestions

Therefore any future improvement in the materials and signage used by the registrar of voters would need to address these factors. It would also be useful to structure more targeted assessment protocols to assess beyond antidotes the impact of the changes that were made.

VI. Conclusions and Recommendations for the Future

A. Coordinated Print and Radio Campaign

Design and implementation of a print and radio media campaign for a registrar of voters can be an effective method of getting a structured message out to the general voting public. This experience suggests the following conclusions in regard to future initiatives:

- To gain a significant reach and frequency from media can be an expensive investment for an advertiser. To use the media wisely, those charged with voter education must be willing to spend the funds necessary to gain the attention of a sizable audience. A specific dollar formula could be appropriated to reach each voter. For example, is it worth $1 per voter to deliver information to their home or car? At such a rate, $1,000 should be allocated to reach each 1,000 voters. This kind of rationale might make it easier for government agencies to justify such expenditures.

- Second, though the use of billboards was not tested here, it should not be ruled out as a viable medium in which to place an ad about voting. The size and location of such outdoor advertising creates significant exposure to simple messages to busy commuters, even if subliminally.

- Third, all media advertising should be coordinated together in a campaign. Unfortunately, here the cable TV spots that ran before the elections did not have the same content as the radio and newspaper ads. Future efforts should ensure a continuity of message.

- Fourth, the Internet as a venue for advertising is largely uncharted, but should not be ignored. More and more voters are getting their mass communication via this new medium. Exposure of ads on a multitude of websites cannot help but generate responses from voters. Even the limited use of tile ads in this experiment appeared to have generated positive results.

- Fifth, an effective media campaign should be run longer than four weeks before an election. To gain the maximum message retention and branding among a population, advertising over a minimum of three months is suggested. Because the cable television ads were run over a month period, they were perhaps more effective in achieving their objectives of encouraging poll-worker participation and the elimination of voter error.

- Sixth and finally, consistent use of identity elements established for print media should be continued across all media including websites.

B. Television Spots

It takes a considerable effort to reach out to the diverse California population when using visual media such as television. Attention to casting, costumes, and location are important in reaching all aspects of the target audience through broadcast media. With care and planning, and of course the funding to produce a series of spots—not just one or two—a county can successfully reach and educate a diverse voting public.

Specific recommendations include:

- Get as much preproduction time as possible. Due to the sensitive nature of attracting and representing the wide diversity of the voting public, several constituencies might be consulted on text and translations, and drafts of original material reworked. Allowing the writer time for revisions and allowing the casting director time to collect a diverse cast of actors will increase the quality of the work presented.

- Utilize the research available through the local television stations. Their detailed demographic data will greatly assist in tracking the accessibility of the message.

- If possible, allow the media team to meet at least eight months in advance of the campaign. Considering all forms of media together can influence the dispersal of budgeted funds. For example, while an attempt was made in San Joaquin County to reach the widest possible range of voters via the television spots, a group might consider utilizing television to reach one segment of voters, and bench ads to reach a different segment. The message, if coordinated, will be the same in all forms of media; but the group might attempt to reach each segment of the demographic using a unique choice of media, one particularly accessible by each segment of the voting public. A billboard ad near the largest employer in the area can reach "the worker," while a strategically placed daytime television ad can reach "the at-home caregiver." Coordinating the overall campaign can assist in using limited funds to reach as wide an audience as possible.

C. The Branding of Official Voting Materials and Signage

Recommendations for future improvements in print media focus on the application of design standards as established by *The American Institute for Graphic Design (AIGA)* in affiliation with *HAVA*. These include similar goals to those used in San Joaquin County and will extend the look of materials to coincide with national standards and conventions. *The Design for Democracy* standards manual developed a best practices approach to use of basic design principles such as type, color, and size, as well as systems for workflow and poll-worker training.[9] The incorporation of these standards will go far in eliminating or correcting a majority of the problems experienced with the current election process and will "fine tune" the work proposed in this project.

VII. An Afterword

The structured media campaign exercise conducted by a class of graduate students in communication at the University of the Pacific provides an interesting glimpse into the development of a marketing plan during an election. Involving Pacific's theatre arts and graphic design students and professionals to produce the marketing products specific to their fields increased the level of expertise on an affordable budget. It provided all students the opportunity to research, create, plan, and implement strategies for the dissemination of messages about voting. It also offers a model for future endeavors by voting agencies and political campaigns.

In other words, those in charge of reforming voter education should think outside the box. If a project can include university students it can generate collateral press and media coverage. It is also critical to get buy-in and trust from all employees and persons involved early on to assure greater success. All participants must have planning time allotted to implement quality work, to get everyone on-board, and to cement a solid collaborative plan and budget. Like many educational and governmental projects, the experiment was limited by time allotment and funding. However, it evolved into a significant interaction of educators, media professionals, and government workers. From such an activity, learning is always enhanced.

---

[9] Marcia Lausen, *Design for Democracy: Ballot and Election Design* (Chicago: University of Chicago Press, 2007).

* * *

End Credits for the video advertisements:

Concept/Writer	Lisa A. Tromovitch, Department of Theatre Arts, University of the Pacific
Director	Lisa A. Tromovitch, Shakespeare's Associates, Inc.
Director of Photography/Editor	Jim Patterson, Comcast Spotlight
Graphic Designer	Brett DeBoer, Department of Visual Arts, University of the Pacific
Story Artist, animated spots	Glynnis Koike
Animator	J. Atwood, T. G. Studios
On-Camera Actors contracted through Shakespeare's Associates, Inc.	Jonathan Cardenas, Stanson Chung, Ochuko Egbikuadje, Susan Giraldez, Nikolai Lokteff, Kathleen Park, Becca Parker, Gloria Betsy Picart, Laura Sudduth, William J. Wolak
Voice-Over Artists	LaShante Churchwell, Johanna Covell, Christopher Dewey, Angela Dunne, Scarlett Eisenhauser, Yunji Johanning, Ginger Mooney, Brian Peccia, Krista Perkins, Danielle Stephens
Translators	Traci Roberts-Camp and her students, Modern Languages Department, University of the Pacific, Gloria Betsy Picart
Sound Editing, animated spots	Gary Scheiding, Department of Theatre Arts, University of the Pacific
Props Masters, *The Cheer*	Brad Enlow and Randall Enlow, Department of Theatre Arts, University of the Pacific

Chapter 6

Methods for Improving Design and Evaluation of Poll-Worker Training

Jon F. Schamber[1]

After the debacle of the 2000 presidential election, policymakers and scholars focused on methods to improve voting procedures in the United States. This attention resulted in the passage of the Help America Vote Act (HAVA) by Congress in 2002. HAVA provided funds for states to replace punch-card voting equipment, established the Election Assistance Commission for assisting with the administration of federal elections, and established minimum standards at the state and the local level for conducting federal elections.[2]

As a result of HAVA, election officials have devoted more time and effort on one of the most neglected parts of the nation's election system—the training of poll workers. Prior to the enactment of this legislation, the recruitment and training of poll workers was primarily a responsibility of more than 10,000 jurisdictions in charge of holding elections in the United States.[3] Section 254(a) of HAVA requires each state to establish plans for implementing new federal voting procedures and allocate HAVA Title II funds for the education of elections officials and poll workers. States such as California subsequently adopted legislation for creating guidelines for the training of poll workers at the county level.[4] As mandated by HAVA, the U.S. Election Assistance Commission has issued a manual titled *Successful Practices for Poll Worker Recruitment, Training, and Retention* that sets forth practical advice for election officials charged with training poll workers.[5] The manual includes "a broad spectrum of 'best practices' . . . for conducting elections" based on the collective advice of experienced election officials and community leaders.[6]

---

[1] Department of Communication, University of the Pacific.

[2] Help America Vote Act of 2002, Public Law 107–252.

[3] Task Force on Poll Worker Training Standards, *Final Report 2005* (Sacramento, California: California State Legislature, 2005), 1; Mary Pat Flaherty, "High Turnout, New Procedures May Mean an Election Day Mess," *The Washington Post*, September 18, 2008, Sept. 21, retrieved from <http://www.washingtonpost.com>.

[4] Task Force on Poll Worker Training Standards, 3.

[5] U.S. Election Assistance Commission, *Successful Practices for Poll Worker Recruitment, Training and Retention* (Washington, D.C.: U.S. Election Assistance Commission, July 2007).

[6] U.S. Election Assistance Commission, i.

The need for federal and state assistance with poll-worker training is documented by continued instances of problems at the polls. Indeed, poorly trained poll workers have been identified as a source of voter frustration and concern on Election Day. During the presidential primary elections conducted during February 2008, poll workers were responsible for many of the things that went wrong at the polls. In Washington, D.C., "poll workers hid electronic voting machines because they didn't like the touch-screen devices."[7] In Chicago, voters at some precincts were given pens for electronic voting machines to mark paper ballots, and when voters complained that the pens could not be used to mark their ballots, some election workers told the voters that the pens "were full of invisible ink."[8] Poll workers in California "mistakenly asked voters to show their driver's licenses before casting a ballot and incorrectly told registered independents they could not vote for a Democratic candidate."[9] Nearly 50,000 ballots in Los Angeles were cast incorrectly by nonpartisan voters as a consequence of a confusing ballot design and poor education of poll workers.[10] These and other instances of poorly trained poll workers adversely affect the conduct of elections in the United States.

This study reports the results of a consulting project to improve the training of poll workers in San Joaquin County, California. Part of the project allowed for testing the effectiveness of an interactive training method from the perspective of poll workers. The project also uncovered institutional impediments that can inhibit the implementation of best practices into the design and evaluation of poll-worker training classes. The results of the consulting project contribute to the growing body of research on interactive training techniques for poll-worker training classes and the importance of evaluation procedures that can be employed by election officials to monitor and improve poll-worker training.

Review of the Literature

Various reasons have been identified in the literature for problems associated with the training of poll workers in the United States. These problems can be organized under three phases associated with the election-worker training process: (1) the recruitment of election workers, (2) the training techniques employed during the training classes, and (3) the evaluation of the effectiveness of the training classes. Each of these phases warrants attention for an understanding of the way that the United States conducts its elections and difficulties confronting poll workers who are on the front lines of the election process.

The recruitment of poll workers represents a significant challenge for government agencies responsible for conducting elections in the United States. On Election Day, a virtual army of volunteers is needed to staff the polls. A survey conducted in 2006 by the National Association of Counties found that 56 percent of election officers "reported that they were unable to fully staff the polls in the last presidential election."[11] In San Joaquin County, California, a "dearth of [poll] workers reached 'crisis levels' during the primary election in June 2006, when there were 200 vacancies the weekend before the election and 35 voting locations had less than 50 percent staffing on the day of the election."[12] For the November 4, 2008, presidential election, nearly two million poll workers were needed across the nation to conduct the election, which was double the number for the 2004 election.[13]

---

[7] Deborah Hastings, "Ever Voted in Invisible Ink?" *The* [Stockton, Calif.] *Record*, February 24, 2008, A1.

[8] *Ibid.*

[9] Hastings, A1, A5.

[10] Joe Garofoli, "L.A. to Try Tallying Ballots Left Out," *San Francisco Chronicle*, February 13, 2008, A8.

[11] U.S. Election Assistance Commission, 7.

[12] Zachary K. Johnson, "S.J. Hopes to Lure Poll Workers," *The* [Stockton, Calif.] *Record*, January 22, 2008, B1-B2.

[13] Ian Urbina, "Influx of Voters Expected to Test New Technology," *The New York Times*, July 21, 2008, A16.

To remedy the problem of attracting sufficient numbers of poll workers, the U.S. Election Assistance Commission offers practical suggestions for recruiting these workers among the general public, college students, and high school students. The commission has also provided useful ideas for recruiting poll workers from businesses, organizations, and government agencies.[14] Moreover, this federal body offers ideas for helping election officials recruit poll workers with disabilities and bilingual capabilities, and people from hard-to-reach communities.[15]

California has also taken a lead in providing recommendations for the recruitment of poll workers to ensure that the minimum number of workers is available to staff each polling place. Although the recommendations offered by the state are "speculative" due to a lack of research on the efficacy of these recommendations, some successful strategies used at the county level include recruiting high school and college students. High school students reportedly have "a good response rate for the effort required to recruit them, and . . . possess attributes that make them . . . valuable at the polls," particularly with respect to serving as bilingual workers.[16] College students are "easy to train . . . and can easily understand how to operate technologically complex voting machines."[17]

There is a limited amount of literature on the education of poll workers through training classes. This literature has focused on such issues as the episodic nature of poll-worker training, the length of training classes, types of training techniques used during the classes, and training techniques for electronic voting equipment. Research on this area emphasizes the fact that well planned and executed training classes for poll workers are essential for elections. Indeed, "effective pre-election training is critical," because "workers need to understand how to address various tasks and problems that may occur on Election Day so that these events do not hamper the overall functioning of the polling place."[18] Poll workers are entrusted with setting up and closing down voting machines, deciding whether a citizen can cast a ballot, and determining if a voter should been given a provisional ballot. As such, poll workers can be regarded as "'street-level bureaucrats' who powerfully affect the experience that voters have on Election Day."[19] In addition, research suggests that the interactions of poll workers with voters affect voter perceptions of the fairness of elections and confidence about whether ballots will be counted.[20]

The episodic nature of poll-worker training represents a special challenge to the trainers of these workers as compared to other types of training programs. Because poll workers do not undertake their work every day and function on the job without the direct supervision of full-time managers, the training provided to these workers is distinctive.[21] On-the-job training for the typical worker often involves the demonstration of job tasks supplemented with general classroom instruction. Training a manager to delegate tasks, motivate employees, and communicate effectively in both interpersonal and small group contexts involves "'tell-show-do' method[s] where supervisory practices are discussed, demonstrated, and the trainees practice each of the skills." Managerial development also typically includes "a debriefing session . . . after practicing the skill in question to answer any questions and clarify supervisory practices."[22]

---

[14] See U.S. Election Assistance Commission, especially Chapters 1, 2, 3, 5, 6, and 7.

[15] See U.S. Election Assistance Commission, especially Chapters 4, 8, and 11.

[16] Task Force on Poll Worker Training Standards, 33.

[17] *Ibid.*

[18] Thad Hall, J. Quinn Monson, and Kelly D. Patterson, "Poll Workers and the Vitality of Democracy: An Early Assessment," *PS: Political Science and Politics* 40, no. 4 (October 2007): 647.

[19] *Ibid.*

[20] *Ibid.*; Lonna Atkeson and Kyle Saunders, "The Effects of Election Administration on Voter Confidence: A Local Matter?" *PS: Political Science and Politics* 40, no. 4 (October 2007): 657.

[21] Hall, Monson, and Patterson, 647; R. Michael Alverez and Thad E. Hall, "Controlling Democracy: The Principal-Agent Problems in Elections Administration," *Policy Studies Journal* 34, no. 4 (2006): 491–510.

[22] W. David Patton, Stephanie L. Witt, Nicholas P. Lovrich, and Patricia J. Fredericksen, *Human Resource Management: The Public Service Perspective* (Boston: Houghton Mifflin, 2002), 327.

Poll workers serving as clerks or inspectors on Election Day necessarily receive a different type of training from that of workers and managers in the real world. Clerks are the frontline employees who process voters while inspectors are responsible for the total operation of voting precincts, including the supervision of clerks. Training clerks for an election cannot follow the prescribed model of on-the-job training "because their job is so episodic in nature." These workers "can be taught through classroom sessions, but these sessions must cover both job function and general information because of the specific kind of work" they do on Election Day.[23] In this respect, the training provided to clerks can be regarded as a one-shot proposition that compresses learning the procedures for processing voters and handling special circumstances such as issuing provisional ballots into a short period of time. Training inspectors to work on the day of an election can utilize a "tell-show-do" method of training, but "the ongoing nature of post-election work, which can last up to one-month after the election, mean[s] that debriefing sessions for [these supervisory] poll workers are likely to be relatively rare."[24] Moreover, voting jurisdictions that use electronic voting systems typically require inspectors to learn how to set up and operate the equipment, and this training often takes place on the same day that inspectors receive instructions for their other duties. Consequently, training poll workers to serve as clerks and inspectors is a challenge for election officials who are responsible for ensuring that the polls are staffed with highly trained workers.

Some research has been conducted on the length of poll-worker training classes. An investigation of the length of poll-worker training classes in California revealed that there was great deal of variation. Three counties relied on training classes that met for one hour or less. Thirty counties used ninety minute to two-hour classes for training poll workers. Eight counties offered classes lasting between two hours and fifteen minutes to three hours. Fifteen counties trained their poll workers in classes that met for three hours or more.[25] Great variation in the length of training was also reported for operating voting systems. Fifteen counties did not devote any time to training workers about the county's voting system. Six counties spent up to 15 minutes on this instruction; four spent 15 to 30 minutes; seven spent 30 to 60 minutes; and 13 spent 60 minutes or more. Ten other counties reported that training time devoted to their voting system "varied."[26]

Although the research about the length of poll-worker classes in California did not address the effectiveness of the training, it might raise concerns about the duration of training on poll-worker comprehension and retention of information. Training classes that are too short might not provide sufficient instruction for trainees to perform their tasks on Election Day, whereas classes that are too long might fatigue trainees and reduce the retention of information. Perhaps for these reasons, the California Task Force on Uniform Poll Worker Standards recommends "training sessions about Election Day processes and procedures should last no more than 60–90 minutes. If more time is needed, the training should be broken into discrete sections with 10–15 minute breaks in between."[27]

Since the passage of HAVA, a limited amount of research has been conducted on various types of poll-worker training methods. These methods can range from a lecture format to a highly interactive training class involving role-playing scenarios. The Task Force on Uniform Poll Worker Training Standards in California undertook a descriptive study of the types of training used by the state's 57 counties for the March 2004 California primary. This study revealed that the traditional lecture format was the most common training method used for poll worker classes. Twenty-one counties, however, employed some nontraditional training methods. These methods included PowerPoint presentations, videos or DVDs, quizzes and/or role-playing exercises. Hands-on training methods were also listed as

---

[23] Hall, Monson, and Patterson, 648.

[24] *Ibid.*

[25] Task Force on Uniform Poll Worker Training Standards, 7. This data was collected for the March 2004 California Primary.

[26] Task Force on Uniform Poll Worker Training Standards, 8. This data was collected for the March 2004 California Primary.

[27] *Ibid.*, 32.

nontraditional instructional techniques, probably reflecting the need for this method of training with electronic voting equipment.[28]

The U.S. Election Assistance Commission recommends that election officials use multiple training methods in the design of their training programs for poll workers. This recommendation is based on the fact that such techniques "have been proved to improve adult learners' comprehension and retention of information."[29] California's Task Force on Uniform Poll Worker Training Standards reached a similar conclusion: "Studies have shown that poll workers, like all adult learners, learn best by short, interactive training sessions."[30]

Studies on adult learning and organizational training emphasize the superiority of interactive training methods over a standard lecture format. Although a lecture format is efficient, a trainee "becomes a passive listener" when instructed through this technique.[31] With lectures, "trainees do not have a chance to find out if they are learning what the trainer wants them to learn."[32] Studies on adult learners also indicate that these learners retain more information when provided with training opportunities to "say and do" what they are being taught.[33] Multimethod training programs involving techniques such as role playing, case studies, and small group discussions have been found to be effective with adults who are learning how to perform tasks and job responsibilities for the first time.[34] These training programs also provide occasions for trainers to monitor what the trainees have learned.

The recent introduction of electronic voting equipment at polling precincts has also stimulated research on training methods. One study compared the effectiveness of different training methods used in two election jurisdictions, both of which were using the Diebold touch screen electronic voting equipment with a voter-verified paper audit trail. In one jurisdiction, poll-worker training classes were conducted with a three-hour lecture format. In the second jurisdiction, the classes were conducted with considerable hands-on practice with the voting equipment, as well as an opportunity for poll workers to return for additional training prior to the election. Survey data revealed that hands-on training classes improved poll-worker perceptions of confidence to work as poll workers on Election Day and job satisfaction as compared to lecture-only classes.[35] The hands-on training classes also reduced problems that poll workers had with setting up and closing down the machines.[36]

The third phase of the poll-worker training process involves an evaluation of the training. At this juncture, an organization reviews the quality of the training, ascertains the learning that occurred from the training, and determines how to improve the training program.[37] The U.S. Election Assistance Commission recommends that election officials evaluate their training programs because this type of assessment can "determine whether the training is effective," "suggest ways to improve the program," "add credibility to the training program," "enable [election officials] to hold trainers accountable," and "provide evidence to support requests for training resources."[38]

Collecting data for evaluating poll-worker training does not require elaborate data gathering methods. Poll workers can be asked to complete an evaluation form after each training class. A post-election evaluation form can also be administered to poll workers to "track weaknesses in training."[39]

---

[28] *Ibid.*, 8.

[29] U.S. Election Assistance Commission, 104.

[30] Task Force on Uniform Poll Worker Training Standards, 32.

[31] Sue DeWine, *The Consultant's Craft: Improving Organizational Communication*, 2d ed. (Boston: Bedford/St. Martin's, 2001), 86.

[32] William E. Arnold and Lynne McClure, *Communication Training and Development*, 2d ed. (Prospect Heights, Ill.: Waveland Press, 1996), 101.

[33] *Ibid.*, 38.

[34] Patton et al., 332–34.

[35] Hall, Monson, and Patterson, 650, 652.

[36] *Ibid.*, 653.

[37] *Ibid.*, 648.

[38] U.S. Election Assistance Commission, 126–27.

[39] Task Force on Uniform Poll Worker Training Standards, 32.

Another useful source of data for the evaluation of poll-worker training is the log of calls placed to election headquarters by poll workers on Election Day.[40] These data are useful for identifying common problems experienced by poll workers in the field on Election Day that might be resolved by revising the content of the training classes. Other data collection methods, such as debriefing meetings held with field technicians after an election, have been suggested for improving training on voting equipment.[41] In addition, debriefing meetings can be held with field inspectors after an election to generate a list of issues that need attention for the training of workers during future elections.

Although data collection methods to evaluate poll-worker training are relatively simple, many election officials who are responsible for training poll workers have not readily embraced a culture of assessment. Hall, Monson, and Patterson explain that "an electoral jurisdiction, like any organization, needs a built-in mechanism that allows it to learn from previous experience to plan for the future. However, public-sector training is often underfunded, largely because it is not seen as central to the organization's mission, and it is difficult to evaluate its impact on the various organizational outputs."[42] Some election officials who are responsible for overseeing the training of poll workers may lack expertise for conducting such assessments and consequently avoid undertaking an evaluation of the program.

Postelection pressures are another impediment for the assessment of poll-worker training classes. After Election Day, election officials can become consumed with postelection work such as verifying and counting provisional and vote-by-mail ballots. In some instances these procedures can take many weeks to complete and consequently reduce the likelihood of holding debriefing meetings with poll workers.[43] Moreover, as time passes, poll workers might not be able to recall problems experienced on Election Day that can be resolved through training.

In summary, research conducted on the recruitment and training of poll workers is incomplete. However, the literature clearly indicates that election officials need to focus on the "assessment, design, delivery, and evaluation" of poll-worker training programs.[44] The point of this attention is to design a training program that maximizes adult learning and to evaluate the training program so that the strengths and weaknesses of the training are revealed for implementing improvements in the training program for future elections. Ultimately, the process of formative assessment based on the collection and analysis of evidence should result in training classes that improve the effectiveness and confidence of poll workers who are empowered with running elections.

Consulting Background and Project Methodology

This consulting project on the effectiveness of poll-worker training in San Joaquin County, California, was undertaken in two phases, both involving mixed methods as the methodology for the project. For the first phase, which evaluated poll-worker training for the February 5, 2008 California presidential primary election, five sources of data were collected and analyzed: (1) field observations of the training classes, (2) a questionnaire administered to poll workers immediately after attending a training class, (3) notes from a debriefing meeting held with field inspectors two weeks after the election, (4) a content analysis of the call center log for the election, and (5) a telephone survey of a stratified random sample of poll workers two weeks after the election. This mixed-methods design was used to strengthen the validity of the findings about the strengths and weaknesses of the county's training program and to formulate recommendations for improving the program.

---

[40] U.S. Election Assistance Commission, 127.

[41] *Ibid.*, 102.

[42] Hall, Monson, and Patterson, 648.

[43] Task Force on Uniform Poll Worker Training Standards, 648.

[44] Hall, Monson, and Patterson, 648.

One of the recommendations, which will be discussed shortly in detail, called for the integration of role-playing exercises and case studies into the design of the training program. It was anticipated that this change would be implemented for the June 4, 2008 California primary election. Since this did not transpire in June, the second phase of the consulting project was postponed until the November 4, 2008 presidential election. For this election, the training program was redesigned to include two case studies involving provisional ballots. Data collected and analyzed for evaluating the second phase of the project included the following: (1) field observations of the training, (2) a questionnaire administered to the trainees immediately after the training classes, and (3) a postelection questionnaire completed by poll workers.

For the February 5, 2008 California presidential primary election, the San Joaquin County Registrar of Voters hired workers to serve as clerks, inspectors, field inspectors, and TSx (Diebold) specialists. For the November 4, 2008 presidential election, the county dispensed with hiring election workers as TSx specialists, but continued the practice of hiring people to serve as clerks, inspectors, and field inspectors. For both elections, small teams of election workers trained as clerks were responsible for processing voters at each precinct. Inspectors were responsible for the overall operation of the voting precincts as well as setting up and operating the Diebold equipment. Field inspectors for both elections were typically assigned to cover four to six voting precincts.

The format of the poll-worker training programs for the February and November elections, with the exception of the inclusion of the two case studies for the later election, was basically the same. Poll workers serving as clerks were trained for approximately 90 minutes using a lecture format supplemented with PowerPoint slides and visual displays of election supplies. The training content for these poll workers included voting supplies, opening the polls, worker duties, special circumstances, and closing the polls. Inspectors and field inspectors were trained separately from clerks, in most instances, using similar lecture materials, PowerPoint slides, and visual aids. However, these workers were also given approximately 90 minutes of additional training. This training covered their duties as election supervisors and hands-on training for operating Diebold touch screen (TSx) equipment with a paper audit trail. For both elections, a head trainer was responsible for designing the training program, training a team of hired trainers to teach the poll-worker training classes, and overseeing the training classes. Paper ballots were used for both elections, but disabled voters were given the option of using the Diebold machines to cast their ballots.

Phase One Results of the Consulting Project

The results of the first phase of the consulting project produced many important findings. A communication professor, one trained graduate student, and nine trained upper-division communication students undertook field observations of the poll-worker training classes. The observations focused on the content of the training classes, the methods used for teaching the training classes, and the communication skills of the trainers. In general, the observations revealed that the training content was appropriate given the tasks and duties of the election workers and that the trainers were effective communicators. Observations of the classes also revealed that with the exception of the hands-on training provided for the Diebold machines for inspectors and field inspectors, the predominant method of the training classes was a lecture presented with PowerPoint slides and visual displays of election supplies that would be used on Election Day.

The questionnaire administered to poll workers after attending a training class yielded both quantitative and qualitative data about trainee perceptions of the training program. Of the 1,771 poll workers attending the training classes, 595 completed the questionnaire. Of those who completed the questionnaire, 549 were clerks, 25 were inspectors, 7 were field inspectors, and 14 were TSx (Diebold) specialists.[45]

Based on nine Likert-type statements rated on a five-point scale (with 5 being "strongly agree" and 1 being "strongly disagree"), the quantitative data indicated high levels of satisfaction with the training in terms of developing confidence as poll workers (see Table 1), trainer credibility (see Table 2), and the quality of training (see Table 3). Inspectors, field inspectors, and TSx specialists who received hands-on Diebold equipment training also reported high levels of satisfaction with this part of the training program in terms of developing confidence and the quality of the training, although the level of satisfaction was slightly lower than that reported for the other part of the training program (see Table 4).

Qualitative data derived from two items on the questionnaire reinforced many of the findings from the quantitative data, but added a richer understanding of poll-worker perceptions about the training program. The first item asked the poll workers to provide additional comments about their trainer. Nearly all of the written comments (203 out of 208) were positive. The trainees noted that the trainers were knowledgeable of election procedures, receptive to answering questions, effective in using humor while presenting the training material, well prepared for teaching the training classes, and excellent public speakers.

The second item on the questionnaire provided an opportunity for the trainees to provide suggestions for improving the training classes. Of 121 comments provided by the trainees, 59 were coded as positive evaluative statements about the training and 62 were coded as areas of training that needed improvement. Positive comments about the training emphasized the clarity of the training information, the quality of the training in terms of organization, and the development of confidence as a result of the training.

The two most important findings from the qualitative data regarding suggestions to improve the training indicated the need for the training to be more interactive and the need for additional training about provisional ballots. Representative comments from a few of the poll workers about the design and content of the training were as follows:

The training session became blurry [or] boring at one point. We need to have interaction of some sort after an hour of [the lecture] presentation to keep our minds active.

I think a mock example of a poll worker and his [or] her team giving out different ballots (i.e., provisional) would be effective. Being able to see a situation may be a lot more helpful than [only hearing] what to do [in that situation].

It would be useful to include role-playing exercises.

We need hands-on training and actual practice instead of just a lecture with PowerPoint slides.

Have us work in groups and work through actual situations.

It would help me if they had us do hands-on training and let us practice what to do in situations.

I needed more examples of provisional ballots.

It would be better to spend more time on provisional votes.

---

[45] The small number of inspectors, field inspectors, and TSx specialists who completed the questionnaire was a consequence of the head trainer's decision not to administer the questionnaire to trainees attending most of the training classes for these positions.

Table 1. Mean Scores of Poll-Worker Confidence

Questionnaire Items	n	Mean
The class helped me understand what I will be doing on Election Day.	592	4.67
The class makes me feel confident that I will do a good job on Election Day.	595	4.64

Table 2. Mean Scores of Trainer Credibility and Effectiveness

Questionnaire Items	n	Mean
The trainer was an effective instructor.	591	4.73
The trainer was knowledgeable of election procedures.	592	4.76
The trainer did a good job explaining the information on the slides.	594	4.74
The trainer was able to answer questions that arose during the class.	592	4.74
The trainer was well prepared for the class.	589	4.62

Table 3. Mean Scores of the Quality of the Training

Questionnaire Items	n	Mean
The information presented during this training class was clear and easy to understand.	593	4.73
The training class was well organized.	579	4.61

Table 4. Means Scores of the Diebold (TSx) Equipment Training

Questionnaire Items	n	Mean
I will be able to assist a voter who needs to use the TSx machine.	61	4.54
I feel confident using the TSx machine.	61	4.44
The information presented during the TSx training was clear and easy to understand.	61	4.62

These comments and others provided initial evidence for changing part of the design and content of the training program. It also prompted the collection of more data to confirm if these changes were warranted.

The debriefing meeting held with a group of field inspectors two weeks after the election provided useful comments about problems that happened on Election Day and suggestions for improving the training program. A graduate student who was a member of the consulting team and who also worked as a trainer and field inspector for the election compiled the list of comments and suggestions. Suggestions for improving the training program were as followings: (1) provide better Diebold equipment training; (2) give more training on tabulating the roster of voters after closing the polls; (3) offer more thorough training for field inspectors, particularly on job responsibilities unique to those working as field inspectors; and (4) hold a field inspector only meeting one week before the election.

Content analysis was employed to analyze the call center log from the February election to ascertain the type and number of calls that might have been resolved through better poll-worker training. Of 358 calls appearing on the log, 141 (39.4 percent) were coded into categories dealing with voting procedures, registration issues, other problems, and operating the Diebold equipment. The results of the content analysis are shown in Table 5. The results of the content analysis of the call center log reinforced the initial finding about the need for more training on provisional ballots. The results also revealed that the training for the Diebold equipment was insufficient. Indeed, of the calls that were placed to the call center on Election Day that might have been resolved through training, more than half involved difficulties with operating this equipment.

The telephone survey of a stratified random sample of poll workers hired by the county for the February election allowed the respondents to evaluate the competence of their co-workers and supervisors on Election Day, to evaluate whether the training classes prepared them for working on the election, and to assess the quality of the training for inspectors and field inspectors for operating the Diebold equipment. Six trained graduate students and seven trained upper-division communication students completed interviews with 183 clerks, 56 inspectors, and 19 field inspectors.

The telephone survey revealed that the poll workers for the February election, for the most part, rated their co-workers as competent election workers. The highest rating was for those who worked as field inspectors, while the lowest was for those who worked as inspectors. Specifically, 91.6 percent of the poll worker who served as clerks rated their fellow clerks as "very competent" or "competent" election workers, and 85.7 percent of the inspectors rated the clerks they supervised as "very competent" or "competent." The competency rating of inspectors by their clerks at the "very competent" or "competent" level fell to 82.4 percent. Field inspectors similarly rated inspectors less favorably, with 78.9 percent reporting that the inspectors they supervised were "very competent" or "competent." On the other hand, inspectors rated the field inspectors as highly competent supervisors, with 94.3 percent indicating that their field inspector was "very competent" or "competent." It is likely that the lower competence rating of the inspectors by the field inspectors was due to the difficulties that many of the inspectors had with operating the Diebold equipment.

The results of the telephone survey also revealed that most of the election workers were satisfied with the training they received prior to Election Day. In fact, 90.0 percent of the clerks, 89.5 percent of the field inspectors, and 81.8 percent of the inspectors reported that they were provided with sufficient information to undertake their duties on Election Day. However, 52.5 percent of the clerks, 66.1 percent of the inspectors, 57.9 percent of the field inspectors affirmed when asked that they wanted the training to be more interactive instead of relying so heavily on a lecture format. When asked for suggestions to improve the training, the three groups of workers stated that they wanted the classes to include role-playing exercises. Inspectors and clerks also reported that they wanted more training on provisional ballots.

The training for operating the Diebold equipment was rated as effective by most of the inspectors and field inspectors. Specifically, 83.5 percent of the inspectors and 83.3 percent of the field inspectors reported that this part of the training program was "very effective" or "effective." However, the telephone survey revealed that there were problems associated with setting up and operating the Diebold machines on the day of the election: 23.2 percent of the inspectors noted that they experienced problems with the machines and 89.5 percent of the field inspectors reported that they needed to help one or more of their inspectors with setting up or operating the machines.

Recommendations for the Training Program

Based on the results of the first phase of the consulting project, two reports were issued to the San Joaquin County Registrar of Voters that included recommendations for improving poll-worker

Table 5. Content Analysis Frequencies by Category

Categories	Frequency
Calls about provisional ballots	28
Calls about mail/absentee ballots or surrendered ballots	9
Calls about cross over voting	9
Calls about voter registration issues	7
Calls about ballot stubs	6
Calls about poll watchers	1
Calls about the final vote tally	2
Calls about TSX set up or shut down problems	50
Calls about TSX printer problems	29

training in San Joaquin County.[46] The recommendations were subsequently summarized in an executive report for a meeting held with election officials in charge of aspects of the training for the county.[47] Four of the recommendations that are instructive for this description of the consulting project were as follows:

> The training of election workers needs to be more interactive, particularly training on election procedures (i.e., provisional ballots, vote-by-mail ballots, cross-over voting, final vote tally, etc.). Role-playing exercises and short case studies about election procedures will help the trainees learn the procedures.

> All inspectors and field inspectors must be trained on the [Diebold] TSx machines. Less experienced inspectors and field inspectors should be provided with more than one opportunity to practice setting up, operating, and breaking down the machines. The size of the TSx classes should be limited to no more than two people per machine.

> An assessment questionnaire should be administered to trainees at the end of all training classes. This questionnaire can provide useful feedback on the trainees' perceptions of the quality of the training and their understanding of election procedures.

> A postelection response form should be completed by election workers at the end of Election Day and collected by inspectors. This form can be used by the registrar of voters to track problems that election workers faced on Election Day as well as gaps in training that need to be addressed in future training classes.

At the meeting held with the small group of election officials in charge of training the county's poll workers, including the head trainer, it was agreed that role playing and case studies would be included in the design of the training program for the June 2008 California primary election. It was also agreed that the assessment questionnaire would be administered to poll workers at all training classes and that a postelection response form would be completed by poll workers at the end of Election Day. No decision was reached concerning the training for the Diebold machines.

Due to time constraints, the design of the training program was not altered for the June 2008 election. It was subsequently decided that the design of the program would be modified for the November

---

[46] Jon F. Schamber, "An Assessment of Poll Worker Training in San Joaquin County," April 2, 2008 (unpublished report); Jon F. Schamber and Mark A. Urista, "Supplemental Report on Poll Worker Training in San Joaquin County," April 21, 2008 (unpublished report).

[47] Jon F. Schamber and Mark A. Urista, "Executive Summary: Recommendations for Poll Worker Training in San Joaquin County," April 22, 2008 (unpublished document).

2008 presidential election. For this election, the consultant met with the head trainer and offered suggestions for the inclusion of case studies about issuing provisional ballots into the design of the training classes. Two case studies on election procedures were subsequently added to the training program near the end of each training class. The consultant also recommended that the training include a role-playing exercise to allow the poll workers to practice processing voters as they would on Election Day. However, this modification for training was not included in the November classes.

The recommendation to administer an assessment questionnaire to poll workers after all of the training classes for the November election was implemented successfully. For the November election 1,850 poll workers completed the questionnaire, as compared to 595 who completed the questionnaire for the February election. The recommendation to administer a postelection response form to election workers at the end of Election Day for the November election was somewhat successful, with 342 poll workers completing this questionnaire.

Phase Two Results of the Consulting Project

Ten upper-division communication students trained by the principal consultant for the project conducted field observations for the November poll-worker training classes. The student observers noted that the training classes were taught using a lecture supplemented with PowerPoint slides, visual displays of election supplies, and two case studies about provisional ballots. With regard to the use of case studies, it was observed that almost all of the trainees were engaged during this part of the class. Some observers suggested, however, that more case studies should have been used to maximize learning and that role-playing exercises could have been integrated into the training classes. This suggestion was based on the students' understanding of literature on adult learning and recommended teaching techniques for training programs.

A questionnaire similar to the one used for the February 2008 California primary election was administered to trainees at the end of the training classes for the November 2008 presidential election. The similarities between the two questionnaires allowed for an inferential statistical analysis to be conducted on the data to determine if there were statistically significant differences between the mean scores of the trainees' evaluation of the training classes conducted in February and November. Independent sample t-tests were used to analyze the data.

The statistical analysis of the data yielded mixed results. For the November poll-worker training program, there were statistically significant and higher mean scores on four questionnaire items as compared to the scores from the February training (see Table 6). There were four additional items on the November questionnaire for which the mean scores were higher as compared to the February training classes, but the differences were not statistically significant (see Table 7). Concerning the Diebold equipment training, the mean scores for the three items from the November poll-worker classes were higher as compared with the February training, but were not statistically significant (see Table 8).

Qualitative data from the questionnaire for the November poll-worker training provided additional information about the poll workers' perceptions of their trainers and the training classes. Of the trainees who provided written comments about their trainers, 548 of the comments were positive and 42 were negative. Representative positive comments from the trainees for the November election about the trainers paralleled the comments of their counterparts for the February election. In particular, the poll workers remarked that their instructors were knowledgeable of election procedures, prepared for conducting the classes, effective communicators, and enjoyable with respect to the use of humor. There were mixed negative comments offered by the poll workers about the trainers' presentations, with some noting that the trainers spoke too fast, while others wrote that the trainers spoke too slowly.

Table 6. Statistically Significant Mean Score Differences for the Two Elections

Questionnaire Items	n	Mean
The trainer was knowledgeable of election procedures.		
November Election Training	1850	4.83
February Election Training	592	4.76
The trainer did a good job explaining the information on the slides.		
November Election Training	1848	4.80
February Election Training	594	4.74
The trainer was well prepared for the class.		
November Election Training	1850	4.81
February Election Training	589	4.62
The training class was well organized.		
November Election Training	1850	4.76
February Election Training	579	4.61

Note: All items were statistically significant at the .05 level.

Table 7. Higher Mean Score Items for the November Training

Questionnaire Items	n	Mean
The class helped me understand what I will be doing on Election Day.		
November Election Training	1850	4.70
February Election Training	592	4.67
This class makes me confident that I will do a good job on Election Day.		
November Election Training	1850	4.65
February Election Training	595	4.64
The trainer was an effective instructor.		
November Election Training	1850	4.78
February Election Training	591	4.73
The trainer was able to answer questions that arose during the class.		
November Election Training	1850	4.81
February Election Training	592	4.74

Table 8. Comparison of Mean Scores on Items for the Diebold Training

Questionnaire Items	n	Mean
I will be able to assist a voter who needs to use the TSx machine.		
November Election Training	225	4.68
February Election Training	61	4.54
I feel confident using the TSx machine.		
November Election Training	224	4.60
February Election Training	61	4.44
The information presented during the TSx training was clear and easy to understand.		
November Election Training	226	4.72
February Election Training	61	4.62

One hundred and ninety-one trainees offered positive written comments about the training classes, while 163 provided suggestions for improvement. Some of the positive comments from veteran poll workers emphasized that the training classes had improved from prior elections. Illustrations of these comments included the following:

Best class yet. Better than the last two classes [for February and June].

[This class was] more informative than the last election class.

I am so pleased to see the process improving.

The training was more informative than the last election class.

Comments such as these might be attributable to the change in the design of the training classes for the November election. Indeed, some of the trainees specifically mentioned the case studies that were included in the design of the training program. Some of these comments were as follows:

Good use of case studies. They are a good way to help [us] understand situations that may arise on Election Day.

Good use of scenarios as examples we need to be prepared for [on Election Day].

I liked the case studies. They allowed us to interact with our co-workers and practice what we are learning.

Good scenarios. Keep up the good work.

Key areas suggested for improving the classes focused on the need to integrate more case studies into the design of the training and the need to include role-playing exercises in the training. The comments that follow exemplify these suggestions:

The information was easy to understand, but [I] would like more case studies.

I liked the case studies but I would like to see more of them.

Make the class more interactive by using more case studies.

Provide more hands-on training. Have more situations for us to go over the steps ourselves.

A mock demonstration of voters casting ballots may clarify some things.

Let us practice what we are supposed to do when a voter comes in to vote.

We should go through an actual hands-on process of checking in voters for those who will be working as clerks.

Have us practice a run through of typical election voting.

Taken together, these and other similar comments of the poll workers clearly suggest that the integration of case studies into the design of the training program helped the trainees learn their duties. Moreover, the qualitative data indicate that the poll workers want more case studies to be used in future training classes and that role-playing exercises should be included as well.

The postelection questionnaire that the poll workers completed immediately after working the polls for the November election also yielded useful data about the challenges confronting these workers on Election Day and the types of training needed to mitigate these problems. The questionnaire included two items: (1) "List two or three problems concerning voting procedures or situations that happened today that were difficult for you to manage or solve." (2) "How could we prepare or train you better to manage or solve these problems?" Three hundred and forty-two workers (290 clerks and 52 inspectors) completed the questionnaire and their comments were coded into patterns of responses.

Of the 342 workers who responded to the questionnaire, 38.3 percent indicated that they did not experience any problems that were worthy of note on Election Day. These poll workers tended to respond to this item on the questionnaire with comments that follow:

I think our team worked very well today. There were not any concerns that we couldn't handle.

We had no problems at all. I can't believe how smoothly it went.

There were no problems today that were difficult for my team to manage or solve.

Everything went very smoothly.

None really. Our inspector was available and helpful. We gained confidence knowing he was around.

Everything was handled quickly. [Our inspector] was great for her first time.

None. Our inspector and our team of clerks worked well as a team.

Our team was very good to work with and we had a very good inspector who was knowledgeable of voting procedures.

For these poll workers, the problems they experienced on Election Day were uneventful or solved through the collaborative effects of their team of workers and their supervisors.

Of the remaining poll workers who indicated that they experienced problems at the polls, their difficulties were coded into 10 categories. The categories and frequency of their responses are provided in Table 9. Some of the problems identified by the poll workers for the November election were exacerbated by the number of voters who turned out for the election. In particular, when listing some of the problems such as processing vote-by-mail ballots and provisional ballots, and voters showing up at the wrong precinct, the poll workers explained that they were not necessarily confused about what to do, but concerned about the amount of time that it took to deal with these situations. However, an analysis of the poll workers' comments regarding how they could be better prepared or trained for Election Day do warrant attention for the design of future training programs.

Of the poll workers who offered suggestions for improving the training program, 59 of the workers actually indicated that they were well trained for the election, whereas 60 offered suggestions for improvement. The training for the Diebold machines received the most frequent attention, with 27 poll workers stating that more hands-on training is required for operating the equipment. The second most frequently mentioned suggestion for improving the training involved making the training more interactive. In fact, 18 poll workers stated that they want the training to be more hands-on, and include role-playing exercises and more case studies. The third most frequently mentioned suggestion dealt with provisional ballots, with 12 poll workers stating that more training is needed to help them understand when to issue these ballots and how to process the ballots correctly.

Discussion of the Results

There are four implications of this consulting project on poll-worker training that deserve further discussion. First, this consulting project demonstrates that poll workers benefit when training pro-

Table 9. Problems Identified by the Poll Workers for the November Election

Categories of Problems	Frequency
Lacked supplies (voting stickers, voting booths, precinct maps, etc.)	42
Problems with the voter registration list	40
Problems setting up or operating the Diebold equipment	32
Problems with processing vote-by-mail voters/ballots	32
Problems with poll watchers	25
Problems with voters going to the wrong precinct	25
Problems with processing provisional voters/ballots	24
Problems with the small physical size of the precinct location	14
Problems with co-workers or supervisors	13
Other miscellaneous problems	42

grams include multiple training methods. Data collected from various sources for the two phases of the project, as well as the literature reviewed for the project, indicate that poll workers need hands-on training. Case studies offer "real-life examples of problems or issues that trainees are asked to analyze" and when used as a small group activity, they can assist trainees with "discovery, problem solving, and collaboration."[48] Role-playing has been recommended for teaching poll workers how to "check in voters, process provisional voters," and "handle special situations such as angry voters [or] lost voters."[49] This training method provides "real-life Election Day experience," establishes "a comfortable environment for [experienced] poll workers to share problems they have encountered" on prior elections, and lowers "anxiety for new poll workers."[50] Many of the poll workers who were surveyed for this consulting project explicitly stated that they want interactive training opportunities such as case studies and role-playing to learn the material they are being taught for performing effectively on Election Day.

Second, the quantitative assessment of the use of case studies for the November 2008 election, although failing to demonstrate the value of this training method unequivocally, should not be regarded as a reason to ignore the use of interactive training methods for poll-worker training classes. The inclusion of the two case studies in the November training program represented, at best, a minimal commitment to the use of interactive training methods. If more case studies had been used, as well as role-playing exercises, the poll workers would have been able to practice more of what they were learning and, in all likelihood, would have experienced and expressed greater satisfaction with the training program.

The third implication of the project deals with training poll workers to set up and operate electronic voting equipment. The first phase of the consulting project found that the election workers who were trained as inspectors needed more training to operate the Diebold voting equipment. This finding emerged from the telephone survey of election workers after the February election in which 89.5 percent of the field inspectors reported that they needed to help one or more inspectors with setting up or operating the machines. The content analysis of the call center log for the February election also revealed that operating the Diebold equipment was problematic. The postelection response form for the November election reinforced the fact that the election workers wanted more training on the equipment. Prior research demonstrates that hands-on training for using this type of equipment and opportunities for election workers to return for additional equipment training can increase poll-worker confidence with operating the equipment and reduce the problems that these workers have on Election Day with operating the machines.[51]

---

[48] DeWine, 95–96.

[49] U.S. Election Assistance Commission, 108.

[50] *Ibid.*, 109.

[51] Hall, Monson, and Patterson, 650, 652, 653.

The fourth implication of the project concerns institutional impediments regarding the use of formative assessment to improve poll-worker training programs. Assessment projects are sometimes misconstrued as a way of criticizing personnel who are charged with designing training programs. Time pressures associated with running elections can prevent agency personnel from making time to revise their training methods. A lack of knowledge about training techniques and adult learning is another impediment that can frustrate the need for modifying poll-worker training programs. But such concerns and misunderstandings about formative assessment should be overcome given the importance of designing effective training programs for poll workers.

Conclusions

This consulting project provides additional evidence in support of efforts that are being undertaken to improve election procedures involving poll-worker training in the United States. The project clearly demonstrates that poll workers want to do a good job on Election Day and want training programs that will help them learn what they need to know. Since the duties and decisions that poll workers make can influence the outcome of an election and the impressions of voters about the voting process, it is imperative that election officials continue to focus on implementing techniques for improving the design and assessment of poll-worker training programs. This project clearly shows that poll workers need to be instructed through interactive training methods such as case studies and role-playing exercises and that the collection and analysis of formative assessment data provides useful information for improving the design of these training programs.

* * *

The following undergraduates enrolled in Dr. Schamber's Community Based Learning course at University of the Pacific assisted with the assessment of poll worker training:

Anthony Brown
Ashley Cookerly
Kimberlee Craig
Chelsea Engle
David Flaherty
Remy Franklin
DeAngelo Garrett
Corin Imai
Jennifer King
Laura King
Victoria Mazal
Kala Mello
Marcus Padilla
Kelly Purcell
Jesus Reyes
Alejandra Ruiz
Tonja Swank
Chad Troyer

Also assisting with the poll worker assessment project were the following graduate students from the Department of Communication at University of the Pacific:

Kathleen Bruce
Christine Callaco

Kasey Gardner
Erin O'Harra
Jeff Toney

A special acknowledgment goes to Mark Urista, a graduate student in the Department of Communication. Mark played an instrumental role in collecting data for the project and assisted Dr. Schamber with writing reports for the Registrar of Voters.

Part III: The Social Science of Ballot Error and Vote by Mail

Chapter 7

Voter Error Analysis

Qingwen Dong and Erin O'Harra[1]

Introduction

The Help America Vote Act (HAVA) of 2002 was passed to address widespread failures in the electoral process. Errors made by voters and voting machines, poor ballot design, and procedural confusion among poll workers were the cause of many past election recounts.[2] In the November 2000 election alone, an estimated four to six million votes were discarded nationwide.[3] Though improvements have been made, problems with accuracy, efficiency, and integrity remain common in voting today, as many HAVA programs are still under development. In order to reduce voting errors and help poll workers provide the best possible service on Election Day, it is critical to develop an understanding of what types of voting errors exist. Analysis of voting errors is an arena in which "research could and should have great practical impact."[4] By exploring voting errors in vote-by-mail and in-person voting, a solid empirical framework can be built to support further research and recommendations for improving the accuracy, efficiency, and integrity of the voting process.

Voter Errors

Greene et al. identified usability as a crucial component of a voting system.[5] In their investigative comparison of voting methods, they defined "usability" as encompassing three traits: effectiveness, efficiency, and satisfaction. Effectiveness is based on the accuracy and completeness with which the system goal is achieved. When the goal is voting, accuracy means that a vote is cast for the intended

---

[1] Both authors are at the University of the Pacific.

[2] Susan A. MacManus, "Implementing HAVA's Voter Education Requirement: A Crisis and a Federal Mandate Improve State-Local Cooperation in Florida," *The Journal of Federalism* 35 (2005): 537–58.

[3] R. S. Collett, B. Goodhue, and N. Monroe, "Helping America Vote in a New Millennium," in *More Votes that Count*, Chapter 1, above.

[4] K. K. Greene, M. D. Byrne, and S. P. Everett, "A Comparison of Usability between Voting Methods," *Proceedings of the USENIACCURATE Electronic Voting Technology Workshop, Vancouver, B.C., Canada* (2006), 1.

[5] *Ibid., passim.*

candidate, without error. When the vote is actually finished and cast, it is complete. Efficiency measures whether a vote was cast without expending an inordinate amount of resources. Finally, satisfaction is the user's subjective response to using the voting system and overall satisfaction with the voting experience.

In their study, Greene et al. pointed out two main issues affecting voting usability: the characteristics of the user population, and the characteristics of the task itself. The voting population is composed of people from diverse backgrounds of different ages, education levels, and socio-economic status. Additionally, there are a large number of voters who are visually impaired, physically disabled, illiterate, or who do not speak English. Greene et al. asserted voting systems should be usable by all voters: "A truly usable voting technology should be a walk-up-and-use system, enabling even first-time voters to cast their votes successfully."[6]

Characteristics of the task of voting differ depending on the method used to vote and the technology involved in the process. The two dominant voting methods are in-person voting at designated precinct locations and vote by mail (VBM). The systemic differences between the two voting techniques suggest voters may face unique usability challenges with each method and consequently make different errors.

In-Person Voting

In-person voting presents opportunities for voting errors caused by both human and mechanical failures. In the 2004 presidential election, Mahoning County, Ohio experienced both varieties of errors firsthand, leading, in some contests, to negative 25 million votes in error.[7] Mark Munroe, chairman of the Mahoning County Board of Elections, attributed the discrepancies to machines malfunctioning and problems with the personal electronic ballot cartridge placed into machines before each vote to count the ballots. Other errors were of a human nature, specifically, "precinct officials getting nervous or overwhelmed by the number of people voting, and then failing to properly follow protocol to count the ballots in the machine."[8]

Common mechanical errors occurring in the voting technology are miss-votes (counting a vote for a candidate other than the one voted for), incorrect tallies, and equipment breakdown during the voting process. These are the fault of the technology and typically lead to revotes, recounts, or using paper ballots instead of more advanced voting technology.

The same human-based voter errors are possible on every type of voting method. Uncounted ballots (cast by voters but not counted by election officials) typically result from undervotes (a voter does not select a candidate for an office) and overvotes (a voter selects too many candidates). These comprise the category of "residual votes," which is the research term commonly used to encompass voter errors.[9]

The type of voting system used in precinct voting varies by state and county, but can include mechanical lever, optical scan, and direct recording electronic (DRE) machines, as well as punch cards and paper ballots. HAVA provided funding to replace older, unreliable voting technology, thus optical scan and DRE machines are most popular today by a wide margin. Optical scan systems employ a paper ballot, upon which the voter records his or her vote by either filling in an oval or connecting the parts of a broken arrow next to the candidate of choice. The ballot is then fed into a computerized

---

[6] *Ibid.*, 2.

[7] "Errors Plague Voting Process in Ohio, Pa.," *The Vindicator*, November 3, 2004. Retrieved April 10, 2008 from <http://www4.vindy.com/print/286876819404835.php>.

[8] *Ibid.*, 1.

[9] M. A. Carrier, "Vote Counting, Technology, and Unintended Consequences," *St. John's Law Review* (2005). Retrieved April 20, 2008 from <http://findarticles.com/p/articles/mi_qa3735/is_200307/ai_n15957783>.

scanner, which reads the ballot and records the votes. The completed paper ballots are retained in the machine in case a hand recount is needed. With DREs, the voter enters his or her candidate selections directly into a computer, often through a touch screen, without first creating a paper record.

A handful of studies have examined error types and rates among the different voting methods. Paper ballots, optical scans, DREs, and lever machines consistently produce around two percent residual votes, while punch cards are typically between two and four percent higher.[10] Not surprisingly, use of punch cards has been all but discontinued in the United States. However, in one previous study, the Caltech/MIT Voting Project found the residual rate among paper ballots, optical scanning devices, and lever machines to be about two percent, while punch cards and DREs rated about three percent.[11] The higher percentage of residual votes for DREs contradicts later research, perhaps because, with time, voters increase familiarity with the DRE technology, thus reducing errors. One reason optical scan, DRE, and lever machines may typically produce fewer voter errors is their ability to alert the voter to errors before the ballot is cast. Optical scanners immediately reject the ballot if it cannot be read, and DRE and lever machines can be similarly programmed. This way, a voter must go back and fix errors before finalizing the vote, thus reducing residual error rates among these technologies.

Herrnson et al. conducted usability tests of optical scan and DRE machines, as well as different ballot designs, and measured voter accuracy on each system according to voter intent.[12] Even when a ballot is technically error-free, it may not be an accurate representation of the voter's preferences. This is the most regrettable type of voting error to commit, because not only does the voter's preferred candidate lose a vote, the opponent gains one. In the controlled experiment, each participant was given a voter guide and instructed to use both types of machine to vote for the choices circled in the guide. The baseline human error rate was then determined for each machine by comparing the actual voting record with the voter's intentions from the guide. On a standard office-bloc ballot, participants voted accurately over 97 percent of the time on both optical scan and DRE machines, though error rates plummeted when using ballots with a straight-party feature. While two or three percent error rates may not seem like a grievous inaccuracy, it can make a big difference in the context of elections. Over 125 million people voted in the 2008 presidential election.[13] With an error rate of three percent, approximately 3.7 million votes would not have been counted. Those uncounted ballots can, at the very least, affect the overall margin by which a candidate is victorious and even have the potential to swing the decision in close races.

When using optical scan and DRE machines, voters commit specific errors that are unique to each system. They are few, but common. With DREs, voters may select the wrong candidate by accidentally touching the selection area onscreen for the candidate above or below the desired candidate. If the ballot is longer than one screen, voters may skip over entire sections when navigating the ballot. Both errors can be identified on the review screen, which displays the voter's selections for the entire ballot before it is cast. Completing a write-in vote is an area in which voters tend to have difficulty in both DRE and optical scan systems. DRE onscreen keyboards pose a challenge when trying to spell a candidate's name correctly, and optical scan voters typically forget to shade in the oval next to the write-

---

[10] *Ibid.*, S. Ansolabehere and C. Stewart III, "Residual Votes Attributable to Technology," *Journal of Politics* 67, no. 2 (2005): 365–89; M. W. Traugott, M. J. Hanmer, W. Park, W., Herrnson, R. G. Niemi, B. B. Bederson, et al., "The Impact of Voting Systems on Residual Votes, Incomplete Ballots, and Other Measures of Voting Behavior." Paper presented at the meeting of the Midwest Political Science Association, Chicago, Ill. (2005).

[11] The Caltech/MIT Voting Project. "A Preliminary Assessment of the Reliability of Existing Voting Equipment." Unpublished manuscript (Pasadena and Cambridge: California Institute of Technology, and Massachusetts Institute of Technology, 2001).

[12] P. S. Herrnson, R. G. Niemi, M. J. Hanmer, B. B. Bederson, F. C. Conrad, and M. W. Traugott, *Voting Technology: The Not-So-Simple Act of Casting a Ballot* (Washington, D.C.: Brookings Institution Press, 2008).

[13] Election Center 2008, "Results," *CNN*, 2008. Retrieved August 30, 2009 from <http://edition.cnn.com/ELECTION/2008/results/president/>.

in option, so the scanner is not alerted to the vote. Optical scan ballots can be invalidated by any stray marks or tears on the ballot, or, most commonly, by not filling in the ovals properly.[14]

Security is an issue of concern with any voting method. As Wallach points out, a system "must provide sufficient evidence to convince the losing candidate that he or she actually lost. Naming the winner is the easy part."[15] Optical scan and DRE machines ensure similar security against voter bribery or coercion, as the voting process is private and controlled, and threatening parties have no way of verifying how someone actually voted. However, optical scanners are vulnerable to software errors, either in the form of program glitches or intentionally fraudulent programming (sometimes referred to as a Trojan horse), which can affect the vote counts registered in the machine. Fortunately, optical scan systems retain the actual ballots cast, providing the ultimate back-up if results are called into question. The biggest threat to the security of optical scanners occurs when the machines are not present at polling locations, but instead exist at a tabulation center, where ballots are sent to be counted. At this point, additional marks can be made by fraudulent officials on ballots so the scanner will reject them and they will not be counted.[16]

DREs, on the other hand, may not leave behind physical evidence for a recount, and the computer elements of the machines are more complex and susceptible to large-scale fraud. According to Carrier, DRE fraud is possible at each stage of the voting process: "before the election (through physically unsecured machines), during voting (through smartcards that allow voters to gain unauthorized access), and after votes have been cast (through votes that are misrecorded when registered or tabulated)."[17] By altering the programming in DREs, organized persons with enough computer knowledge could make the screen display the voter's intended selections on screen, while internally recording a different vote. This alteration can even be programmed to disappear and eliminate any traces of its presence after the votes have been changed, making it virtually undetectable.[18] Herrnson et al. illuminated two methods of protection against DRE fraud: parallel testing and vote verification systems.[19] Parallel testing is done by having election officials cast votes and then check the machine tally for the accuracy of the recording. Vote verification systems provide an independent record of machine votes, which voters can visually inspect when casting their ballots. If the voter accepts the printed record as accurate, the vote is completed and the paper is deposited within the machine for use in the occurrence of a recount. The printed page is displayed behind a glass screen for voter inspection, so the ballot cannot be tampered with or removed. Currently, vote verification is not widely used, as loading the paper and clearing jams pose challenges for poll workers, and the printed ballot can be hard for voters to read.[20] However, with further development and adoption, they could provide an added element of security to DRE voting.

Poll workers are an integral part of in-person voting and are accountable for all aspects of the voting experience. Though they are hired to do a job that only occurs a few times per year, the responsibilities and demands of poll workers are intense, and consequently, sometimes poorly executed. Poll workers are expected to set up and close down voting machines, provide voter assistance and education, decide whether a citizen can cast a ballot and in which instances a provisional ballot can be issued, maintain security of the polling place and machines, keep machines functioning and manage the overall voting procedure.[21] Undertrained or overwhelmed poll workers can commit a variety of mistakes, from forgetting to plug the voting systems into electrical outlets to misplacing memory chips

---

[14] Herrnson, et al., *loc. cit.*

[15] D. Wallach, "Electronic Voting: Accuracy, Accessibility, and Fraud." Unpublished manuscript, Rice University, Houston, Tex. (n.d.), 3.

[16] *Ibid.*, 4.

[17] Carrier, *loc. cit.*

[18] Wallach, *op.cit.*, 5

[19] Herrnson, et al. *loc. cit.*

[20] *Ibid.*

[21] J. Schamber, "An Assessment of Poll Worker Training in San Joaquin County." Unpublished manuscript, University of the Pacific, Stockton, Calif., 2008, 4.

that store the cast ballots and forgetting to distribute access cards needed to activate some DRE machines.[22] In some cases, poll workers have hidden voting machines, informed voters that empty pens were marking the ballots with invisible ink, and told registered independent voters they could not vote for a Democrat candidate.[23] The importance of good poll-worker training is obvious, and can lead to greater accuracy, efficiency, and integrity of the voting process.

Regardless of voting method employed, in-person voting does offer some distinct benefits that support the effectiveness of the voting process. As Greene et al. pointed out, there are a considerable number of voters who are disabled or vision-impaired, are unable to read, do not speak English, are first-time voters or are unfamiliar with digital technology and rely on the assistance of poll workers to help them effectively cast their votes.[24] DRE voting technology provides the ability to present the ballot in a different language, enlarge text size on the screen for readability, and even offers audio guidance for voters with vision impairment. However, some factors of in-person voting also work to erode the effectiveness and efficiency of voting. Cost is commonly cited as an area of concern, in the form of time and effort expended by voters to vote in person, as well as the monetary cost to hire and train poll workers for Election Day. Voting machines themselves are expensive, costing around $3,000 for one DRE and $4,000 for an optical scanner, and each precinct typically requires five to ten DREs or one optical scanner.[25] Additionally, the technical problems that occur in voting machines create errors in the count and slow down the voting process. The technical aspects of voting machines also present a challenge to some voters, especially those of older generations and first-time voters, who are unfamiliar with the mechanized voting systems, thus resulting in voting errors.[26]

In-person voting relies on the coordination of poll workers and election officials, ballot design and technology, and voters to achieve effectiveness and efficiency. Though technological advancements have made voting more accessible, problems still exist with the security of voting machines and accuracy with which people use them. Numerous studies have found the average voting error rate to be around two to three percent; however, even 98 percent accuracy allows for the corruptibility of election results. Action must be taken to significantly reduce error rates to maintain the integrity of the voting process.

Vote by Mail

Vote by mail has been mentioned widely as a way to streamline voting and alleviate some of the organizational and mechanical pitfalls of poll voting. To vote by mail, voters request a ballot to fill out and return, which will be fed into an optical scanner at a tabulation center. This allows voters to avoid missing work to stand in line at a precinct on Election Day and provides the conveniences of choosing when to vote. This way voters can take as much time as needed to complete the task. However, many VBM ballots still go uncounted due to ballot errors and other problems.

In the 2004 presidential election in Trumbull County, Pennsylvania, election officials rejected 53 out of 13,000 VBM ballots, due to problems with signatures. Some were unsigned, while others had been signed by someone other than the person casting the ballot.[27] While many voting errors in VBM are unique to the system, it is still possible to commit overvoting and undervoting errors, as seen in voting at the polls. Also, since VBM uses optical scan ballots, similar problems occur with regards to shading in ovals and making stray marks. When voting by mail, people do not have the option of re-

---

[22] Herrnson, et al., *op. cit.*, 112.

[23] Schamber, *loc.cit.*, 2.

[24] Greene, *loc.cit.*

[25] K. Zetter, "The Cost of E-Voting," *Wired,* April 4, 2008. Retrieved August 30, 2009 from <http://www.wired.com/threatlevel/2008/04/the-cost-of-e-v/>.

[26] Herrnson et al., *loc.cit.*

[27] *The Vindicator*, *loc.cit.*

voting if the counting machine rejects their ballot, like those who vote in person. Other common VBM mistakes include sending in the ballot late, failing to include adequate postage, not including adequate identifying information, or not signing in the right place.

Fraud is also possible in regard to mail-in ballots, partly because the vote is not anonymous. This allows the possibility of people selling their votes, being bribed, or suffering coercion.[28] Vote by mail also creates opportunities for interception while a ballot is on its way from election authorities to the voter and back again. Tokaji points out that though Oregon has used all-mail elections for over a decade, with little-to-no history of corruption, Florida has experienced fraud with mail-in ballots.[29] In 1997, a Miami mayoral election was tainted by officials paying citizens for their votes. Completed absentee ballots were found at the home of a local political boss. Seven years later, in 2005, an Orlando mayor paid other politicians to collect absentee votes. Wallach counters that VBM fraud is expensive to perform at a large scale, especially without being caught. Features of the ballot make tampering hard to disguise, though once the ballot reaches the tabulation center it is subject to the same vulnerabilities of the optical scan machine in similar circumstances.[30]

Cost savings, in the form of time and money, is cited as a primary benefit of VBM.[31] Gronke, Galanes-Rosenbaum, and Miller report the state of Oregon saved an estimated 17 percent of the costs of holding elections when it began conducting them entirely through the mail.[32] VBM alleviates some costs to the county in the form of money saved on machines, poll workers and technical support on the day of the election. High levels of procedural coordination are necessary in order for voters to complete a precinct vote in a timely fashion, and long lines put pressure on voters and poll workers to speed things along, sometimes at the cost of voting accuracy. VBM saves time by eliminating the need to recruit and train poll workers and maintain machines, and county businesses can avoid sacrificing productivity by letting employees leave the workplace to go vote. This efficiency translates to the voter by allowing him or her to vote at a convenient time and take as long as needed to fill out the ballot. However, a procedural burden also falls on voters in some counties, as they must be registered to vote well in advance of the election (provisional ballots are currently available only in precinct voting), obtain and send in a form to request a VBM ballot ahead of time, and then be sure his or her ballot is completed and mailed in by a specific day.

A unique shortfall of VBM occurs for people who have moved or are homeless, for the visually impaired or those who are illiterate, or for those who do not speak English. These populations may be expected to have trouble with the VBM system, some of which could be alleviated with the assistance of a poll worker or DRE machine in precinct voting situations. On the other hand, those with limited mobility or demanding schedules will likely enjoy the convenience of voting by mail.

Initial Efforts to Reduce Errors

HAVA funding may be used at the discretion of a state and county to improve the accuracy, efficiency, and integrity of the voting system. To devise effective solutions, some counties are collaborating with local institutions of higher education to gain a better understanding of voting problems through research. The Vote Smart project conducted by the University of the Pacific for San Joaquin

---

[28] R. M. Alvarez, T. E. Hall, and B. Sinclair, "Whose Absentee Votes Are Returned and Counted: The Variety and Use of Absentee Ballots in California," *Electoral Studies* 27 (2008): 673–83.

[29] D. Tokaji, "The Problems with All-Mail Elections," *The Ohio State University Moritz College of Law Equal Vote blog,* March 12, 2008. Retrieved April 10, 2008 from <http://moritzlaw.osu.edu/blogs/tokaji/index. html>.

[30] Wallach, *loc. cit.*

[31] N. Monroe and D. Sylvester, "Who Converts to Vote-By-Mail? Evidence from a Field Experiement," *Election Law Journal* 10, no. 1 (March 2011): 15–35.

[32] P. Gronke, E. Galanes-Rosenbaum, and P. A. Miller, "Early Voting and Turnout," PS. *Political Science and Politics* (October, 2007): 639–45.

County in California is one such venture. The research has been multifaceted and delved into voter errors, the design of voter communications, precinct voting improvements, and the VBM system. Several departments from the University of the Pacific worked together to implement voter education efforts, to review balloting procedures for absentee voting, to observe polling place behaviors, and to improve the understanding of voter rights and responsibilities by improving the distribution of sample ballots and the use of public service announcements. This study examines data collected as part of the Vote Smart project to measure the effectiveness of a campaign to improve voter performances by tracking voter errors in elections before and after implementation. Examining differences in voter errors by election type may also provide insight into differences in voter habits and errors in the primary, general, and special elections.

After conducting an assessment of poll-worker training in San Joaquin County, Schamber recommended numerous improvements, suggesting the training instruction seemed "insufficient to ensure that voters will fill out their ballots properly so they can be counted."[33] He suggested the training classes be more interactive, especially in regard to teaching how to operate voting machines. Also, role playing and case-study exercises, and a question-and-answer game with nominal prizes could better engage the workers, help trainers assess the progress of the trainees, and better prepare them for real-life situations. It may be beneficial to pair experienced poll workers with first-time trainees for exercises. Take-home study materials may be most helpful to trainees if they contain specific notes, rather than generalized materials, such as pictures, as supplements to an oral lecture. Schamber reported that telephone calls to the call center during Election Day indicated that many voting errors could be prevented with better training. Schamber recommends field inspectors and machine specialists attend multiple, targeted training classes, and assessment questionnaires be used after training and Election Day to gauge and improve the effectiveness of classes.

Ray undertook voter education through outreach in the form of advertising.[34] A series of cable television commercials and public service announcements were developed to "create an opportunity for every voter to feel invited into the conversation about voting effectively."[35] The process was guided by the concept of identification: if a voter identifies with the character portrayed, they are more likely to want to do what the character is doing. Because California is particularly noted for the diversity of its population, special attention was paid to costuming, casting, and style of the ads produced. Another aim of the advertising efforts was to encourage use of VBM. Demographic analysis led to the targeting of commuters as a key population likely to adopt and benefit from VBM. From this conclusion, it was decided the best way to reach commuters would be through billboard and radio advertisements. Newspaper advertising was also employed, but placements on news and radio station Web sites proved to be especially effective and cost efficient.

In his recommendations to the San Joaquin County Registrar of Voters, Turpin emphasized the necessity for clear copywriting and graphic design in materials aimed to educate voters, specifically the sample ballot sent out for each election.[36] An increase in the information-processing costs may improve the degree to which voters make sense of issues and voting procedure, thereby increasing the likelihood they will choose to vote, and to vote accurately (without committing errors). DeBoer and Tromovitch redesigned the sample ballot booklet and polling place and voting booth signage to increase accessibility and accuracy in voting.[37] Accessibility was addressed by creating all materials in English and Spanish, and promoting VBM by creating a branded logo. Education to improve voting

---

[33] Schamber, *loc.cit.*

[34] A. Ray, "A Structured Media Marketing Campaign Using Radio, Newspaper, and the Internet." Unpublished manuscript, University of the Pacific, Stockton, Calif., 2008.

[35] *Ibid.*, 2.

[36] P. Turpin, "Voter Education and Information Delivery: From the Rationality of Voting Behavior to the Political Economy of Elections." Unpublished manuscript, University of the Pacific, Stockton, Calif., 2009.

[37] B. DeBoer, and L. Tromovitch, "Voter Education: The Message through the Media." Unpublished manuscript, University of the Pacific, Stockton, Calif., 2008.

accuracy was communicated by improving the clarity of voter information, adjusting typographic variables, grouping and organizing information in a hierarchy, varying the method of delivery, as well as the sequence and frequency of information. Design standards were adopted from *The American Institute for Graphic Design (AIGA)* in affiliation with *HAVA* and *Design for Democracy*.

A related tactic for increasing efficiency was to send postcards to registered voters before the election, encouraging them to request a VBM ballot by signing the postcard and mailing it back with prepaid postage. Monroe and Sylvester found that by doing this, more people signed up to vote by mail and actually voted in the election than those using traditional methods to request a VBM ballot.[38] Using the VBM system eases the labor cost for election officials by allowing them to process the ballots over a longer period of time than in-person votes made on Election Day, thereby leading to greater accuracy in the process.

This research illuminates the need for improvement in poll-worker and voter information and optimism for the possibility of increasing voting accuracy, efficiency, and integrity through education and structural reform. Remaining questions, which this study seeks to answer, are: what types of errors do people tend to make by either VBM or vote in person (VIP), and what are the best means through which to overcome such errors?

Summary and Research Questions

In reflecting upon in-person and VBM systems, each carries significant benefits and drawbacks. VBM alleviates some monetary and temporal costs to counties, and makes the act of voting more convenient for the voter. However, a procedural burden is transferred to the voter, in the form of multiple registrations to receive a VBM ballot and the managing deadlines for returning these forms and the ballot.

Fraud is always a concern in voting, and though both VBM and precinct voting promote safeguards against fraud, neither system is infallible. In-precinct DREs' voter-verifiable paper trails provide a means for voters to visually confirm that the machine recorded their intended choices, and provide a hard-copy record if the security of the computer system is called into question. The procedures of the mail system make large-scale fraud difficult in VBM, but there is greater opportunity for voter coercion and local election fraud than with in-person voting.

The general accessibility of in-person and VBM are high, though each offers contrasting benefits and restrictions for certain populations. The homeless, visually impaired, illiterate, and non-English speaking populations will likely face challenges with an all-VBM system, while less mobile voters are apt to appreciate the ability to vote from home. Precinct voting offers the benefit of personalized assistance, while VBM provides personal convenience, with room to improve the efficiency of each.

There is obvious variation in the types of errors committed in precinct voting and VBM systems, though certain errors are possible on any ballot. Current average error rates are dangerously high and threaten the integrity of the electoral process. The potential for error is aggravated by a number of common occurrences: by unfamiliar or confusing ballot or machine design, unprepared poll workers, uninformed voters, and anxiety from the stress of precinct voting environments. These can compound each other and eventually result in cumulative inefficiencies. These factors and error rates may differ according to election type. In order to successfully improve the accuracy, efficiency, and integrity of the voting process, it is crucial to first understand the specific reasons in which the problems occur. This study seeks to further that knowledge by exploring the nature of voter error through pursuit of the following research questions:

Research Question 1: What errors do voters make using VBM and in-person systems? What are their relative frequencies and how do they differ?

---

[38] Monroe and Sylvester, *loc.cit.*

Research Question 2: To what extent does the nature of the election (primary or general) influence the type of errors voters make?

Research Question 3: What educational and/or structural reforms might reduce voter error?

Method

Voter Population and Characteristics

In San Joaquin County, there were 434 precincts and 245,781 registered voters out of the 407,636 eligible voters[1] in January 2008; 441 precincts and 253,148 registered voters in June 2008; and 515 precincts and 268,476 registered voters in November 2008. During the February 5, 2008 early primary election, 131,964 people cast their ballots with 77,140 (58 percent) in-person voters and 54,824 (42 percent) vote by mail voters; during the June primary election, 71,233 people cast their ballots with 25,963 (36 percent) in-person voters and 45,270 (64 percent) VBM voters; during the General Election in November, 212,214 people cast their ballots with 110,447 (52 percent) in-person voters and 101,767 (48 percent) VBM voters. The statewide VBM average was 42 percent in Early primary election, 59 percent in primary election in June and 42 percent in general election in November.

Data and Conceptualization

Data for this study consist of error ballots from the three elections in San Joaquin County, California in 2008: the early primary election (Feb. 5, 2008), the primary election (June 3, 2008), and the general election (Nov. 4, 2008). The San Joaquin County Registrar of Voters Office provided the error ballots for this investigation. All error ballots were stored in the researcher's office, and only the researcher and research assistants had access to the ballots.

Three types of error ballots were examined during this investigation. The first type of error is "duplicate ballots," which were rejected by the tabulation machine for various reasons. The voting officials made a copy of these ballots with errors, and the copied ballots were used for ballot counting for the election. The original error ballots were kept as a record and used for this study. The error ballots were classified by the voting procedure used (VBM vs. VIP) so the type and rate of errors could be compared.

The second type of error ballots is "spoiled ballots." By definition, "spoiled ballots" are those on which voters make errors in filling them out at the voting place, and return them to poll workers in exchange for a new ballot. Each voter may have three new ballots during Election Day. The "spoiled ballots" are not counted, and they are returned to voting officials and used for this investigation.

The third type of ballots is "surrendered ballots," which are stored in a plastic bag by precinct. These "surrendered ballots" are vote by mail ballots that were brought to a polling location and surrendered by the voter, either because the voter does not wish to cast a ballot in the election or was dissatisfied with how he or she filled out the ballot and wanted to instead vote in person. Surrendered ballots are not counted in the vote. In this investigation, the researchers conducted a comparative analysis of "spoiled ballots" vs. "surrendered ballots" in order to contrast ballot errors between VBM and VIP procedures.

Coding Procedures and Items

Before coders began coding the ballots, a pilot study was conducted to develop a preliminary understanding of the types of errors extant in the primary election. The pilot study included ballots containing all three types of errors, from 20 precincts. Based on the errors found within these precincts, a coding sheet was developed. The coding sheet included identification number, precinct group, number of spoiled ballots, number of surrendered ballots, party affiliation, types of errors and surrendered ballots. The types of errors include "ovals not filled in completely," "ovals filled in with a check mark," "ovals filled in with an 'X' mark," "ovals not filled in clearly," "write-in overvoting," "other overvoting," "partially empty ballot," "completely empty ballot," "signed ballots," "cannot tell," "others" and "multiple errors." (Examples of each error type can be found in Appendix C on the CD included with this book).

One of the critical variables in this study is "vote type," which is used to describe whether individuals cast their ballots at a polling place (vote in person, or VIP) or through vote by mail (VBM). In operationalizing the vote type in "duplicate ballots," investigators followed the marks (vote by mail or poll) made on the right top corner of each ballot to distinguish the two vote types. In operationalizing the vote type in "spoiled ballots," researchers used "spoiled ballots" (errors made by people at the polling place) and "surrendered ballots" (ballots surrendered by VBM voters to voting officials, due to various errors).

Five research assistants were involved in ballot error coding and content analysis for the three elections. Explanations including training about coding ballots were explicitly provided before coding started. The coding procedures were supervised, and answers to individual questions about the coding procedures were provided to the coders throughout the coding process.

Data Analysis

Data were entered in to both Excel and SPSS (Statistical Package for Social Sciences) for data analysis. Descriptive analysis was generated to provide answers to the research questions.

Results

Results were generated through frequency and cross-tabulation analysis and are displayed in eight tables and eight graphs in this section. Results were used to answer the three questions raised in the study.

Research Question 1: What frequencies of errors do voters make using vote by mail (VBM) and voting in person (VIP)? What are the types of errors made by vote by mail and voting in person?

Results showed that VBM voters made fewer errors than VIP voters during the three elections of 2008 in San Joaquin County, California (details can be found in Tables 1 and 2 as well as Figures 1 and 2). In the category of duplicate errors, there were 1,832 error ballots for VBM over the three elections, which is 0.9 percent of the total VBM population. For VIP, there were 8,767 error ballots, which is 3.15 percent of the total in-person voting population. The same pattern was found in the category of spoiled ballots versus surrendered ballots (VBM). There were 1,286 surrendered ballots (0.73 percent) and 2,833 spoiled ballots (1.31 percent).

Data from Tables 1 and 2 also showed VBM voters made fewer errors than in-person voters during each of the elections in both the duplicate and spoiled ballots, and surrendered ballots. Results provide a clear pattern of errors resulted from vote type.

People using VBM had fewer errors than VIP voters in the top three errors over the three elections in the category of duplicate ballots. These errors include "ovals not filled in completely," "ovals not filled in clearly," and "partially empty ballot" (See Appendix A, Tables 3a, 3b, and 3c). However, the results also showed that VBM voters generated more multiple errors than VIP voters, though the total errors made by VBM are far fewer than VIP.

In the category of spoiled versus surrendered ballots, the results are mixed between VBM and VIP, though the total of errors made by VBM were far less than VIP. Results indicated that in "ovals not filled in clearly," and "partially empty ballot," VBM made fewer errors when compared to VIP. In

Table 1. Trends of Duplicate Errors by Vote Type

Total	spoiled	total vote	error %
VBM	1,832	201,861	0.90%
VIP	6,935	213,550	3.15%
SUM	8,767	415,411	2.07%
Early Primary	spoiled	total vote	error %
VBM	324	54,824	0.59%
VIP	3,224	77140	4.01%
SUM	3,548	131,964	2.62%
Primary	spoiled	total vote	error %
VBM	536	45,270	1.17%
VIP	488	25,963	1.84%
SUM	1,024	71,233	1.42%
General	spoiled	total vote	error %
VBM	972	101,767	0.95%
VIP	3,223	110,447	2.84%
SUM	4,195	212,214	1.94%

Figure 1. Trends of Duplicate Errors by Vote Type

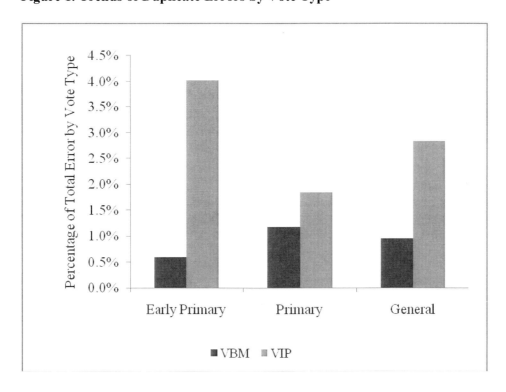

Table 2. Trends of Spoiled Errors by Vote Type

Total	spoiled	total vote	error %
VBM	1,486	201,861	0.73%
VIP	2,833	213,550	1.31%
SUM	4,319	415,411	1.03%
Early Primary	spoiled	total vote	error %
VBM	596	54,824	1.08%
VIP	1,431	77,140	1.82%
SUM	2,027	131,964	1.51%
Primary	spoiled	total vote	error %
VBM	140	45,270	0.31%
VIP	216	25,963	0.83%
SUM	356	71,233	0.50%
General	spoiled	total vote	error %
VBM	750	101,767	0.73%
VIP	1,186	110,447	1.06%
SUM	1,936	212,214	0.90%

Figure 2. Trends of Spoiled Errors by Vote Type

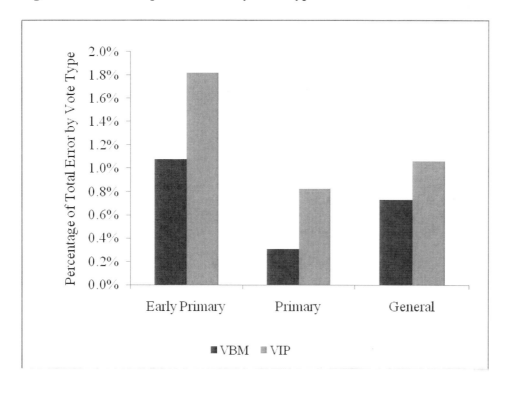

addition, both groups had a significant percentage of "complete empty ballots" (see Appendix A, Tables 4a, 4b, and 4c). One explanation of this result is that some of the VBM voters surrendered empty ballots at the polling place and chose to cast their ballots there. For VIP voters, empty ballots may indicate that poll workers initially gave voters the wrong ballots, which the voter then returned empty and sought a second ballot.

Research Question 2: To what extent does the nature of the election (primary or general) influence the type of errors voters make?

Results showed that the primary election (June 3, 2008) had a relatively higher "duplicate errors" in VBM, compared to the other two elections. This error may result from the low turnout rate, as well as a high VBM rate in the election. In terms of spoiled versus surrendered ballots, the primary election showed fewer errors by VBM, compared to VIP.

In terms of specific errors, there was not a significant difference across the three elections, except multiple errors showed a higher rate by VBM in the general election (11.9 percent) than the primary election VBM (3.6 percent) and early primary VBM (4 percent).

One result stands out and should be further investigated: the early primary showed a high number of signature problems, while very few occurred in the primary and none in the general election. It is unclear why this difference occurred.

Research Question 3: What educational and/or structural reforms might reduce voter error?

As is shown in Tables 1 and 2, combined voter error for vote-by-mail and in-person voting totals about two percent, on average. However, even 98 percent accuracy is insufficient to prove a winning candidate, especially in a close race. Increasing vote-by-mail usage may increase overall voting accuracy because, as shown in Tables 1 and 2, VBM error rates were consistently and significantly lower than in-person voting error rates for this study.

The data for this study was originally gathered as part of the University of the Pacific Vote Smart project to test voter behavior before and after implementation of a voter-education and poll-worker training campaign. Conclusions about the effectiveness of such efforts can be extracted from Tables 1 and 2, which show a significant reduction in voter errors between the February primary election, before the program launched, and November, after all elements had been executed. The program consisted of poll-worker training, voter literacy education, and VBM education and recruitment. A pilot study revealed the primary types of ballot errors committed by voters, which the education efforts specifically addressed. A complete inventory of these errors can be seen in Appendix A. Another possible result from the campaign is revealed in Tables 1 and 2. Clearly, VBM usage, which was one of the subjects of the campaign, increased from February to November, and this shift contributed to the overall drop in errors.

Discussion

Analyzing the types and frequencies of voting errors in actual elections introduces a new area for voting research, especially in the context of evaluating a specific voter and poll-worker education campaign. This study found an overall voting error rate of around two percent, which is consistent with similar studies. Errors of this magnitude have the ability to markedly affect the outcome of an election, and it is necessary to strengthen efforts to improve the accuracy, efficiency, and integrity of the voting system. This study provides evidential grounds for achieving such improvements through increasing use of VBM and targeted and comprehensive voter and poll-worker training efforts. Results show VBM consistently produces significantly fewer voting errors than in-person voting. Increasing VBM use will predictably lead to greater accuracy and efficiency overall. Decreasing the number of people voting at polling places will necessitate fewer poll workers and voting machines and shorter lines to vote at precincts. With greater assistance available from poll workers and less pressure to vote quickly because of long lines, accuracy of in-person voting will likely improve. Also, decreasing the number of people voting in person will have a positive impact on air pollution by lessening the use of vehicles to reach precincts and reduce the loss of business productivity by workers taking time off to vote.

This study also revealed specific types of errors committed on VBM ballots and in-person ballots, and the prevalence of such errors threatens the integrity of the voting system. Based on the success of the Vote Smart project in reducing the occurrence of errors in VBM and in-person voting, targeted voter education and poll-worker training methods as elections approach can be highly recommended. Vote Smart focused on increasing VBM use and voter literacy through advertisements on television, the Internet, and radio and in newspapers. Poll-worker recruitment and training efforts were analyzed and augmented. Efforts also focused on improved precinct signage and ballot design, and a program for increasing VBM turnout was tested and proven effective. In most of the aforementioned tactics, the common error types were considered and incorporated, especially in education through voter out-reach.

The researchers noted differences in possible causes of voter errors in VBM and vote in person. Though not included as a variable in the data, it was observed that a large number of VBM ballot errors were associated with postmarks close to the submission deadline, or VBM ballots surrendered at polling places. Rushing while trying to vote may increase errors, and voter education campaigns could encourage voters to complete their ballots early. In-person voting errors seem attributable to problems with voter literacy and may be improved through voter education campaigns targeting specific error types.

Limitations and Suggestions for Future Research

The design of content analysis procedures used here could benefit from further replication. Also, conducting such research solely in one county, San Joaquin County, limits its applicability. Such analysis could be profitably expanded and with such expansion new explanatory variables could be tested.

One of the limitations of the study is that there were a large number of unanswered questions raised through this study, regarding human motivations: "why did people make specific types of errors," "why did people surrender their ballots," "how and why did election officials deal with 'duplicate ballots' as they did?" For future study, focus groups and experimental designs that tap voter and poll-worker attitudes could help explore why ballots errors are committed and what are the best ways for voters and poll workers to guard against them. Future research should also focus on the peripheral effects of using specific voting systems, so counties can optimize accuracy, efficiency, and integrity in devising voting methods to best serve their individual electorates.

Appendix A

Tables & Graphs

Table 3a. Early Primary Election Duplicate Error

	VIP		VBM		Total	
	n	**%**	**n**	**%**	**n**	**%**
Ovals not filled in completely	1,518	47.1%	150	46.3%	1,668	47.1%
Cannot tell	580	18.0%	34	10.5%	614	17.3%
Ovals not filled in clearly	401	12.5%	28	8.6%	429	12.1%
Partially empty ballot	235	7.3%	19	5.9%	254	7.2%
Torn ballot	185	5.7%	17	5.2%	202	5.7%
Others	95	3.0%	44	13.6%	139	3.9%
Multiple errors	75	2.3%	13	4.0%	88	2.5%
Ovals filled in with an x mark	63	2.0%	10	3.1%	73	2.1%
Ovals filled in with a check mark	42	1.3%	4	1.2%	46	1.3%
Other overvoting (except writing in)	10	0.3%	5	1.5%	15	0.4%
Writing-in overvoting	12	0.4%	0	0.0%	12	0.3%
Complete empty ballot	4	0.1%	0	0.0%	4	0.1%
Total	3,220		324		3,544	

Figure 3a. Early Primary Election Duplicate Error

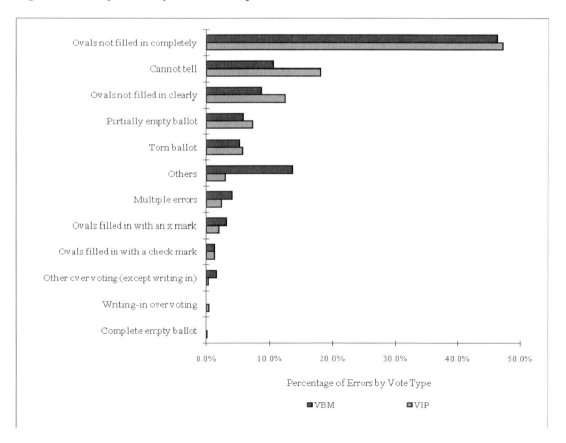

Table 3b. Primary Election Duplicate Error

	VIP		VBM		Total	
	n	**%**	**n**	**%**	**n**	**%**
Ovals not filled in completely	171	35.1%	136	25.5%	307	30.1%
Ovals not filled in clearly	90	18.5%	66	12.4%	156	15.3%
Partially empty ballot	44	9.0%	51	9.6%	95	9.3%
Others	18	3.7%	68	12.7%	86	8.4%
Writing-in overvoting	16	3.3%	64	12.0%	80	7.8%
Torn ballot	43	8.8%	30	5.6%	73	7.1%
Ovals filled in with an x mark	35	7.2%	25	4.7%	60	5.9%
Other over voting (except writing in)	17	3.5%	41	7.7%	58	5.7%
Cannot tell	17	3.5%	27	5.1%	44	4.3%
Multiple errors	10	2.1%	19	3.6%	29	2.8%
Ovals filled in with a check mark	18	3.7%	5	0.9%	23	2.3%
Complete empty ballot	8	1.6%	2	0.4%	10	1.0%
Total	487		534		1,021	

Figure 3b. Primary Election Duplicate Error

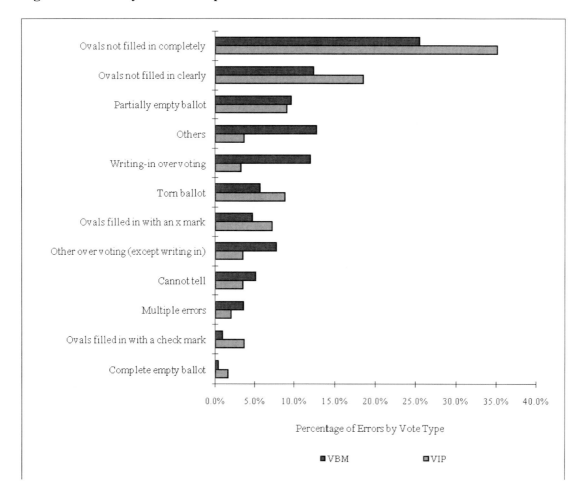

Table 3c. General Election Duplicate Error

	VIP		VBM		Total	
	n	**%**	**n**	**%**	**n**	**%**
Ovals not filled in completely	1,164	36.1%	287	29.5%	1,451	34.6%
Ovals not filled in clearly	1,120	34.8%	274	28.2%	1,394	33.3%
Partially empty ballot	523	16.2%	143	14.7%	666	15.9%
Cannot tell	145	4.5%	44	4.5%	189	4.5%
Multiple errors	27	0.8%	116	11.9%	143	3.4%
Writing-in overvoting	82	2.5%	20	2.1%	102	2.4%
Torn ballot	27	0.8%	30	3.1%	57	1.4%
Other overvoting (except writing in)	44	1.4%	12	1.2%	56	1.3%
Ovals filled in with a check mark	38	1.2%	4	0.4%	42	1.0%
Ovals filled in with an x mark	33	1.0%	7	0.7%	40	1.0%
Others	9	0.3%	30	3.1%	39	0.9%
Complete empty ballot	8	0.2%	5	0.5%	13	0.3%
Total	3,220		972		4,192	

Figure 3c. General Election Duplicate Error

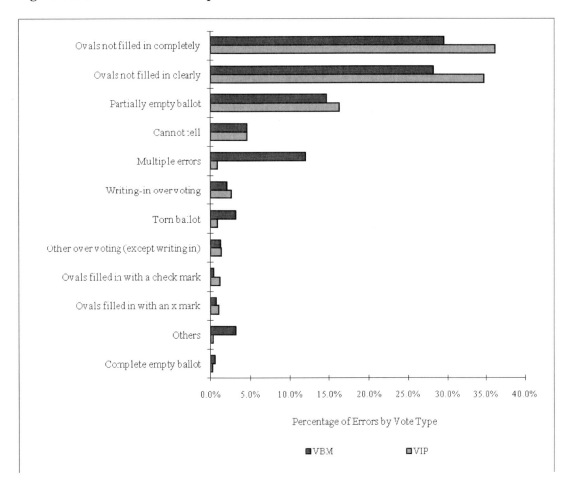

Table 4a. Early Primary Election Spoiled Error

	VIP		VBM		Total	
	n	**%**	**n**	**%**	**n**	**%**
Partially empty ballot	382	26.7%	36	6.3%	418	20.8%
Complete empty ballot	261	18.3%	101	17.5%	362	18.1%
Ovals not filled in completely	240	16.8%	37	6.4%	277	13.8%
Ovals not filled in clearly	217	15.2%	20	3.5%	237	11.8%
Cannot tell	113	7.9%	122	21.2%	235	11.7%
Signature problems	7	0.5%	197	34.2%	204	10.2%
Others	64	4.5%	30	5.2%	94	4.7%
Multiple errors	66	4.6%	22	3.8%	88	4.4%
Other overvoting (except writing in)	51	3.6%	5	0.9%	56	2.8%
Ovals filled in with an x mark	15	1.0%	2	0.3%	17	0.8%
Ovals filled in with a check mark	7	0.5%	4	0.7%	11	0.5%
Writing-in overvoting	6	0.4%	0	0.0%	6	0.3%
Total	1,429		576		2,005	

Figure 4a. Early Primary Election Spoiled Error

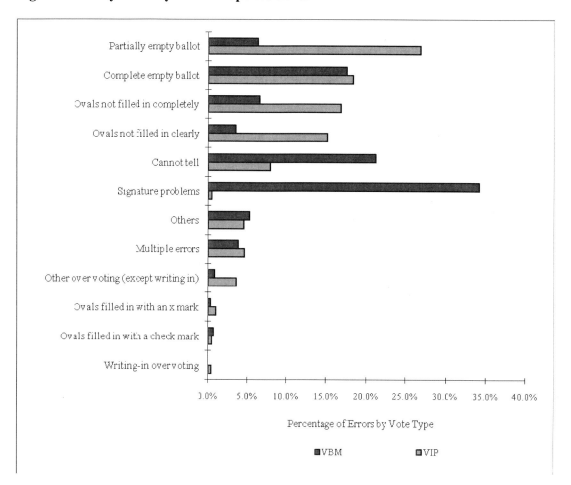

Table 4b. Primary Election Spoiled Error

	VIP		VBM		Total	
	n	**%**	**n**	**%**	**n**	**%**
Complete empty ballot	35	16.5%	31	22.3%	66	18.8%
Partially empty ballot	53	25.0%	11	7.9%	64	18.2%
Others	10	4.7%	35	25.2%	45	12.8%
Cannot tell	9	4.2%	34	24.5%	43	12.3%
Ovals not filled in clearly	35	16.5%	6	4.3%	41	11.7%
Ovals not filled in completely	31	14.6%	5	3.6%	36	10.3%
Other overvoting (except writing in)	19	9.0%	3	2.2%	22	6.3%
Multiple errors	8	3.8%	8	5.8%	16	4.6%
Ovals filled in with an x mark	8	3.8%	3	2.2%	11	3.1%
Writing-in overvoting	3	1.4%	1	0.7%	4	1.1%
Signature problems	0	0.0%	2	1.4%	2	0.6%
Ovals filled in with a check mark	1	0.5%	0	0.0%	1	0.3%
Total	212		139		351	

Figure 4b. Primary Election Spoiled Error

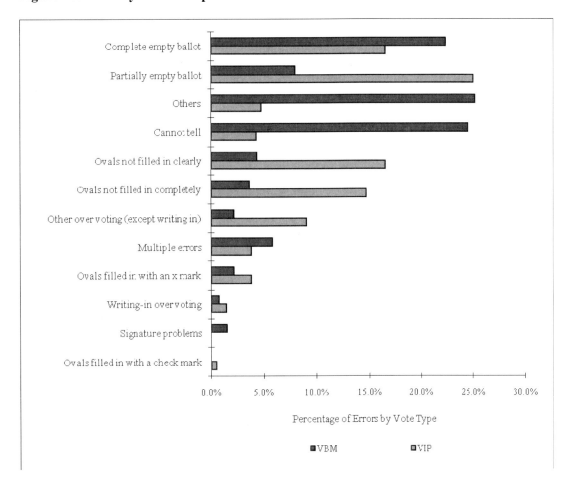

Table 4c. General Election Spoiled Error

	VIP		VBM		Total	
	n	**%**	**n**	**%**	**n**	**%**
Others	475	40.1%	209	27.9%	684	35.3%
Partially empty ballot	228	19.2%	88	11.7%	316	16.3%
Complete empty ballot	71	6.0%	200	26.7%	271	14.0%
Ovals not filled in clearly	153	12.9%	71	9.5%	224	11.6%
Ovals not filled in completely	76	6.4%	81	10.8%	157	8.1%
Other overvoting (except writing in)	49	4.1%	39	5.2%	88	4.5%
Multiple errors	64	5.4%	17	2.3%	81	4.2%
Cannot tell	28	2.4%	34	4.5%	62	3.2%
Ovals filled in with an x mark	15	1.3%	9	1.2%	24	1.2%
Writing-in overvoting	16	1.3%	1	0.1%	17	0.9%
Ovals filled in with a check mark	11	0.9%	1	0.1%	12	0.6%
Total	1,186		750		1,936	

Figure 4c. General Election Spoiled Error

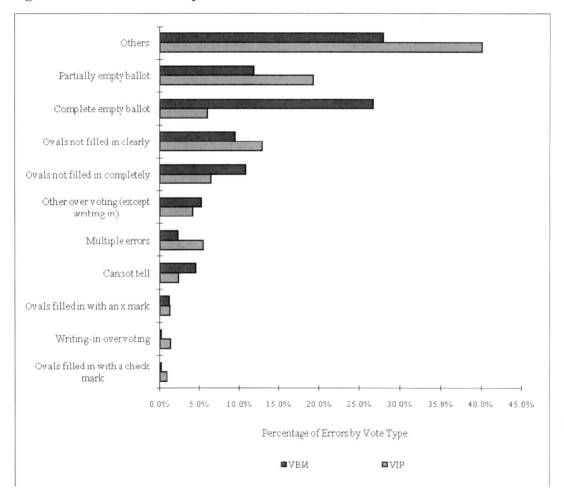

Appendix B

Coding Sheet

Coding sheet (spoiled and surrendered ballots)
1 Identification number
2 Group (precinct group)
3 Precinct number
4 Number of spoiled ballots
5 Number of surrendered ballots
6 Party affiliation
7 Type of errors
8 Surrender ballots

Party affiliation: 1= Dem; 2=Rep; 3=Nonpartisan; 4=Ind; 5=Peace; 6=Green; 7=Libertarian
Type of errors
1 "Ovals not filled in completely"
2 "Ovals filled in with a check mark"
3 "Ovals filled in with an x mark"
4 "Ovals not filled in clearly"
5 "Writing-in overvoting"
6 "Other overvoting (except writing in)"
7 "Complete empty ballot"
8 "Signature problems"
9 "Cannot tell"
10 "Others"
11 "Partially empty ballot"
12 "Multiple errors"

Vote type: 1 "VIP" Vote in person; 2 "VBM" Vote by mail

Coding sheet (Duplicate ballots)
 Identification number
1 Precinct numbers
2 Party affiliation
3. Type of errors
Party affiliation: 1= Dem; 2=Rep; 3=Nonpartisan; 4=Ind; 5=Peace; 6=Green; 7=Libertarian

Type of errors
1 "Ovals not filled in completely"
2 "Ovals filled in with a check mark"
3 "Ovals filled in with an x mark"
4 "Ovals not filled in clearly"
5 "Writing-in overvoting"
6 "Other overvoting (except writing in)"
7 "Complete empty ballot"
8 "Partially empty ballot"
9 "Torn ballot"
10 "Cannot tell"
11 "Others"

12 "Multiple errors"
Vote type: 1 "VIP" Vote in Person; 2 "VBM" Vote by mail

Chapter 8

Cutting Costs: An Assessment of Vote by Mail

Dari E. Sylvester and Nathan W. Monroe[1]

Introduction

Election Administrators (EAs) are tasked with the substantial responsibility of conducting fair, open elections and maintaining the integrity of each person's vote. While EAs are not explicitly in the business of increasing voter turnout, the culmination of their duties reflects a fundamental belief in "one person, one vote" such that all eligible citizens are effectively empowered to participate. Popular participation in government is, by definition, critical to democracy, and the legitimacy of a democratic government is partially determined by the extent to which the people can and do participate. Despite the salience of political participation, voting—one of the most important and symbolic political acts—is currently performed by around 60 percent of the voting age population during national presidential elections and is lower than 50 percent during less salient election years.[2]

Numerous scholars have grappled with the question of why citizens do not vote, from social network influence[3] and parental conditioning,[4] to education[5] and rational weighing of the costs and bene-

[1] The authors wish to acknowledge Social Science Research Center at the California State University, Fullerton for administering our three-wave survey and Jess Cervantes of Leading Edge Data for his help and good advice. Nathan W. Monroe is in the School of Social Science, Humanities, and Arts at the University of California, Merced. Dari E. Sylvester is in the Department of Political Science at the University of the Pacific. This paper was prepared as part of the Vote Smart Project at the University of the Pacific, under the umbrella of the Harold S. Jacoby Center. The authors gratefully acknowledge the financial support of the San Joaquin County Registrar of Voters, the comments of Bob Benedetti, Lisa Tromovitch, Paul Turpin, and the research assistance of Kristen Chang.

[2] File, Thom, "Voting and Registration in the Election of November 2006," *U.S. Census Bureau*, retrieved March 12, 2009, <http://www.census.gov/population/www/socdemo/voting.html>.

[3] Bernard R. Berelson, Paul F. Lazarsfeld, and William N. McPhee, *Voting: A Study of Opinion Formation in a Presidential Campaign* (Chicago: University of Chicago Press, 1954).

[4] Angus Campbell, Philip E. Converse, Warren E. Miller, and Donald E. Stokes, *The American Voter* (New York: Wiley, 1960).

[5] Raymond E. Wolfinger and Steven J. Rosenstone, *Who Votes?* (New Haven: Yale University Press, 1980).

fits of voting.[6] Empirically, though rational choice explanations of voting clearly fail to explain general patterns of turnout,[7] it is clear that the variable "costs" of voting do influence voters' decisions to go to the polls under some circumstances. Thus, the purpose of this chapter is to consider one of what we see as the most efficient and appropriate parts of the voting decision that EAs *can* affect: the cost-benefit tradeoff faced by citizens deciding whether to turnout. That is, by encouraging voters to vote by mail (VBM), EAs can change the calculus of voting for some voters, moving them from passive observers to active democratic participants.

Although there is some preliminary evidence that the introduction of VBM has a positive effect on voter turnout, there has been no research on the extent to which EAs can continue to promote VBM as a means of boosting turnout even further, after its initial introduction. In particular, here we ask, will promoting the VBM option, beyond its initial adoption, convert significant numbers of new voters to become permanent VBM voters? And, going one step further, will a new wave of VBM voters be more likely to actually turn out?

To answer these questions, we use a combination of voter survey data and a field experiment from the June 3, 2008 election conducted in California's San Joaquin County. We find that citizens who receive information on and opportunities to become VBM voters are more likely to convert to that voting method and are then more likely to cast a vote in the subsequent election. Per our theoretical expectations, we find that citizens who face higher costs for going to the polls are also more likely to convert to VBM.

The remainder of this chapter proceeds as follows. In the next section, we lay out previous literature on voting, providing the foundation for our theoretical framework and hypotheses, which occupy the section that follows. With predictions in place, we then proceed to a description of our field experiment and results, as well as our supplementary analysis using survey data. In the final section, we briefly summarize and conclude.

Why Don't People Vote?

Early voting scholars attempted to identify the most important factors in the voting decision, contending that voting is a decision rooted in a number of sociological or psychological variables. The Columbia studies of the 1940s and 1950s concluded that friends, family, and religious influences form the foundation of one's social network, which is ultimately the primary force in determining the voting decision.[8] Later, the Michigan school developed around the theory that a symbolic attachment to one's political party, formed very early in life, was not only stable throughout adulthood, but also had a major impact on voting decisions.[9] These studies were particularly influential in explaining why some voters vote the way they do; nevertheless, it was not until the watershed work of Anthony Downs that scholars began to think more about why individuals might chose *not* to vote. Anthony Downs's theory concluded that rational individuals weigh the relative costs and benefits of voting,

---

[6] Anthony Downs, *An Economic Theory of Democracy* (New York: Harper & Row, 1957); William H. Riker and Peter C. Ordeshook, "A Theory of the Calculus of Voting," *American Political Science Review* 62, no. 1 (1968): 25–42.

[7] In general, the rational "Calculus of Voting" presents what is commonly referred to as the paradox of voting. As defined in rational choice, the cost-benefit tradeoff implies that voters should almost never vote in any election. The "paradox" is that many voters vote in every election.

[8] Paul F. Lazarsfeld, Bernard Berelson, and Hazel Gaudet, *The People's Choice: How the Voter Makes Up His Mind in a Presidential Campaign* (New York: Columbia University Press, 1944); Bernard R. Berelson, Paul F. Lazarsfeld, and William N. McPhee, *Voting: A Study of Opinion Formation in a Presidential Campaign* (Chicago: University of Chicago Press, 1954).

[9] Angus Campbell, Philip E. Converse, Warren E. Miller, and Donald E. Stokes, *The American Voter* (New York: Wiley, 1960).

and given the low probability of any one person's vote deciding an electoral outcome coupled with the high (nonzero) costs of voting, choosing *not* to vote was a most rational decision indeed.[10]

Since that time, researchers and practitioners have struggled to explain why turnout rates continue to be so low and how they might increase, insisting that proper representation in a democracy is ultimately contingent on near perfect voter participation. If we accept the Downsian notion that prohibitively high costs of voting can reduce turnout, then efforts aimed at lowering costs can have a positive impact on turnout. In the U.S. certain election officials have modified structural rules of voting ostensibly in an effort to lower these costs. For example, studies have been conducted on administrative procedures or modifications such as improving the availability of voter registration through motor voter acts,[11] restrictive registration rules,[12] or centralizing polling place locations.[13] Furthermore, federal legislation under the Help America Vote Act (HAVA) 2002 has increased funding for measures aimed at improving voting administration.

VBM is one of those institutional measures created largely to lower the costs associated with voting at a polling place by allowing individuals to vote ahead of time and mail in their ballot. It has been touted by many academicians and practitioners to be a possible remedy to the relatively high levels of nonvoting that plague the country. Gaining momentum in the late 1980s and into the 1990s when the Oregon citizens approved the initiative to conduct all elections by VBM, the VBM movement has become a highly controversial electoral change in the voting literature. A variety of scholars sing the praises of VBM, citing cost savings, increased turnout, improved convenience of voting, and increasing acceptance among the electorate and election administrators. For instance, elections conducted by mail reduce costs of conducting an election by as much as one-third to one-half of what a polling place election costs.[14] Second, many scholars believe that VBM increases the percentage of registered voters turning out to vote,[15] but this is not a foregone conclusion, as some studies have found a small but significant reduction in turnout rates.[16] Third, in her analysis of the Oregon VBM system, Southwell finds widespread majority support for the system, five years after the adoption of the system for all elections.[17] Her findings seem to cast doubt on the notion that high initial rates of support for VBM were based on the novelty of the system rather than true satisfaction.

On the other hand, some analysts insist that VBM is far from a panacea and that, in the words of E. E. Schattschneider, the "heavenly chorus sings with a strong upper-class accent."[18] First, certain

[10] Anthony Downs, *An Economic Theory of Democracy* (New York: Harper & Row, 1957).

[11] Benjamin Highton and Raymond E. Wolfinger, "Estimating the Effects of the National Voter Registration Act of 1993," *Political Behavior* 20, no. 2 (1998): 79–104.

[12] Raymond E. Wolfinger and Steven J. Rosenstone, *Who Votes?* (New Haven: Yale University Press, 1980); Jonathan Nagler, "The Effect of Registration Laws and Education on U.S. Voter Turnout," *American Political Science Review* 85, no. 4 (1991): 393–405; Benjamin Highton, "Easy Registration and Voter Turnout," *The Journal of Politics* 59, no. 2 (1997), 565–75.

[13] Henry E. Brady and John E. McNulty, "The Costs of Voting: Evidence from a Natural Experiment" (presentation, annual meeting of the Midwest Political Science Association, Chicago, Ill., April 7–10, 2005).

[14] Patricia L. Southwell, "Five Years Later: A Re-Assessment of Oregon's Vote by Mail Electoral Process," *PS: Political Science and Politics* 37, no. 1 (2004): 89–93.

[15] Paul Gronke, Eva Galanes-Rosenbaum, and Peter A. Miller, "Early Voting and Turnout," *Political Science and Politics* 40 (2003): 639–45; Patricia L. Southwell and Justin I. Burchett, "The Effect of All-Mail Elections on Voter Turnout," *American Politics Research* 28, no. 1 (2000): 72–79.

[16] Thad Kousser and Megan Mullin, "Does Voting by Mail Increase Participation? Using Matching to Analyze a Natural Experiment," *Political Analysis* 15, no. 4 (2007).

[17] Patricia L. Southwell, "Five Years Later: A Re-Assessment of Oregon's Vote by Mail Electoral Process," *PS: Political Science and Politics* 37, no. 1 (2004): 89–93.

[18] Elmer E. Schattschneider, *The Semisovereign People: A Realist's View of Democracy in America* (New York: Harcourt Brace College Publishers, 1975).

analysts argue that VBM "has not changed who makes up the electorate, but only how they vote."[19] Rather than adding new voters to the pool of voting Americans, VBM seems to improve the convenience of voting for those who were already inclined to vote, and this effect seems fairly robust across election types such as special elections[20] as well as primary and general elections.[21] Berinsky et al. add that any increase in the voter pool is strictly based on better retention of previous voters, rather than mobilization of new recruits.[22] Furthermore, additional pernicious effects may accrue from the institution of VBM. Berinsky, for instance, found evidence that VBM may contribute to widening socio-economic gaps in turnout.[23] Kousser and Mullin found a slight, but statistically significant reduction in voter turnout when comparing VBM districts to traditional polling place districts.[24]

This chapter looks at the relationship between the promotion of VBM and voter turnout utilizing a field experiment in which a voter education/VBM conversion campaign was conducted and a randomized telephone survey of registered San Joaquin County, California voters. Our findings provide further evidence for Berinsky's[25] findings, that while VBM does increase turnout, the increase is likely to widen socio-economic gaps in turnout.

Cutting Costs for Voters: A Theory

If our aim is to provide a framework for thinking about how EAs can improve turnout through VBM, then in setting up the theoretical foundation, we will do well to begin with the calculus of the decision to cast a vote:[26]

$$R = B(P) - C$$

where R is the payoff (or "reward") to the citizen for casting a vote, B is the benefit of having your candidate(s) win (compared to that of the opponent(s)), P is the probability that your vote matters (i.e., is decisive), and C is the cost of voting borne by the voter. Certainly, as discussed above, there are many reasons for voting and nonvoting that are not captured here. But, for both parsimony and clarity, our assumption that at least *part* of many voters' decision process is approximated by this calculation sets us off in the right direction.

To start down that road, we make a very simple observation about the conditions under which a citizen will decide to vote: the R term must be positive. That is, citizens only have an incentive to vote if the net rewards for doing so warrant the action. There are obviously several moving parts in the right hand side of the equation, and thus several ways a positive R might result. Stated in terms of comparative statics, as the $B(P)$ product increases and/or the C term decreases, a positive R value be-

---

[19] Subcommittee on Elections of the Committee on House Administration, Expanding and Improving Opportunities to Vote by Mail or Absentee: Hearing before the *Committee on House Administration* (testimony of John Fortier), 110th Cong., 1st Sess., 2007.

[20] Patricia L. Southwell and Justin I. Burchett, "The Effect of All-Mail Elections on Voter Turnout," *American Politics Research* 28, no. 1 (2000): 72–79.

[21] Adam J. Berinsky, Nancy Burns, and Michael W. Traugott, "Who Votes by Mail? A Dynamic Model of the Individual-Level Consequences of Voting-By-Mail Systems," *Public Opinion Quarterly* 65, no. 2 (2001): 178–97.

[22] *Ibid.*

[23] Adam J. Berinsky, "The Perverse Consequences of Electoral Reform in the United States," *American Politics Research* 33, no. 4 (2005): 471–91.

[24] Thad Kousser and Megan Mullin, "Does Voting by Mail Increase Participation? Using Matching to Analyze a Natural Experiment," *Political Analysis* 15, no. 4 (2007).

[25] Adam J. Berinsky, "The Perverse Consequences of Electoral Reform in the United States," *American Politics Research* 33, no. 4 (2005): 471–91.

[26] Anthony Downs, *An Economic Theory of Democracy* (New York: Harper & Row, 1957).

comes more probable. Let us consider what this means in plain English for a moment, taking each of these variables in turn.

The *B* term captures the cumulative value of any given voter getting their preferred candidate in every race, as compared to the other candidate(s) in those races. Put another way, *B* captures how much better off a voter is under her preferred electoral outcome than the alternatives. For illustration, let us imagine an election with only one item on a ballot, a choice between two candidates for governor. If, from a given voter's perspective, those two candidates were exactly the same, then this *B* term is 0. That is, they derive no benefit from electing one candidate over the other. On the other hand, one could imagine a very liberal voter considering a choice between one very liberal candidate and one very conservative candidate. In that case, *B* is going to be relatively large. The point here, however, is not to determine the precise size of *B* for any given voter (after all, it is much more complicated than the example, since we would have to aggregate over all races and compare all candidates). Rather, for the moment, simply notice that it is the *candidates* (or other ballot alternatives) that affect the size of the *B* term.

Of course, that benefit only really comes into play insomuch as a voter thinks that he or she is likely to cast the deciding vote, which is captured by the *P* term. *P,* very simply, represents the probability that a given voter will break a tie and decide the outcome of an election. Consider an election in which a voter knew with certainty that they would cast the deciding vote (i.e., *P* = 1). In that case, their vote would allow them to realize the full benefit captured by *B*, based entirely on their own decision to vote. On the other hand, if that voter was certain she would *not* cast the deciding vote (i.e., *P* = 0), then, though her preferred candidate may win, it will not have anything to do with whether or not she voted. Thus, they should not count that benefit as part of their reason for voting (that is, no matter how large *B* is, if *P* is 0, then the product of the two will be 0 as well).

Indeed, this is where the rational calculus of voting is said to fall flat. Though the probability of being the deciding vote is probably not 0, it is *very* small in most elections, even at the local level. Thus, critics argue that voters should virtually never vote, and the fact that they do nullifies the usefulness of the calculation framework. As a solution, Riker and Ordeshook[27] add a "*D* term" to the equation, which has an additive effect and is intended to capture a voter's sense of civic duty, satisfaction from participation, chance to affirm partisan identification, and other benefits of the act of voting that do not depend on the outcome of the elections. Formally, their modified equation takes the form,

$$R = B(P) + D - C$$

Our intent here is certainly not to sort out this debate. Instead, we want to direct the reader's attention to two further points at this juncture. First, even if we believe that *P* is always 0, thus negating the impact of *B* in increasing the likelihood of a positive *R*, the *D* term is a plausible addition that still creates a benefit for voting. In other words, regardless of the outcome of the election (and a given voter's perceived impact on that outcome), there are still potential "rewards" from the act of voting. Second, to the extent that the probability of a person casting the deciding vote *is* a key factor in that person's calculus, it is primarily *other voters* (and that person's own perception) that determine the size of *P*.

So, taken together, the key point is that changes in the *B(P)* variable are *not* in the hands of EAs. Indeed, by law and by strict practice, EAs cannot do much to affect the *B* or *P* terms. One only needs to consider the hypothetical situation of a registrar of voters trying to boost turnout by recruiting extreme candidates (thus increasing the *B*'s) or making an effort to create or portray a close race (thus increasing the *P*'s) to see that this would be both odd and illegal behavior.

---

[27] William H. Riker and Peter C. Ordeshook, "A Theory of the Calculus of Voting," *American Political Science Review* 62, no. 1 (1968): 25–42.

Thus, if EAs are to change turnout, according to the calculus of voting, they are left with cutting the costs of voting. This is intuitively appealing as, in a sense, this is in perfect harmony with the basic job of most EAs: to administer elections as efficiently and effectively as possible and to bring to life the constitutional guarantee that each citizen be allowed to exercise their right to vote. Encouraging voting by making that process less burdensome for voters seems to further that mission. So how might they be most effective in cutting costs?

Returning to our equation, assume $B(P)$ is fixed for all voters. Assume further that the difference in cost between voting at home and voting at the polls is a value of size h.[28] Perhaps a better way to think of h is as a "discount" that the voter gets by voting at home. Now, we can divide voters into three subsets, which are exhaustive of the entire population:

Subset 1: $B(P) + D - C + h > 0$ & $B(P) + D - C > 0$
Subset 2: $B(P) + D - C + h > 0$ & $B(P) + D - C < 0$
Subset 3: $B(P) + D - C + h < 0$ & $B(P) + D - C < 0$

The first subset is those citizens for whom the cost benefit tradeoff, even if they have to pay the cost of showing up at the polls, dictates that they are regular voters. That is, the benefit is so large, that it offsets the full cost of voting, even without the discounted voting at home option. Accordingly, these voters may find it beneficial to adopt VBM, but it is not pivotal in terms of their participation in the voting process.

Skipping ahead to the third subset, these are citizens for whom the costs of voting are so large, or the benefits so slight, that they will likely never vote even if they could do it from home. Thus, even with the discount of VBM, these inactive voters will not see participation as a desirable option. So VBM is not pivotal in this case either.

The second subset, however, is confronted with a tradeoff that is sufficiently "close" that the discount from voting at home will push them over the edge utility wise, making their R term positive, and compelling them to cast a ballot. In this case, adoption of VBM is crucial in turning potential voters into active voters. This categorization, however, is largely a conceptual point. That is, because we have a difficult time identifying voters that fall into Subset 2, we would have a difficult time testing the hypotheses that incorporate that sorting. However, it *is* crucial, from a broader theoretical perspective, to establish that such a group exists. For, even if we cannot separate them out empirically, it is this group that we expect to be most affected by the efforts of EAs in lowering the cost of VBM.

This is a critical point when we consider that signing up for VBM is not a costless action itself. It is, however, a one-time cost (it takes attention and effort and knowledge, typically), which makes it difficult to incorporate formally into the "calculus of voting" equation above. But the basic intuition is straightforward. The up front, "fixed cost" of signing up for VBM must be made up for in "savings" over all the future instances where the voter uses VBM instead of paying the extra cost to go the polls. You might think of it like buying a membership to Costco. You pay an upfront cost, but get it back with the savings on all your future purchases. Still, the cheaper the membership, the more likely members are to expect to be able to "make up the difference" in savings. Thus, in the case of VBM, the comparative static is evident: even for voters who would benefit most from the VBM option (subset 2), the cheaper it is to convert to VBM, the more likely voters are to convert.

Two predictions follow from the logical framework laid out above. First, we predict that:

H1: By reducing the costs of signing up for vote by mail, more voters will become permanent absentees.

---

[28] Of course, here we are assuming that this difference between voting at home and in person at the polls is uniform across all voters. We realize that this is a simplification that doesn't hold, and perhaps in the future we'll want to try to model this. Indeed, some voters will live further from the polling station, some will not have good transportation, and some will even get a social "benefit" from going to the polling place.

Second, when we take away the costs of going to polls, h, by converting some in-person voters to VBM voters, then R is more likely to be positive; and thus these voters are *more likely* to cast a ballot. Stated in plain language:

H2: When voters become vote-by-mail participants, their rate of voter turnout will increase, *ceteris peribus*.

In the next sections, we submit these hypotheses to empirical testing.

Research Design: A Field Experiment

To test our hypotheses, we ran a field experiment[29] using the entire registered voting population of California's San Joaquin County as our pool of subjects.[30] Our efforts were focused on the June 2008 election. Using this as our election of interest is ideal insomuch as field experimental studies on voter turnout have been shown to be more effective in less salient nonpresidential elections.[31] We began by using an algorithm to randomly identify 60 percent of the voting precincts within the county as our treatment group. This consisted of approximately 250 precincts, containing a total of 101,553 registered voters, leaving a control group of approximately 160 precincts and 82,903 voters.[33] On April 15, 2008, all registered voters in the treatment group who were not already signed up for permanent VBM were sent a postcard. The postcard informed them about the option of permanent VBM status, was preprinted with their name and other information, already had the box check-marked to indicate their desire to become a permanent VBM voter, and included return postage (see Figure 1 for a picture of an example postcard). Voters needed only to sign their name and put the postcard back in the mail in order to gain permanent VBM status.

Of course, we cannot be certain that the voters actually got the postcards, paid attention to them, understood them, and considered the VBM option. However, it seems safe to assume that, since none in the control group got a postcard, the rate of voters who, in the fullest sense, "received" the treatment, was much higher in the treatment group.

We turn first to consider Hypothesis 1, that by reducing the start up costs of VBM, more voters will obtain permanent VBM status. For those in the control group, becoming a permanent VBM voter would have required considerably more effort than simply returning a precompleted postcard with their signature.[34] Certainly, then, voters in our treatment group who received our postcard had a sig-

---

[29] One could debate the characterization of our research design as an "experiment" rather than a "quasi-experiment." Though our design has true random assignment—a hallmark of a true experiment—it is not conducted in a controlled environment. Moreover, one could object that because our treatment was "sent" to our treatment group (though we can't be certain it was received in every case), it violates the requirements for a true experiment. We acknowledge these objections, but still would argue that our design falls closer to an experiment than a quasi-experiment.

[30] This experiment is part of a larger project run through the Jacoby Center at the University of the Pacific, by contract and in conjunction with the San Joaquin County Registrar for Voters. Funding for the project originated with the Help America Vote Act (HAVA) and was directed to the SJC Registrar by way of the California Secretary of State's office. Other parts of the project include efforts to reduce voter errors and improve poll-worker training.

[31] Harold F. Gosnell, *Getting Out the Vote: An Experiment in The Stimulation of Voting* (Chicago: University of Chicago Press, 1927); Donald P. Green, Alan S. Gerber, and David W. Nickerson, "Getting Out the Vote in Local Elections: Results from Six Door-to-Door Canvassing Experiments," *Journal of Politics* 65, no. 4 (2003): 1083–1096.

[33] More precisely, there were originally about 116,000 voters who were mailed postcards, but roughly 15,000 were returned as undeliverable.

[34] Note that between the time the postcard was sent out and the June 3 election (when we assessed the number of new permanent VBM voters), there were television ads running on local cable stations that aimed to make voters more aware of VBM, thus lowering the information cost for signing up for VBM. However, any affect these ads had should have been evenly distributed across treatment and control groups.

Figure 1: VBM Postcard Mailed to Treatment Group

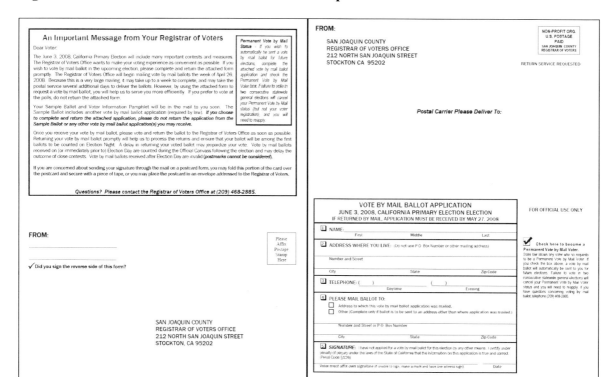

nificantly lower cost of signing up for vote by mail. Thus, based on Hypothesis 1, we should expect to see a significantly larger proportion of voters signing up for permanent VBM status in the treatment group than in the control group.

Directing our attention to Figure 2, that is just what we find. Of the 101,553 individuals that received the postcard treatment, 20,400 (20 percent) subsequently converted to permanent VBM status prior to the June election. The 82,903 control group subjects, on the other hand, yielded only 8,151 (10 percent) new permanent VBM voters during the same time period. The conversion rate in the treatment group was approximately double that of the control group, and the difference of proportions is significant at better than .001. From this, it seems clear that by lowering the start-up cost of entry into permanent VBM status, voters are substantially more likely to take advantage of this option.

Turnout and VBM

Next, consider Hypothesis 2, that switching to VBM should lead to higher turnout rates. Of course, there is a potential problem with the inference drawn here. Unlike our experimental evaluation of Hypothesis 1, where we used random assignment to eliminate selection bias in who got the VBM postcard, we cannot be sure that VBM voters and non-VBM voters are sorted without bias. Indeed, it seems hard to believe that there is not bias, such that those who take the time to sign up for VBM are more predisposed to turn out in the first place. Thus, this threatens the inference that can be drawn about the positive VBM impact on turnout based on our field experiment. Still, it may be informative to look at the relationship between VBM and turnout here, with caution in mind as we draw our conclusions.

Figure 2. Voters Converted to VBM by Postcard Mailer

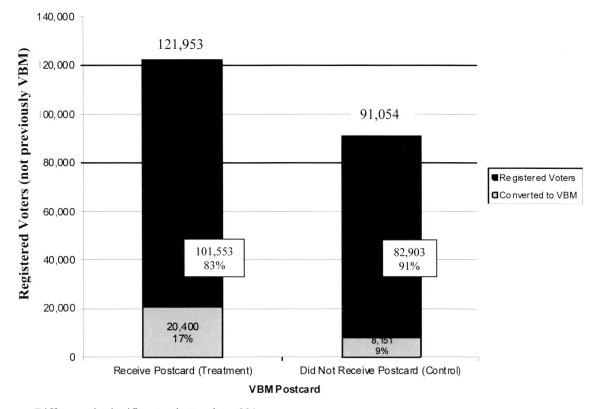

Difference is significant at better than .001.

As a first cut, Figure 3 compares turnout rates of VBM voters to that of non-VBM voters. Of the 162,967 registered voters who were *not* signed up for permanent VBM status, just 23,376 (14 percent) physically showed up at the polls and voted. This is a staggeringly light turnout when compared to permanent VBM voters: of the 89,610 VBM registrants, 41,542 (46 percent) mailed in ballots in June 2008 (the difference of proportions is significant at better than 99.9 percent confidence). So, while there were nearly twice as many "walk-in" voters registered, nearly twice as many "mail-in" voters cast ballots. Though we are hesitant to draw strong conclusions given the threats to internal validity, the magnitude of this difference is impressive, and suggests support for Hypothesis 2.

Perhaps more interesting, however, are the results that show up in Figure 4. Here, we look at turnout *only* among VBM voters. However, we subdivide into three groups: converts from our treatment group, converts from our control group, and individuals who were already VBM voters prior to our field experiment. Of the 20,400 new VBM voters from our treatment group, 9,974 (49 percent) voted in the June election. This represents the *highest* turnout rate of the three groups, with just 40 percent (3,091 of 8,151) voting from the control group, and just under 47 percent (28,477 of 61,059) voting from the group of previous VBM voters. These groups are all significantly different at better than .001 by difference of proportions tests.

In some sense, this is a very surprising result. One would think that those voters from the control group, who were motivated enough to pay the higher cost of signing up for VBM, might also be more motivated to cast a ballot. Yet, the opposite seems to be true. It appears that the postcard treatment not only made voters more likely to sign up for permanent VBM status, but for those who converted, at

Figure 3. Turnout in Person and By Mail

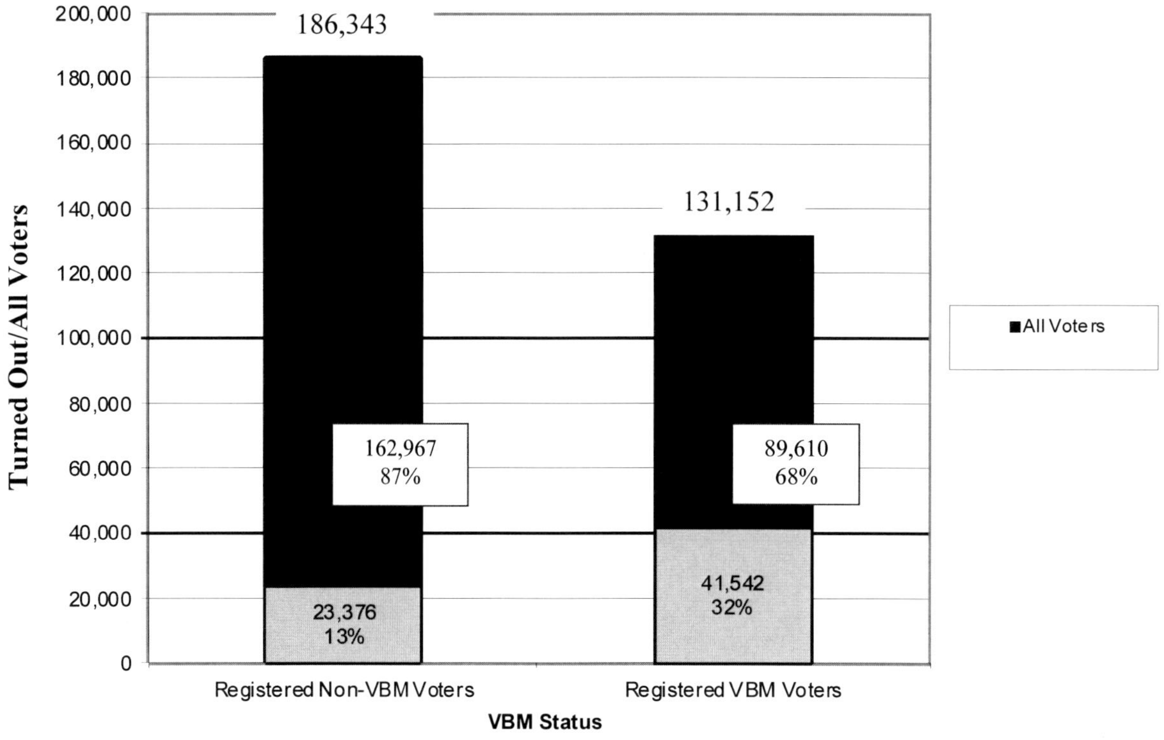

Difference is significant at better than .001.

least in the short run, it also made them more likely to vote. Thus, with this result, we might tentative-ly add a corollary to Hypothesis 1, stating that those who pay lower costs to sign up for VBM will also turn out at a higher rate once converted.

Survey Supplement

To supplement our field experiment, we also ran a survey of voters in San Joaquin County in May 2008, leading up to the June election. The Social Science Research Center (SSRC) at California State University, Fullerton conducted a telephone survey completing interviews with 542 registered voters in San Joaquin County. Five hundred and nine (93.9 percent) interviews were completed in English and 33 (6.1 percent) in Spanish.[35] Select items from the actual survey instrument can be found in Appendix 1.

---

[35] Telephone surveys were administered between May 5 and May 29, 2008. The survey questionnaire was programmed for administration utilizing computer-assisted telephone interviewing (CATI) software. The SSRC utilizes the Ci3 CATI software package; the same system supported by the Centers for Disease Control and Prevention (CDC) for their statewide and national surveys. Interviews were conducted between 4:00 p.m. and 9:00 p.m. local time Monday through Thursday, and between 11:00 a.m. and 7:00 p.m. local time Saturday and Sunday. The sample frame for this study is the roster of registered voters in San Joaquin County. The voter registration file was annotated to indicate voters who had received an educational mailing antecedent to the study (*n* = 101,558), those slated to receive a mailing in the future (*n* = 82,909), and those already registered as "Per-

Figure 4. New VBM Voters, Old VBM Voters, and Turnout in June 2008

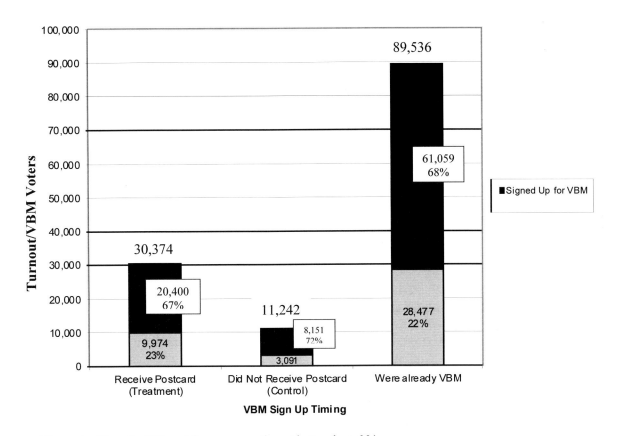

All are significantly different from one another at better than .001

One of the key premises of our argument about conversion to VBM is that for some voters, the costs of voting in person are sufficiently high that they are kept from voting often. Thus, we expect that these "high-cost" voters should be more likely to take advantage of the VBM option. To assess this expectation, we estimate a probit model to gauge whether respondents that received our post card and high-cost voters were more likely to convert to VBM.[36]

---

manent Absentee" ($n = 61,061$). Because one goal of this study was to investigate the effect of a voter education mailing upon intentions to vote by mail, "permanent absentees" (those already voting by mail) were excluded from the sample frame. Subtracting voters for whom telephone numbers were either missing or incomplete from those who had already received the educational mailing ($101,558 - 12,449 = 89,109$) and from those scheduled to receive a future mailing ($82,909 - 8,697 = 74,212$) produced a sample frame consisting of 163,321 voters with valid telephone numbers. From this pool, a random sample of 2,012 was selected. Of these, 993 (49.5 percent) had received the mailing and 1,019 (50.6 percent) had not.

[36] We estimated the following equation:

$\text{ConvertVBM}_i = \alpha + \beta_1 \text{Treatment}_i + \beta_2 \text{HighCost}_i + \beta_3 \text{Treatment*HighCost}_i + [\beta_{4..n} \text{Controls}_i] + \varepsilon_{ik}$

where the dependant variable *ConvertVBM*$_i$ equals 1 if an individual converted to VBM during the treatment period, and 0 otherwise. Our three main independent variables are: *Treatment*$_i$, which equals 1 if an individual received the postcard treatment (as described above), and 0 otherwise; *HighCost*$_i$, which equals 1 if an individual reported lack of transportation, child care issues, or too many hours of work on Election Day as difficulties related to going to the polls; and *Treatment*HighCost*$_i$, which is an interaction of the two previous variables.

The dependent variable in our analysis is a dichotomous indicator of whether the respondent converted to VBM during the treatment period, and our main independent variables are dichotomous measures of whether the respondent received our postcard treatment (as described above), had "high costs" to get the polls (e.g., reported a lack of transportation, child care issues, or too many hours of work on election day as difficulties related to going to the polls). In one model, we add a series of control variables, which capture respondents' marital status, education level, home language, political ideology, homeowner status, ethnicity, and religiosity.[37]

Table 1 includes results from three probit models, all variations on the same basic design. In each model, we include our treatment variable indicating whether or not the individual received the post-card treatment. Unsurprisingly, this is highly significant in each case. That is, the basic result from the entire population in our experiment also shows up in our sample: lowering the cost of signing up for VBM significantly and substantially increases the conversion rate.

Of central interest here, however, are the coefficients on the high-cost variable. As our theory presumed, high-cost voters were significantly more likely to have converted to VBM. Interestingly, however, where we include an interaction variable to capture the combined effect of high voting costs with our postcard treatment (in Model 2), we find no significant effect. This seems to suggest that though high-cost voters were generally more likely to convert to VBM, they were no more susceptible to the low-cost conversion option than other voters. It does, however, speak to the basic intuition behind Hypothesis 2. If part of the choice to vote is driven by cost, then the voters with the highest cost should be more likely to seek out low-cost voting options. This is what our results suggest.

All control variables fail to reach significance in Model 3, and this is not especially surprising. We would be more concerned if the dependant variable were simply whether individuals were VBM voters at all. Certainly, we would expect many of these variables to be significant, and this is precisely why we chose to include them here. But since we are instead looking at *conversion* to VBM during a very specific period, it is not clear that any of the control variables should be predictive.[38]

To give a sense of magnitude to our multivariate results, we have constructed Table 2, a two-by-two representation of predicted probabilities that reflect the various intersections of the high-cost and treatment variables.[39] Starting with the difference between treatment and control groups, the predicted probabilities almost perfectly mirror the percentages in the raw population data (from our field experiment, discussed above), with low-cost voters in the control group having about a .10 probability of conversion, while low-cost voters that received the postcard are twice as likely to convert to VBM. The effect of the treatment is slightly smaller among high-cost voters, going from .32 to almost .50. Still, as expected, we see an across the board increase in probability. The increases are even more dramatic when we look at the impact of high cost on conversion. For those in the control group, the effect of being a high-cost voter more than triples a respondent's probability of conversion, from .10

---

[37] The control variables were coded as follows:

Married equals 1 if a respondent is married, and 0 if not.

Education equals an ordinal variable, ranging from 1 ("less than high school diploma") to 6 ("a graduate or professional degree").

English equals 1 if only English is spoken in the respondents home, and 0 otherwise.

Ideology equals a five-point scale, rescaled from 0 to 1, where 0 is very liberal and 1 is very conservative.

Homeowner equals 1 if the respondent owns his/her home, and 0 otherwise.

Caucasian equals 1 if the respondent is Caucasian, and 0 otherwise.

Religiosity equals an ordinal variable indicating the frequency of attending religious services, ranging from 0 ("less than a few times per year") to 1 ("every week").

[38] We also ran models that include a control for income and found no substantive difference in our variables of interest. Since using income cut our observations in half, and it was not significant, we decided to exclude it from the models presented here.

[39] These predicted probabilities were generated using Clarify (Tomz, Wittenberg, and King 2003), and are based on Model 1.

Table 1. The Effect of Postcard Treatment and High Voting Cost on Switch to VBM

	Model 1	Model 2	Model 3
Treatment	.472***	.487***	.524***
	(.131)	(.141)	(.157)
High Cost	.794***	.849***	.841***
	(.195)	(.272)	(.226)
High Cost x Treatment		-.110	
		(.388)	
Married			-.224
			(.181)
Education			.082
			(.054)
English			.078
			(.247)
Ideology			.476
			(.305)
Homeowner			-.072
			(.203)
Caucasian			-.006
			(.209)
Religiosity			-.041
			(.222)
Constant	-1.270***	-1.279***	-1.741***
	(.103)	(.108)	(.358)
Pseudo R^2	0.055	.056	.079
N	542	542	404

Table displays coefficients, with standard errors in parentheses
*Significant at .10
**Significant at .05
***Significant at .01
Dependant Variable: Switched to VBM
Estimation Technique: Probit

to .32. Among voters who received postcards, the effect is only slightly smaller, with an increase from .21 to 50.

Discussion

Though in recent years, we have seen modest increases in rates of voter turnout, explaining and improving these rates continues to be a goal of many social scientists and EAs alike. Armed with the ability and resources to structurally modify individuals' costs associated with voting, EAs can have a significant impact on rates of voter turnout. Using an innovative, mixed-method approach, this study has demonstrated the powerful impact of an active VBM campaign conducted at the county level. Our field experimental and survey research results lend strong support to our hypotheses that (1) decreas-

Table 2. Predicted Probability of Converting to VBM, by High Cost and Postcard Treatment

	Low Cost of Voting	High Cost of Voting
Did not receive postcard (Control)	.1032 (.0719 – .1450)	.3203 (.2042 – .4645)
Received postcard (Treatment)	.2141 (.1658 – .2641)	.4997 (.3423 – .6490)

Confidence intervals in parentheses

ing the costs associated with registering for permanent VBM will lead to greater rates of permanent VBM registration; and (2) when voters become vote-by-mail participants, their rate of voter turnout will increase. Furthermore, the notion that changes in the cost of voting may even trump individual motivation levels seems to gain some initial support given the finding that those who pay lower costs to sign up for VBM will also turn out at a higher rate once converted. To the extent that VBM is often a lower-cost alternative to in-person voting both in terms of voter costs *and* EA costs, we recommend that government officials consider implementing similar programs universally.

Appendix 1: Selected Items from Survey Instrument Included in the Statistical Analysis

[SCHEDULE CALLBACK]

TRANS1   I'd like to begin by asking you a few general questions about some voting information that you may have seen or heard recently. When I mention a "sample ballot," I'm referring to an official booklet sent to you by the San Joaquin County Registrar of Voters a few weeks before the election. This booklet contains information about the upcoming election and candidates for office.

Q1   Do you recall seeing or hearing any information in the last three months about voting by mail?

    1. Yes   [CONTINUE]
    2. No   [SKIP TO Q2]
    7. Don't know/no response   [SKIP TO Q2]
    9. Refused   [SKIP TO Q2]

Q4   Did you vote in the last election, in February?

    1. Yes   [CONTINUE]
    2. No   [SKIP TO Q12]
    7. Don't know/no response   [SKIP TO Q12]
    9. Refused   [SKIP TO Q12]

Q5   Did you vote . . .

    1. In person at a polling place, or   [SKIP TO Q7]
    2. by mail?   [CONTINUE]
    7. Don't know/no response
    9. Refused

Q6   Did you vote using . . .

    1. An absentee ballot, or   [SKIP TO Q12]
    2. Permanent vote by mail?   [SKIP TO Q12]
    7. Don't know/no response
    9. Refused

    7. Don't know/no response

Q19   Some people find a variety of things about casting their vote in person at a polling place to be difficult or inconvenient. Is there anything about voting in person at a polling place that is difficult or inconvenient for you?
[RECORD UP TO THREE RESPONSES]

    a. Yes, specify>
    b. Yes, specify>
    c. Yes, specify>

        1. Lack of transportation

    2. Child care issues
    3. Working too many hours on Election Day
    4. Don't know how to vote
    5. Don't know anything about politics
    6. Other, specify>
    7. No, nothing about voting in person at a polling place is difficult or inconvenient
   77. Don't know/no response
   99. refused

Q20   The way you see it, are there any specific advantages to voting by mail?
       [RECORD UP TO THREE RESPONSES]

    a. Yes, specify>
    b. Yes, specify>
    c. Yes, specify>

    1. General convenience
    2. Can vote when I want to
    3. Have as much time as I need to read/think it through/talk to others
    4. Don't have to worry about child care
    5. Don't have to take time off from work
    6. Other, specify>
    7. No, there are no specific advantages
   77. Don't know/no response
   99. refused

Q21   Are there any particular problems with, or disadvantages to voting by mail?
       [RECORD UP TO THREE RESPONSES]

    a. Yes, specify>
    b. Yes, specify>
    c. Yes, specify>

    1. Concerns about confidentiality and privacy
    2. Like the feeling/get something out of voting in person
    3. Too easy to lose or accidentally destroy the mail ballot
    4. Too easy to forget deadline for voting by mail
    5. Have to vote before the campaign is over
    6. Other, specify>
    7. No, there are no specific problems or disadvantages
   77. Don't know/no response
   99. refused

Q33   Are you registered to vote as a Democrat, Republican, another political party, or are you
       registered with no party affiliation?

    1. Democrat
    2. Republican
    3. Other, specify>
    4. No party affiliation
    7. Don't know/no response

9. Refused

Q34   Politically, do you consider yourself to be . . .

1. Very liberal
2. Somewhat liberal
3. Middle-of-the-road
4. Somewhat conservative, or
5. Very conservative?
7. Don't know/no response
9. Refused

Q35   Which of the following best describes your present situation? Are you . . .
[CHECK ALL THAT APPLY]

1. Retired
2. A student
3. A homemaker [not employed outside the home]
4. Disabled,
5. Currently employed full time,
6. Currently employed part time,
7. Self-employed, or
8. Currently unemployed, laid off, or looking for work?
77. Don't know
99. Refused

Q36   What was the last grade in school that you completed?

1. Less than high school diploma/GED
2. High school diploma/GED
3. Some college, no degree
4. Associate degree
5. Bachelor's degree
6. A graduate or professional degree (i.e., Teaching Credential, Masters, Ph.D.)
7. Don't know/no response
9. Refused

Q37   What is your marital status? [READ ONLY IF NECESSARY]

1. Married
2. Single, never married
3. Divorced
4. Widowed
5. Separated
6. Cohabiting with a partner/domestic partnership
7. Other
8. Don't know/no response
9. Refused

[IF INTERVIEW IS IN SPANISH, SKIP TO Q39. IF INTERVIEW IS IN ENGLISH, CONTINUE]

Q38   Do you speak a language other than English at home?

           1.   Yes, specify>   [CONTINUE]
           2.   No   [SKIP TO Q36]
           7.   Don't know/ no response
           9.   Refused

Q40   Do you own or rent your home?

           1.   Own
           2.   Rent
           7.   Don't know/ no response
           9.   Refused

Q41   In what year were you born?

           19__
           777. don't know/no response
           999. refused

Q43   How do you describe your race or ethnicity?

           1.   Asian, specify>
           2.   Black or African American
           3.   Latino or Hispanic
           4.   Caucasian or White
           5   Other, specify>
           7.   Don't know/no response
           9.   Refused

Q44   How many children younger than 18 years of age currently reside in your household?

           1.   Number
           7.   Don't know/no response
           9.   Refused

Q45   Not including weddings and funerals, how often do you attend religious or spiritual services? Would you say . . .

           1.   Every week (or more often)
           2.   Almost every week
           3.   Once or twice a month
           4.   A few times per year, or
           5.   Less often than that?
           7.   Don't know/no response
           9.   Refused

Q46   Which of the following categories best describes your total household or family income before taxes, from all sources?

   1. Under $20,000
   2. $20,000 to $29,999
   3. $30,000 to $39,999
   4. $40,000 to $49,999
   5. $50,000 to $59,999
   6. $60,000 to $69,999
   7. $70,000 to $79,999
   8. $80,000 to $89,999
   9. $90,000 to $99,999
   10. $100,000 to $124,999
   11. $125,000 to $149,999
   12. $150,000 to $174,999
   13. Over $175,000
   77. Don't know/no response
   99. Refused

ADDRESS   Lastly, the San Joaquin County Registrar of Voters lists your address as [READ ADDRESS]. Is this accurate? Your address information will not be included with your survey responses, just a "yes" or "no" to indicate whether it is accurately recorded.

   1. Yes
   2. No
   7. Don't know/no response
   9. Refused

References

Berelson, Bernard R., Paul F. Lazarsfeld, and William N. McPhee. 1954. *Voting: A Study of Opinion Formation in a Presidential Campaign.* Chicago: University of Chicago Press.

Berinsky, Adam J. 2005. "The Perverse Consequences of Electoral Reform in the United States." *American Politics Research* 33(4): 471–91.

Berinsky, Adam J., Nancy Burns, and Michael W. Traugott. 2001. "Who Votes By Mail? A Dynamic Model of the Individual-Level Consequences of Voting-By-Mail Systems." *Public Opinion Quarterly* 65(2): 178–97.

Brady, Henry E., and John E. McNulty. 2005. "The Costs of Voting: Evidence from a Natural Experiment." Presentation at the annual meeting of the Midwest Political Science Association, Chicago, Ill., April 7–10.

Campbell, Angus, Philip E. Converse, Warren E. Miller, and Donald E. Stokes. 1960. *The American Voter.* New York: Wiley.

Downs, Anthony. 1957. *An Economic Theory of Democracy.* New York: Harper & Row.

Expanding and Improving Opportunities to Vote by Mail or Absentee: Hearing before the Subcommittee on Elections of the Committee on House Administration. 2007. U.S. House, 110th Cong., 1st Sess., 2 (testimony of John Fortier).

File, Thom. 2009. "Voting and Registration in the Election of November 2006." *U.S. Census Bureau,* retrieved March 12, < http://www.census.gov/population/www/socdemo/voting.html>.

Gosnell, Harold F. 1927. *Getting Out the Vote: An Experiment in the Stimulation of Voting.* Chicago: University of Chicago Press.

Green, Donald P., Alan S. Gerber, and David W. Nickerson. 2003. "Getting Out the Vote in Local Elections: Results from Six Door-to-Door Canvassing Experiments." *Journal of Politics* 65(4): 1083–1096.

Gronke, Paul, Eva Galanes-Rosenbaum, and Peter A. Miller. 2003. "Early Voting and Turnout." *Political Science and Politics* 40: 639–45.

Highton, Benjamin. 1997. "Easy Registration and Voter Turnout." *The Journal of Politics* 59(2): 565–75.

Highton, Benjamin, and Raymond E. Wolfinger. 1998. "Estimating the Effects of the National Voter Registration Act of 1993." *Political Behavior* 20(2): 79–104.

Kousser, Thad, and Megan Mullin. 2007. "Does Voting by Mail Increase Participation? Using Matching to Analyze a Natural Experiment." *Political Analysis* 15(4).

Lazarsfeld, Paul F., Bernard Berelson, and Hazel Gaudet. 1944. *The People's Choice: How the Voter Makes Up His Mind in a Presidential Campaign.* New York: Columbia University Press.

Nagler, Jonathan. 1991. "The Effect of Registration Laws and Education on U.S. Voter Turnout." *American Political Science Review* 85(4): 393–405.

Riker, William H., and Peter C. Ordeshook, 1968. "A Theory of the Calculus of Voting." *American Political Science Review* 62(1): 25–42.

Schattschneider, Elmer Eric. 1975. *The Semisovereign People: A Realist's View of Democracy in America.* New York: Harcourt Brace College Publishers.

Patricia L. Southwell, and Justin I. Burchett. 2000. "The Effect of All-Mail Elections on Voter Turnout." *American Politics Research* 28(1): 72–79.

Southwell, Patricia L. 2004. "Five Years Later: A Re-Assessment of Oregon's Vote by Mail Electoral Process." *PS: Political Science and Politics* 37(1): 89–93.

Tomz, Michael, Jason Wittenberg, and Gary King. 2003. "CLARIFY: Software for Interpreting and Presenting Statistical Results." *Journal of Statistical Software* 8.

U.S. Congress. House. Subcommittee on Elections of the Committee on House Administration. 2007. *Expanding and Improving Opportunities to Vote by Mail or Absentee: Hearing before the Committee on House Administration (testimony of John Fortier).* 110th Cong., 1st Sess.

Wolfinger, Raymond E., and Steven J. Rosenstone. 1980. *Who Votes?* New Haven: Yale University Press.

Part III: The Social Science of Ballot Error and Vote by Mail

Chapter 9

When Registrars of Voters and Academics Talk

Robert Benedetti and Austin Erdman[1]

A Registrar Reflects[2]

Elections officials care deeply about the right to vote in America and go to great lengths to afford every legally eligible voter a chance to participate in the electoral process. Academics can help by uncovering new ways to help registrars of voters fulfill this commitment. Educating others and attention to detail is a way of life for registrars. We are continually engaged in educating constituents, the general public, poll workers, staff, voters, and others about ever-changing laws, rules, and regulations in the elections industry and reflecting on how these practices can best be implemented.

As governmental leaders, registrars must also maintain a "big picture" vision of the future of the elections industry. One could say that academicians and registrars share a common commitment to life-long teaching and learning. It seems only natural, then, that formal researchers and educators specializing in the political policy sciences could assist elections officials in improving the education process surrounding elections, while suggesting new tools for envisioning the future of elections. Collaboration with university-level faculty engaged in studying voting processes is a relatively new concept in San Joaquin County—one of which is now being fully embraced by both parties.

What registrars know and academics come quickly to realize about the phenomena of elections is that every election is unique. While a prescribed methodology (the law) dictates the manner in which elections must be run, there is a set of special circumstances that shapes each election day to be like no other. These unique and sometimes unwelcome circumstances can be summed up in *Murphy's Law*: *"Anything that can go wrong will go wrong."* Voting systems require constant attention to detail to minimize the laundry list of potential pitfalls that must be addressed in order to ensure a successful outcome—a legally and properly run election.

If any tasks are left undone or not done correctly, these failures become increasingly apparent as the election process wears on. Generally, by the time one discovers a problem and if not acted on quickly, it is too late for corrective action. For instance, if poll workers are not trained properly and thoroughly, Election Day can result in call center mania—phones ring off the hook from poll workers experiencing panic and uncertainty. Given the large number of special circumstances surrounding elections, acade-

---

[1] Robert Benedetti is executive director of the Jacoby Center for Public Service and Civic Leadership and professor of political science at the University of the Pacific. Austin Erdman is registrar of voters for San Joaquin County, California.

[2] This section was written by Austin Erdman.

micians who would join with registrars in examining this process must pay heed to the long checklist of variables; else, *Murphy's Law* overwhelms both the election and any research that focuses upon it.

Both registrars and scholars can learn from the history of voting systems. Changes in voting technology have been largely driven by perceived and real needs of voters themselves. For instance, the initial move from voice voting (calling aloud one's vote yay or nay) to secret paper ballots addressed the problem of voters being influenced by external pressures such as threats and intimidation. Secret paper ballots gave each citizen the comfort of voting without everyone knowing how they cast their vote.

Technological advances in voting continued with the use of Greek tokens, Italian round black and white balls, mechanical lever machines, paper ballots, punch cards, optical scanners, and direct recording electronic voting machines. Preprinted ballots solved the problem of interpreting handwriting of voters in the mid-1800s, solving the issues of secrecy and one person—one vote. In the late 1890s, lever machines solved the problem of human misconduct during tabulation of the vote. In the 1960s, punch card voting addressed the tabulation issues associated with manual tally and enhanced the speed and accuracy of results that voters and the press demanded on election night.

Problems interpreting voter intent from inspecting Vote-A-Matic punch card ballots during the Florida debacle in 2000, gave rise to the increased use of optical scanning and touch screen voting. Almost two million ballots were disqualified in the 2000 election because they registered multiple votes or none when run through vote-counting machines. The result was the *Help America Vote Act* (HAVA) signed in to law by President Bush in 2002. HAVA mandates that all states and localities upgrade many aspects of their election procedures, including their voting machines, registration processes and poll worker training. The specifics of implementation have been left up to each state, which allows for varying interpretations of the federal law. The goals of HAVA are to replace punch-card and lever-based voting systems, create the Elections Assistance Commission to assist in the administration of federal elections, and establish minimum standards in the elections administration.

As voting systems continued to evolve, so did the technology to support them. Optical scan equipment helped address problems of an increased number of names on ballots and addressed voting confidence levels for those who did not feel comfortable with punch cards. Touch-screen voting systems introduced unlimited ballot size, reduced the costs associated with ballot printing, and simplified the creation of ballots in multiple languages for ethnic communities that had grown to at least 5 percent of a jurisdiction. Touch screen technology could also assist voters with disabilities such as visual impairments. Voters with hearing impairments could listen to their ballots and vote unassisted for the first time in history. Severely physically disabled voters could now use alternative devices designed for use with the touch screen voting machine such as the "sip and puff," which allowed voters to control the touch screen alone, unassisted.

Every advance in voting has its roots in a perceived problem or issue. Today's new voting technologies are a response to financial and security concerns as well as concerns about access and accuracy as the numbers of voters increases. Registrars and academicians have made contributions regarding the design of such systems and assessing their successes. Decisions to continue funding new technologies for voting in the future will be preceded by serious cost/benefit accounting including analyses of what is gained by implementation. It is clear that local, state, and federal governments are under increasing pressure to spend less. Objective scholarship can assist elections officials who make decisions on what to spend and what to expect from their investments.

In the recent past, both registrars and scholars have reacted to the efforts of manufacturers to adapt machines to changing national and state legislation. A more basic focus on the essential mission of elections systems should address whether social and structural solutions might be more cost effective than technological ones. Scholars and registrars are well suited to the framing of pointed questions such as: What are, in fact, the most significant voting-related challenges today? Are these challenges best addressed by the application of newer technologies such as the web, encryption, and smart phones, or should more effective communication and organizational strategies be the priority? When is outsourcing a preferred alternative, or by what standards should vendors' products be judged?

Advances in voting systems, while fixing one problem, lead to other issues or problems. Given the challenges presented by voting machines at this time (security, expense, and maintenance, to name a few) perhaps it is time to seriously consider expanding the system of voting by mail. The vote-by-mail system addresses real-world economic problems being experienced today. All-mail voting is significantly less expensive than polling-place voting, easier to administer (no lugging around machines to hundreds of different polling places), and faster to produce results.

The use of complex voting machines could continue to be used in registrars' offices and other strategic locations for individualized services enabling all voters with disabilities the opportunity to exercise their constitutional right to vote.

Social scientists can assist the elections industry in developing a mail ballot that takes into account the diversity of citizens and the variety of potential errors. They could also help structure any evolution in this direction in such a way that a change to vote by mail would be informed by the opinions of as many citizens as possible. Registrars of voters need academic assistance in devising ways to dialogue with the public about the structure of the voting system as well as in the construction of the system itself. It is not only important that a system work, but that all those it serves perceives the system in a positive way.

For scholars to best assist registrars of voters, they must become ever more aware of real-world expectations. Only "on-the-job training" leads to a full understanding of the performance goals with which a registrar must be satisfied. For example, it is possible to misinterpret the concept of an error rate. While all registrars strive for an election without errors, they anticipate that an error-free election is an impossibility given the humanity of the staff and the electorate. Even if an office could afford to implement a fail-safe system for an election, it would be highly repressive. One cannot possibly expect that every voter or poll worker will not make a mistake, nor would one want the regime needed to guarantee such a result. Scholarly analysis, however, implies that even one error is too many, that all errors have causes that are worth pursuit. Elections officials, on the other hand, are fully satisfied when receiving a report indicating a minimal error rate. While "zero errors" may signal an ideal system within the world of academia, this cannot be a "real world" expectation.

Experiences of elections staff can open new areas of scholarship. For example, the research reported here interprets over- and undervoting as an error. It has occurred to elections staffers that voters may be intentionally marking their ballots in a way to send a particular signal. Such is the case when voters are presented ballots with multiple choices for an elected office. A voter may believe that there are not enough qualified candidates for whom to vote and signal dissatisfaction by voting for only two candidates where three may be listed on the ballot. In the case where a measure may require a yes or no vote, a voter may feel neutral, and signal no preference by marking both options. At any rate, scholars and registrars can benefit from increased dialogue between these groups.

II

The ferment surrounding the electoral process occasioned by recent federal and state legislative and administrative interest provides challenges that both registrars and academics may find profitable to explore together. There are no consistent standards between states and the federal government, between states, or even between states and their counties. Each jurisdiction operates differently—in some cases very differently as many states and counties today are awash in debt. Everywhere revenues are shrinking, while costs to conduct elections continue to rise dramatically. There is a great need for cost-effective reforms that will also improve accuracy of the system.

Inconsistency and changing state and federal regulations also cause stress for vendors and, in some cases, are causing them to withdraw from the business. The mass exodus of elections vendors has increased market share for those that survived. From an economic perspective of supply and demand, costs of elections systems have risen sharply while service levels have declined as a result of diminished competition in the industry.

California's Proposition 41 (the Voting Modernization Bond Act of 2002) and the Help America Vote Act (HAVA) stimulated a brisk business in the sales of voting machines. However, now that the funds for the purchase of new equipment have nearly all been spent to comply with changing federal requirements, the voting machine industry has been forced to move from sales to service.

At this point, technology is not a primary concern, in part because there is no funding to change what exists. Before spending more, it is important to take time to develop consistent standards that could provide a stable foundation for more technology. The current economic downturn is providing an opportunity to focus on cost-savings measures. Some of these measures may investigate human interactions that surround the voting act and may lead to improvements that cost little, such as those that require training and education rather than new hardware. In this quest, elections officials, legislators, social scientists, and experts in technology all have their part to play.

To better understand the types of clarification needed before any future technology is selected, it is useful to review the impact of recent federal and state policy on county voting systems. This history is replete with lessons for the future and can assist any who would uncover foundational standards on which a renewed development of voting systems could be built.

Proposition 14, HAVA, and Kevin Shelley

While California Secretaries of State Dr. March Fong Eu and Bill Jones laid the groundwork for Proposition 41, it was Kevin Shelly who administered its passage. Proposition 41 and HAVA gave California and its counties the ability to fund and purchase modern voting systems. Prior to this time, most of the existing voting systems were over 20 years old, paper-based, and antiquated.

Proposition 41 funding required a three-to-one match with county funds for the purchase of voting-related machines, while HAVA required no match at all. In fact, California counties could, and did, efficiently use HAVA funds as the match to obtain Proposition 41 funding; but, there was a catch—HAVA required counties to purchase their systems by 2006.

The purchase timeline requirement caused buyer frenzy and a seller's market with jurisdictions across the country scrambling to rush into purchasing systems that could comply with HAVA regulations. As local governments scrambled, vendors ramped up production and hired sales people. Many jurisdictions wanted to move slowly but were forced to act to meet impending deadlines. The United States Department of Justice threatened to enforce HAVA, making it costly for jurisdictions not to meet deadlines or to comply with HAVA requirements. New York, for example, did not move fast enough and was threatened by the Department of Justice with a lawsuit for noncompliance. Since no vendor was capable of serving the largest jurisdiction in the United States—Los Angeles County—the vendor was only able to modify a paper-based system ("Ink-a-Vote") within the legislated time constraints. Still, Los Angeles needed to get Department of Justice approval to do so.

Given the short time frame for implementation, local governments were unable to solicit academic assistance even though it was desperately needed. Registrars of voters were dependent on information from the professional sales force hired by the companies providing their voting systems. Some sales personnel pressured local leaders to purchase equipment, anticipating a continuing revenue stream for service and upgrades from the jurisdictions using their products.

HAVA also established the Elections Assistance Commission (EAC), which immediately began to issue opinions and guidelines toward standardizing federal elections in the United States of America and its territories. However, just as members of the EAC came and went, so did their opinions, particularly regarding how HAVA funds could be spent. HAVA was not written clearly in regard to such matters.

Another provision of HAVA was the creation of a centralized registered-voters database at the state level that was anticipated to ultimately feed a national database. Centralization of voter information was believed necessary because of the ever-increasing mobilization of American society. Such a database could eventually minimize fraud and facilitate crosschecks by various government agencies. However, implementation of such a system would prove difficult and costly.

Subsequently, Kevin Shelley introduced and passed legislation that mandated voter-verified paper audit trails (VVPAT) for electronic votes cast in California. Before the passage of this legislation, vendors had developed and deployed voting machines that captured and recorded votes electronically. Voters' electronic information was stored on memory cards, which were kept in a vault with paper-cast ballots. Several groups, including the Black Box Voting coalition, came forward to challenge this method of storing electronic votes. While votes that were changed by software or a virus would always be detected, the coalition argued that at the electrical engineering level, changes to memory cards could be made undetectable by simply changing the gates on how the memory was stored.

In any case, the impact of the VVPAT legislation was that vendors were forced to invent or retrofit and install technology that produces an actual printed piece of paper that recorded votes cast. The new mandated technology was to be produced and implemented at the expense of vendors, which dropped their profit margins. Because VVPAT technology was an afterthought, vendors were sent scrambling to produce printed-paper technology that would satisfy the new legislative requirement to record votes as inexpensively as possible. The new paper audit trail technologies added dramatically to the length of time for training poll workers, as well as setting up electronic voting machines at polling places on Election Day. Election administrators hurriedly searched for younger poll workers who were "savvy" regarding technology.

Secretary of State Shelly held public hearings in Sacramento to give those opposed to electronic voting a forum to voice their opinions. The hearings fostered a circus-like atmosphere with election watchdog groups such as the Black Box Voting coalition and others using the forum to promote their books and literature about paper ballots and open source coding in elections. They argued that electronic voting was unsafe in a variety of ways. Still, at this writing, there have been no proven incidents of corruption or misconduct linked to the use of touch screen voting systems themselves. With proper setup, calibration, and maintenance, the machines appear to have worked flawlessly and as designed at each election where they were used in San Joaquin County.

It would seem, then, that Kevin Shelly allowed a vocal minority using arguments without adequate support to sway his decision to decertify electronic voting systems. He actively encouraged interest groups to speak negatively about electronic voting systems, which he would eventually decertify and, subsequently, conditionally recertify once the VVPAT technology had been added.

As a result of a misappropriation of campaign funds scandal not directly linked to voting systems, but soon after his decision on VVPAT, Kevin Shelly resigned his position as secretary of state. The Democratic Committee paid monies owed to the federal and state government, and Kevin Shelly was never indicted on these charges.

After the resignation of Kevin Shelly, California Governor Arnold Schwarzenegger appointed Bruce McPherson, a Republican, to finish Shelly's term. McPherson quickly recertified all of the approved electronic voting systems in California. To our delight, registrars suddenly found ourselves able to actually use the electronic voting equipment we had feverishly purchased with the "HAVA bucks." The summer before the next election, I asked Secretary McPherson why he was not actively campaigning. He responded that Governor Schwarzenegger's re-election bid was consuming most of the Republican Party's resources and that his campaigning would have to wait. That wait may have cost him the election he subsequently lost to Debra Bowen.

Debra Bowen and the Decertification of Electronic Voting

Debra Bowen was elected by a narrow margin with the same electronic voting machines she so quickly moved against once her election was certified. Bowen cited lax protection of security-sensitive information as the basis for ordering a "top-to-bottom review" of all electronic voting systems in California. Ultimately, several voting systems were issued a withdrawal of approval notice, with conditional re-approval. Such re-approvals would be based on conditions to be announced after extensive testing that was never finished.

The partial limited nature of the testing and the nature of its results may have been partially the result of the idealized conditions assumed by the academic researchers who were assigned the task of examining voting machines. It is unclear whether those who undertook the testing fully understood the context under which the voting machines would be employed in the field. In any case, testing was performed on voting equipment without input from those who actually conduct California's elections—the registrars of voters.

The testing that was completed claimed to have uncovered serious flaws. These flaws were prematurely made public on the California Secretary of State's web site and, as a result, vendors found it increasing difficulty to predict how they would survive decertification and conditional recertification procedures. It became painfully apparent that certifying voting equipment in California would be prohibitively expensive for most vendors. Vendors were required by the state to pay for their certification testing and ordered to deposit about $300,000 in an escrow account before their product would be eligible for testing. There was no guarantee that a product would pass California's rigorous testing process, and the funds deposited in an escrow might be insufficient if further testing was required.

Bowen's sudden decertification of electronic voting pushed California counties back toward paper, a process that she deemed safer. Counties put thousands of expensive touch screen machines in equally expensive HAVA-compliant storage mothballs. Since it was unclear whether these machines could be recertified, local jurisdictions could not dispose of their inventories. With the reversion back to paper elections, counties suddenly found themselves with a huge investment in electronic voting machines that they could not fully utilize. In a much-appreciated administrative action, Bowen allowed counties to use HAVA money to help prepare for the return to paper ballots.

The Call for Academic Assistance in San Joaquin County

While most registrars of voters in California's 58 counties are elected, there are approximately 14 counties that currently have appointed officials. Those agencies include some of the largest jurisdictions in California such as Los Angeles, San Diego, San Joaquin, and Orange counties. For those who are appointed, it is particularly important to be ahead of the curve regarding change because of the need to report regularly to a political body, a county board of supervisors.

Facing the shift back to paper balloting in San Joaquin County—a highly diverse demographic—I sought out the assistance of academia from faculty drawn from a local university. I hoped to investigate alternatives to voting machines that would improve the accuracy and efficiency of the voting process. Such alternatives included improving poll-worker training, educating the public about ballot errors, increasing vote by mail, using advertising to reach the public, and recruiting poll workers who could embrace new technologies, other reforms, and the old paper voting system. As the San Joaquin County Registrar of Voters, I subsequently contracted with the Jacoby Center for Public Service and Civic Leadership at the University of the Pacific to develop an applied research program that embodied the new alternatives.

The Jacoby Center developed a program that included experiments in poll-worker training designed to modify behaviors resulting in successful poll workers. To give our experiments the greatest chance of success, I recruited a group of volunteers as diverse as the overall population using specially prepared advertisements. Participants were carefully screened by my office staff to ensure that the pool of volunteer poll workers was not only varied in socio-economic status and education, but that they were also of a nonpartisan mindset. The latter condition proved to be more difficult to flesh out than the others. As diverse as the group of volunteers, so were their political opinions. An ever-changing political playing field and partisan politics complicated both the recruitment and training of these critical volunteers. Ultimately, the behavior-modification training proved to be successful in quelling personal political preferences and developing strong poll-worker skills to be able to appropriately assist voters.

Our team of University of the Pacific partners and my office staff worked tirelessly together to implement a variety of training programs. Training sessions varied in length and technical teaching skills depending on the type of position in which poll workers were being trained. For instance, personalized sessions included those for "judges" or "inspectors" who were trained to be in a leadership role. The leadership training sessions were very lengthy—over four hours of class time, with additional reading—due to the extra duties of touch screen voting machine assembly instruction, information concerning paper ballots, and polling place set-up. It is important to note that voting machines were conditionally recertified by the secretary of state due to a federal HAVA requirement that at least one machine be used at all polling places to comply with Americans with Disabilities Act.

Most class instructors were able to impart sufficient training in about two hours. Strict training schedules were enforced to accommodate the approximately 2,400 community volunteers and poll workers. While the majority of poll workers are returning volunteers, continuing education is an important part in developing effective polling skills. Without well-trained volunteers, elections would be impossible to operate. Stipends continue to be a critical attractor in recruiting such a large army of adaptable volunteers.

San Joaquin County also implemented a county poll-worker program. However, this program was subsequently discontinued amid criticism that employees were "double-dipping." County workers were allowed to volunteer as poll workers on Election Day and also accept the stipend associated with being a poll worker. While some criticized the county poll-worker program, the stipend was allowed as volunteers customarily work about 16 hours on Election Day. County staff was typically well-suited to poll-worker duties as most were skilled in dealing with the public.

Looking to the Future

Expanding federal and state requirements post-HAVA continue to slow the purchasing and servicing of voting machines while increasing costs to vendors, states, counties, and, ultimately, tax payers. Vendors changed their business models attempting to accommodate new and changing requirements and mitigate their business risk. Still, many firms who have been unable to adapt to the continually changing requirements, have been acquired by others, or simply have gone out of business. Constant changes to federal and state regulations make it difficult for vendors to adapt their products to lengthy timeframes required to bring new products and features to market. Additionally, in response to budget constraints and the pressures of investors, vendors may be pressed to bypass the "right" fix, for the "cheapest" alternative.

A change that could help alleviate pressure on vendors to produce inadequate systems would be to address inconsistencies in federal, state, and county procedures. Once the current economic downturn is over and a renewal of voting systems can again be contemplated, a strong, consistent foundation of regulations is necessary to allow the vendors to help implement new systems. Rather than relying strictly on engineers and computer scientists to design voting systems, it may be wise to seek out the assistance of policy and legal scholars as well as the registrars who implement voting regulations to work cooperatively in crafting requirements for acceptable standard policies regarding voting systems. Policy analysts from centers of academic knowledge along with experts in practical elections administration should quickly be pressed into service to improve voting in America.

Voting solutions need to be particularly sensitive to cost, a factor not well appreciated when Proposition 14 and HAVA were implemented. Resources can only be saved through approaches that attempt to minimize administrative and hardware costs. For this reason, implementing vote by mail provides a promising cost-effective solution that may also be designed to address the needs of disabled voters without unreasonable costs.

With HAVA, Congress created a sellers' market by injecting $3.5 billion into the voting-systems marketplace. Manufacturers hurriedly responded with fragmented voting systems not thoroughly planned out. HAVA's regulations forced jurisdictions to buy quickly despite the fact that some manufacturers had better hardware while others had better software. Jurisdictions too often were pushed to base the adoption of systems on little more than personal preferences or sales tactics. HAVA also forced manufacturers to come to market with equipment that may not have been ready. Put on the spot by politicians, some manufacturers were tempted to change names or model numbers rather than upgrade equipment.

Complicating vendor relations was the federal Elections Assistance Commission's decision that favored "off the shelf" parts for voting machines. While manufacturers tried to forecast which parts would need to be replaced, and to house those parts for 10 years or longer, the EAC's decision caused unanticipated confusion because of the rapid evolution of technology. For example, memory cards that were manufactured in 2002 did not carry the same components as memory cards manufactured in 2010. If a county tries to replace outdated memory cards that were produced eight years later, the commission requires a complete retest of the entire voting system. In addition, because each jurisdiction adopts their own different election-system requirements, manufacturers must incorporate the requirements from all jurisdictions into their equipment. This consuming adaptation became overwhelmingly expensive for both manufacturers and clients. In some cases, parts can cost more than an entire unit's original cost. As a result, jurisdictions are left with antiquated systems for which they can no longer get parts at a reasonable price, if at all.

Before rethinking future voting systems, whether they are Internet based, vote by mail, or others, it is equally critical to respond to the current economic system. For example, vote by mail costs about half as much as polls voting. Local jurisdictions can no longer afford to place specialized machines at each polling place with the limited number of replacement parts available to keep the devices working. The full costs of training poll workers, voters, staff, and constituents can no longer be borne by the local jurisdictions alone.

We hope to build on a secure system of voting in the future, but not based on the antiquated expectations of current laws, rules, and regulations of outdated voting systems and old voting methods. Academics can help in the short run by creating training tools to develop competent poll workers and assist registrars in developing procedures to standardize the counting and recounting of votes. I believe that registrars and academia should work together to explore less expensive organizational changes and voting systems that include vote by mail while awaiting the return of economic prosperity. Lessons learned from the past can help us to structure implementation of future elections technology in the most cost-effective and orderly conduct possible. The future of voting requires a new standardized regulatory foundation. This will include new rules and regulations that account for new technology, some of which has not been invented or implemented, to allow for fair, accurate, transparent, and comprehensive election systems that are accessible to voters. The future of voting is here and now.

An Academic Responds[3]

The interdisciplinary team from the University of the Pacific who authored the chapters above benefited mightily from the full cooperation of Austin Erdman and his staff. In fact, the funding for much of the project was secured through the San Joaquin County Office of the Registrar of Voters, later to be supplemented by support through the Pew Foundation.

While team members have shared their research findings in the separate chapters of this book, their observations of voting in San Joaquin County generated insights that went beyond their particular research questions. Each team member was, in reality, a participant observer for three elections from a vantage point within the Office of the Registrar of Voters. Based on their informal contacts, members of the team were asked to provide tips for a savvy voter (see Appendix A). Twenty-five distinct tips were generated.

---

[3] This section was written by Robert Benedetti.

This exercise allowed the team to debrief from their experience and to offer up areas for future investigation. However, this list also reflects a growing awareness by the team that current levels of voter education are not adequate. Elections are complex and occur over substantial intervals. The teams doubt that the voting system can be made increasingly fail-safe without the cooperation of the voter, including preparation before Election Day. One of the expectations of voting machines was that they would eliminate error from the process of voting. As Austin Erdman suggests above, such a perfect system may be an academic pipedream, but cannot be a reasonable expectation for the Office of the Registrar of Voters. Rather, our team concluded that education rather than engineering may provide the best protection for reasonably fair elections that stay within governmental budgets.

That is, rather than focusing on voting machines, the team envisioned an interactive system in which the registrar of voters further embraces the role of teacher with the citizens as learners. Through a variety of media, the registrar should communicate with voters before, during, and after elections providing helpful tips and instructions. This relationship should be conceived as a continuous one, not just a channel for basic information before Election Day. We believe that such a communications network would be of particular use to voters with special needs, but also to voters who wish to vote early, by mail, or outside of their assigned precinct.

Clearly the recruitment of poll workers from a more diversified sample of the public would be made easier if such a communications network was generated. The more citizens actually participate in the electoral system, the greater the recognition by the public at large that voting is an important responsibility. In fact, it might be beneficial to view service at the polls as a civic duty, much like we view jury duty. In any case, it is a significant opportunity for citizenship training and for spreading the word about one's obligation to vote.

Thus, the tips for a savvy voter were meant to begin to evolve a curriculum for voters, a curriculum to be developed and presented by a registrar of voters. The team continues to be skeptical that any machines can so discipline the electoral process as to eliminate human error at a reasonable cost with minimum burdens being placed on the individual voter.

In any case, we think it is worth the effort to mount increasing educational campaigns, enlisting citizens' help in improving our system of voting. Appendix A is a first cut at what all of us need to know before, during, and after we go to the polls.

Appendix A

Twenty-Five Tips for a Savvy Voter

Before Election Day

1. Frequent the registrar of voters' website for up-to-date information. **1**

2. Keep your registration current, including any changes of address. **2**

3. Use any media (emails, cards, newspaper ads, magazine articles, etc.) as reminders of the Election Day or day to return vote-by-mail ballots. Post them on a bulletin board or refrigerator. **1**

4. Share media received that relate to the election with others so they remember as well; email relevant materials to family and friends. **1**

5. Volunteer to be a poll worker to gain a better understanding of the voting process. **1**

6. Know where your precinct polling place is located. **2**

7. Read the instructions on your sample ballot; they are the same as will be on the actual ballot and should tell you everything you need to know about making your vote count. It also allows you to familiarize yourself with propositions and candidates. **3, 4, 5**

8. You may wish to mark your sample ballot before you mark your official ballot to ensure accuracy. You can take your sample ballot into the voting booth. **5**

9. In preparing your selections, it is perfectly fine to use a voting guide prepared by media or an organization that you trust rather than investigating each contest fully yourself. **6**

Vote by Mail

1. Voting by mail is the new name for absentee voting. **4**

2. Voting by mail allows you extra time to consider voting decisions, is convenient, and saves gas and time on Election Day. Consider it seriously. **3, 5**

3. Be sure to sign your vote-by-mail ballot envelope. **2, 5**

4. Vote-by- mail ballots can be turned in on Election Day at any polling place in the county. **2, 6**

5. Remember all valid vote-by-mail ballots are counted. **6**

6. Vote-by-mail ballots returned before Election Day are among the first results released after the polls close. **6**

Election Day

1. Vote during midday to avoid long lines at the polling places. **2**

2. Make sure your vote counts by following the instructions for filling out ballots carefully. It is possible that some rules may have changed since the last time you voted. If asked to use a black ballpoint pen, not a pencil, do it! It may help the machine to read your vote clearly. **2, 3, 5, 7**

3. Ask for assistance from a poll worker if you need to. Though they are ordinary citizens who have volunteered for this task, they have been trained to help you. **2, 7**

4. Completely fill in the oval on your paper ballot when voting; do not mark the oval with an X or check mark. Incorrect marking in and around an oval may invalidate your vote about the ballot item in question. Extraneous markings or doodles on the ballot can "spoil" a ballot and disqualify it entirely. **4, 5, 7**

5. You do not have to vote in every contest. There is no shame in not voting if you really do not have a preference. **6**

6. Writing the name in the space for write-in candidates of a candidate you have already marked as your vote will make it appear that you are voting twice, and your vote may be rejected. **7**

7. Remember that we are all human. If you make a mistake marking your ballot, ask a poll worker for a new one. Do not attempt to correct the ballot. You may request up to three fresh ballots. **3, 5, 7**

8. While you need to sign the address registry at your polling place, you should not sign your ballot, as it will disqualify your vote. Signing the ballot itself violates the basic principle of a secret ballot. **4, 5**

After Election Day

1. Voters should be interacting with their registrars of voters, contacting and communicating often to ensure full understanding of the electoral process. **1**

2. Do not hesitate to voice a concern or complaint about poll workers or other observed irregularities in voting procedures at the polls or in the Office of the Registrar of Voters. **2**

Note: These tips were generated by several of the authors of the chapters in this book. The numbers next to each tip indicate the author who suggested it. Where several authors supported the same tip, several numbers are listed. The following key associates numbers with authors:

1. Alan Ray, Professor of Communication
2. Jon Schamber, Professor of Communication
3. Dari Sylvester, Assistant Professor of Political Science
4. Brett DeBoer, Associate Professor of Visual Arts
5. Paul Turpin, Assistant Professor of Communication
6. Keith Smith, Assistant Professor of Political Science
7. Lisa Tromovitch, Assistant Professor of Theatre Arts